Calling Acade
Account

SRHE and Open University Press Imprint
General Editor: Heather Eggins

Current titles include:

Catherine Bargh, Peter Scott and David Smith: *Governing Universities*
Ronald Barnett: *Improving Higher Education: Total Quality Care*
Ronald Barnett: *The Idea of Higher Education*
Ronald Barnett: *The Limits of Competence*
Ronald Barnett: *Higher Education: A Critical Business*
John Bird: *Black Students and Higher Education*
Jean Bocock and David Watson (eds): *Managing the Curriculum*
David Boud *et al.* (eds): *Using Experience for Learning*
Angela Brew (ed.): *Directions in Staff Development*
Anne Brockbank and Ian McGill: *Facilitating Reflective Learning in Higher Education*
Ann Brooks: *Academic Women*
Robert G. Burgess (ed.): *Beyond the First Degree*
Frank Coffield and Bill Williamson (eds): *Repositioning Higher Education*
John Cowan: *On Becoming an Innovative University Teacher*
Rob Cuthbert (ed.): *Working in Higher Education*
Heather Eggins (ed.): *Women as Leaders and Managers in Higher Education*
G.R. Evans: *Calling Academia to Account*
David Farnham (ed.): *Managing Academic Staff in Changing University Systems*
Sinclair Goodlad: *The Quest for Quality*
Diana Green (ed.): *What is Quality in Higher Education?*
Robin Middlehurst: *Leading Academics*
Sarah Neal: *The Making of Equal Opportunities Policies in Universities*
David Palfreyman and David Warner (eds): *Higher Education and the Law*
Moira Peelo: *Helping Students with Study Problems*
John Pratt: *The Polytechnic Experiment*
Michael Prosser and Keith Trigwell: *Understanding Learning and Teaching*
Tom Schuller (ed.): *The Changing University?*
Peter Scott (ed.): *The Globalization of Higher Education*
Peter Scott: *The Meanings of Mass Higher Education*
Harold Silver and Pamela Silver: *Students*
Anthony Smith and Frank Webster (eds): *The Postmodern University?*
Imogen Taylor: *Developing Learning in Professional Education*
Paul R. Trowler: *Academics Responding to Change*
David Warner and Elaine Crosthwaite (eds): *Human Resource Management in Higher and Further Education*
David Warner and Charles Leonard: *The Income Generation Handbook* (Second Edition)
David Warner and David Palfreyman (eds): *Higher Education Management*
Graham Webb: *Understanding Staff Development*
Sue Wheeler and Jan Birtle: *A Handbook for Personal Tutors*

Calling Academia to Account

Rights and Responsibilities

G.R. Evans

The Society for Research into Higher Education
& Open University Press

Published by SRHE and
Open University Press
Celtic Court
22 Ballmoor
Buckingham
MK18 1XW

email: enquiries@openup.co.uk
world wide web: http://www.openup.co.uk

and 325 Chestnut Street
Philadelphia, PA 19106, USA

First published 1999

A catalogue record of this book is available from the British Library

ISBN 0 335 20194 6 (pb)   0 335 20195 4 (hb)

Library of Congress Cataloging-in-Publication Data

Evans, G.R. (Gillian Rosemary)
Calling academia to account : rights and responsibilities / G.R. Evans.
p. cm.
Includes bibliographical references (p.) and index.
ISBN 0-335-20195-4 (hardbound). – ISBN 0-335-20194-6 (pbk.)
1. Education, Higher – Aims and objectives – Great Britain.
2. Universities and colleges – Great Britain – Evaluation.
3. Education, Higher – Great Britain – Administration. 4. Academic freedom – Great Britain. 5. Educational accountability – Great Britain. I. Title.
LA636.8.E83 1998
378.41 – dc21 98-16399
CIP

Typeset by Graphicraft Limited, Hong Kong
Printed in Great Britain by St Edmundsbury Press Ltd, Bury St Edmunds, Suffolk

For the members of the
Council for Academic Freedom
and Academic Standards

Contents

Acknowledgements

To members of the Council for Academic Freedom and Academic Standards, those who have allowed me to try to help with the disputes in which they have found themselves involved in their own universities and colleges, numerous colleagues within the University of Cambridge, academic lawyers who became interested, supporters and good friends, I owe various kinds of debt of gratitude. There is also a debt to those with whom I have worked on ecumenical committees over the last two decades. There I learned 'transferable skills' which have had to be stretched a good deal in battles where there is no underlying presumption of mutual charity. But that presumption can be sustained by one side even if not always by both; and I should say in fairness to the administrative officers of the University of Cambridge, that they have mostly behaved with decency and courtesy. For challenge is always uncomfortable and when things have been done a certain way without anyone asking awkward questions those questions are likely to be unwelcome when they come.

Preface

Higher education is about to come face to face for the first time with what openness really means. The Public Interest Disclosure Act has received the Royal Assent as this book goes to the printers in the autumn of 1998. In the months while it has been in production many of the cases on which it has been based have moved towards their happy or unhappy conclusions, some in the full light of media coverage. A number of fresh public policy issues arising from the exposure of what has been happening in universities have also entered the public domain. These have raised profound questions about both the ethics and the pragmatics of confidentiality for universities as they set up codes of conduct for dealing with whistleblowing, and for members of their academic staff as they debate with themselves whether and how to raise concerns.

The whistleblower is not always a hero. Sometimes he is a damn nuisance. But he should never become a victim as a result of conscientious raising of substantive concerns. Universities should be as fearless in accepting challenge about their conduct of their affairs as it is the duty of scholars to be in teaching and research.

The Committee on Standards in Public Life in its *Second Report* called for a change of climate and public expectation. Transparency and accountability are shining words but it is painful to have muddled attempts to deal with day-to-day problems exposed even internally, let alone in the newspapers. Those running universities and academics working within them need to find the courage to be honest and to publish what they learn from rigorous examination when something goes wrong. They can only benefit in the end from thinking big about what is at stake beyond the immediate interests of individual institutions and their officers. Only in that way perhaps can they inhabit the wider world of intellectual endeavour in which I have tried to set this study and in which scholars in every century have felt at home. It has proved durable.

Abbreviations

AUT	Association of University Teachers
BBSRC	Biology and Biological Sciences Research Council
CAFAS	Council for Academic Freedom and Academic Standards
RAE	Research Assessment Exercise
CVCP	Committee of Vice-Chancellors and Principals
HEFCE	Higher Education Funding Council for England
MRC	Medical Research Council
HEQC	Higher Education Quality Council
QAA	Quality Assurance Agency
RAE	Research Assessment Exercise
UGC	University Grants Commission

Introduction

During the 1990s in the UK two national committees have met and reported: the Nolan Committee (the Committee on Standards in Public Life) published its *Second Report* in 1996 and the Dearing Committee its own *Report* in 1997. Both Committees had a concern for the future governance of higher education, and both looked at the matter in the context of the wider public scene, considering universities and their connected colleges and institutes engaged in higher education partly or largely in terms of their place in public life.

This approach was timely. It helped to focus attention on problems with patterns of governance which were calling into question the very purpose of universities. This was not mere grumbling in the common room. Sir Richard Scott, reflecting on his experiences while conducting the Scott Inquiry, commented, 'I learned of the tenacity with which officialdom can strive to avoid publicity for manifest mis-management.'[1]

In *Ex parte Forster re University of Sydney* the court put faith in: 'the good sense and wisdom of the Senate acting as a responsible body charged with an important public function, exposed to public criticism, and subject to the measure of public control'.[2] That does not allow for a situation where good sense and wisdom desert decision-makers who are not, in practice, easily thus accountable in the public arena. It is not even clear that there are the same duties of fairness in domestic decisions as in public ones. The problem is not lack of goodwill, lack of good intentions (as a rule) or lack of structures. Instead, there is a gap between the platform and the train, through which individuals can fall to their destruction when mistakes are made, and an institution's officers seek to cover those up or to justify their actions.

Thus, numerous complaints and disputes are arising as a result of failures of fairness under the internal rules of universities. The question where, or even whether, there is jurisdiction to deal with them is urgent. In the UK, the Education Reform Act 1988 and the Further and Higher Education Act 1992 have moved the boundaries between public and private as they relate to universities, and have brought about changes in the legal status of universities and in their powers to run their own affairs, thus creating a minefield in the arena of accountability, legally speaking.[3]

It is time for some stocktaking. No one, especially post-Nolan, has much trouble with the general idea that transparency and accountability are good things. However, it is by no means easy to say what that means in practice. To love such shining ideas is not a guarantee of willingness to hand over the papers or explain a decision when it is challenged.

The interest in trying to write such a book at the present time lies not only in the intrinsic importance of getting right a system of higher education within which the best minds can do their best work. The 'embarrassment potential' of the Scott Inquiry was not realized; his report is a devastating indictment, but the practices it condemns are not noticeably changed by it. Public consciousness also needs to be kept alert if that is to change. The price of freedom continues to be eternal vigilance.

The training of minds is, perhaps, the supreme distinctive task of universities. In the 'old' universities there was a culture which took it for granted that whatever happened in a university happened also in the wider community of scholarship, and that was where it ultimately mattered. It will be a main theme of this study that universities ought still, consciously, to set a duty to the universal community of scholarship over against their duty to themselves; that they ought, indeed, to understand their duty to themselves in that wider manner. It will be taken as an implication of that duty that they ought to treat those who teach and do original work in their employ 'collegially', as 'peers'.

In UK law, the freedom of speech of academic staff enjoys a special protection under the Education Reform Act 1988, in recognition that it is inseparable from their doing their job properly. Universities are unique in the kind of person who works in them, for the outcomes of education are unpredictable. To train a human mind to a high level of sophistication and competence in thinking, to show its owner where to go to find things out, to make it a sharp tool, is to let something loose in the world which it may subsequently be difficult to control. Academics have a professional responsibility to use their intellectual tools, and a further duty to create more such tools in the minds of the students they teach. Thus, inherent conflicts of interest are set up within universities and between universities and the wider world where independence meets control.

Moreover, one person's freedom to speak may be another person's incitement to racial hatred. With rights go responsibilities, and such correlation creates tensions central to the concerns of this book, for responsibility is also accountability.

This book is about calling to account. Much of the recent reflection on accountability has been concerned with accountability upwards, and especially to those who hold purse-strings. However, it is equally, if not more, important to ensure that persons in positions of authority are accountable to those over whom they have powers, that there are means by which the weak in any organizational structure can be protected, and that the general good is looked after when someone gives the wrong steer: 'It is not discreditable to get it wrong. What is discreditable is a reluctance to explain fully what has occurred and why.'[4]

> Authorities whose decisions are challenged . . . should have a common interest with the courts in ensuring that the highest standards of administration are maintained and that, if error has occurred, it should be corrected . . . When challenged they should set out fully what they did and why, so far as is necessary, fully and fairly to meet the challenge.[5]

Accountability need not, in principle, be always upwards. Indeed, it ought to be downwards too, or there will be no satisfactory check on the use of powers. But if it is to be argued that those in authority ought to be accountable to those *over* whom they exercise authority, that will have to be on a different basis, because they may have no reward they can withhold, no sanction to bring to bear.

In its recognition that a gap exists in the provision of remedies, the Committee on Standards in Public Life, in its *Second Report* (1996) places the problem squarely in frame: 'It is no longer sufficient for public bodies to take good decisions. They must be seen to do so, and be prepared to let an independent person or body review their activities if necessary.'[6]

There can be no accountability where mistakes and misbehaviours can be hidden, so this book is also about transparency: 'Just as the judges of the inferior courts when challenged on the exercise of their jurisdiction traditionally explain fully what they have done and why they have done it, but are not partisan in their own defence, so should be the public authorities.'[7]

The bodies with which we shall be chiefly concerned are the universities, but the lessons are of much wider application. The ordinary human failings of people in charge of decision-making in any context can run out of hand where the natural checks upon them are removed. The broader balancing mechanisms in a system can fail to operate or disappear altogether where there is in practice nothing to stop bureaucratic covering-up of mistakes. Even such checks as exist in principle may prove ineffective where management structures make it difficult for individuals to criticize or make suggestions for change without placing themselves in professional jeopardy.

This book is not comfortable reading. Something of the first importance is at stake, not only in catching up before they go beyond recall some of the problems which are running away with the future of higher education, but also in keeping in being something old and deep and necessary to the best in human endeavour of which the present-day university student is lucky to get a glimpse. The encounter with minds engaged in a lifetime's purposeful inquiry marks the apprentice to learning for life. This inwardness is hard to see where all that a university does is placed face up for inspection by visible measures which do not look below the surface. So it is the central paradox of this study that those engaged in the running of higher education must be accountable precisely so that those engaged in the teaching and research which are its real 'business' may be in some measure unaccountable or, at least, accountable only to the truth and the verdict of history.

This is not, by any means, a study solely of the British scene. One must, however, begin from what one knows, and I shall take that arena as the source of many of my illustrations of the internal economy of the problems with which this book is concerned. I hope the universality of many of them will be apparent to readers struggling with them elsewhere in the world.

Part 1

Calling to Account in the Wider World

Introduction

What do universities owe by way of accountability to the wider world which is their setting? Much depends on how wide their field of work, their influence and their impact is deemed to be. A good deal of what the British Government-commissioned *Dearing Report* of 1997 has to say about accountability and responsiveness to 'external constituencies' assumes that a university is a local institution meeting local needs. In the case of the leading universities of the world, the 'relevant constituency' must include the world (15.53). That the Dearing Committee's remit was specifically restricted to the interests of the UK was an important limitation, because it discouraged the Committee from looking at the broader international, or even the European, dimensions. It turned overseas students into a source of fee income. This is in contrast to the generosity of the assumption of Shirley Williams, 20 years earlier, that Britain should welcome overseas students not for its good but for theirs. In 1978–9 there were 50,000 overseas students in the UK. At that date, the natural question to ask was whether 'the very substantial resources that are spent on overseas students . . . are spent in a way that reaches the students most in need and the countries most in need'.[1] In other words, whether Britain was serving an international need as well as it could.

There is, however, an altogether different way of understanding 'wider world', and that is to look at what academics and universities do which is of enduring, and not necessarily financial or practical, value or use. There are high themes here; themes of contribution to the human endeavour and the moving forward of the boundaries of knowledge. These things are not consistently valued at the same level over time. Twenty or 30 years ago active researchers were often hired by universities for their scholarly standing and then expected to turn almost entirely to teaching and administration, with research coming third as a 'selfish' activity. The advent of funding by research profile in UK universities has meant that the climate of expectation has changed and active researchers have become heroes not villains. At the same time a premium is placed by governments on research with applicable outcomes. The deep purposes are easily lost sight of in such discussions on the allocation of funding. That does not mean they go away. They provide the inner drive for the labours of academics and the work of universities. However, account needs to be rendered for them, too, because unbridled inner drives to learn can lead to the making of dangerous and damaging discoveries.

In this part of the book I shall take first the inward realities, the values and inner purposes and assumptions of academic research and scholarship; and second, the issues which arise about accountability for investment to fund that work, the 'games' which can be played in the process of giving it and withholding money. It is important that these games are recognized for what they are and that everyone can see them being played. Otherwise there is no control over 'fixing' things.

1

Values and the World of Scholarship

The sharing of knowledge

One way of sharing knowledge is by teaching it to others. Another is through meeting and talking with fellow students and scholars, for example, by 'giving papers' at conferences. Another is by publishing books. Even if the originator of the ideas or the discoveries thus shared keeps the credit, this is an act of openness. The modern scholarly scene is international in this respect, and that was also true in the geographically smaller world of the mediaeval universities of Europe. What is important about this characteristic of scholarship is not the scale or distance of the exchange but its generosity. One gives account of one's work by communicating it.

In the ancient world, learning already involved a shared search, though the emphasis tended to be on the intimate personal exchanges of friends. Cicero's *Academica* is set in a country house at Cumae. Varro arrives, and the assembled friends excitedly want him to join them at once if he is not too tired after his journey.[1] Their reason is a strong sense of fellow-feeling; he is 'joined' with them in common study, which has become the foundation of friendship.[2] Augustine's Cassiciacum treatises, also placed in a setting of 'philosophical retirement' in a country house, are dialogues, recording a sustained inquiry made by a group of friends meeting in an informal seminar over a period of time, so that they can explore an intellectual problem together. In the early twelfth century, Gilbert Crispin, the scholarly Abbot of Westminster, tells of a philosophical club he used to attend. This does not mean there was not also rivalry (from the earliest period), and jealousy, and the other negative counterparts of a sense that the getting of knowledge is a shared endeavour. Still, it is plain what the common ideal was, and that it had to do with a pooling or trading or exchange of knowledge.

There must also be, inescapably, a sense of having a 'common cause' with those who have worked on a subject before.[3] It is no more logical for scholars to seek to keep the results of their inquiries from their contemporaries than it would be for them to destroy all the outcomes of their work on their deathbeds.[4] The modern sciences still build on earlier discoveries, or challenge received assumptions which are there to be challenged only because they are taken from previous work.

There has been recent reflection on the argument that there exists a veritable 'moral obligation to convey the results of research to others, that there is an imperative of communicating that corresponds to the indicative of knowing'. 'Both the results of university research and the data on which it is based should be public',[5] insists Jaroslav Pelikan.

This is a statement about accountability. It is not a new idea, but as we shall see, it is an increasingly thorny area in modern scientific research. Yet, arguably, the principle ought not to be different, just because financial or commercial interests are involved, from that which governs the sharing of, for example, knowledge about recipes for Byzantine 'porridge' in mediaeval Greek studies.

The conscious sense of a continuity of endeavour in a continuing community of scholarship which marks the first universities of the Middle Ages, was made possible by the continued use of books written in the Greek and Roman world. They were read as textbooks or as the subject of study in lectures, or as the starting point for disputations, but above all as 'authorities' (*auctoritates*). Their authors were seen as giants on whose shoulders later scholars stood like dwarfs.[6] In this way, an encounter of minds continued over time as well as between contemporaries. Once printing was invented that went on in a manner less precarious as to the transmission, but with a changing and less solid respect for past authorities. It began to become possible to see them as merely fellow scholars from another age.[7]

That was, perhaps, a healthy change. A community of scholarship requires mutual respect, mutual freedom of speech and even some fear of being challenged by other scholars' opinions. And that depends upon an assumption of equality. It is essential for a scholar to be prepared to say, 'my opinion is as good as yours'.

The lesson of the past is that a university or the individual scholar has stewardship, rather than ownership, in the community of 'shared' knowledge. The stewardship is not, either at institutional or at individual level, merely a function of custodianship. It is a trust, and the current holders ought to seek to hand it on intact and with interest.

The desire for learning

Cicero asks himself why he is writing his book on 'the nature of the gods' now. He makes a list of reasons. He has the time (*otium*). Reading books and writing about problems have cheered him at a difficult time in his life.[8] The public interest requires it. An autocratic government is holding sway, and in such circumstances he thinks it his duty (*ad decus et ad laudem civitatis*) for the good of the community to help make philosophical ideas available in Greek also accessible in Latin.[9] Experience suggests he is being proved right. Others are being stimulated to study and to write. These last two factors are connected in his mind with the duty to share knowledge, and also with its innately universal character.

In Cicero's mixed list of motivations a scholar of any century would find things to recognize. There is an inner drive and an inner satisfaction. There is an inhabiting of a mental space in which there is room to walk about and stretch the intellectual legs. There is a sense of contributing to the totality of the human endeavour. A modern scholar, too, might see coming out of his work benefits for himself and the public good, and an enlargement of the sphere of knowledge. Yet, he does it not solely for those reasons, but because he 'has to'; curiosity drives him on much more strongly than the carrot of promised rewards. For what other reason will a subject area first explored by new graduates in their early 20s still have the same men and women working on it eagerly in their 80s, when professional achievement has gone as far as it is going to?

There ought, also, to be an element of risk-taking. The door, says Augustine, is set wide open, so wide that it may let in error, or changes of opinion on the way, although the seeker is looking for solid ground.[10] This is a means of differentiating the serious seeker after knowledge from the 'hobbyist' enthusiast who, perhaps chiefly, seeks to add to his own knowledge about the subject and not to challenge – indeed precisely not to challenge, since the instinct at play is different. A 'Jane Austen' society (to take an example) would perhaps enjoy or celebrate the novelist's work rather than criticize it. Interest in a subject does not, in itself, make a scholar. On the foundations of true scholarship can be built something more rigorous, and perhaps specific to a given discipline, involving conviction that it matters to extend knowledge about something even if the extension of knowledge has no perceptible application at any foreseeable time.

Teaching and research: the adult community

The *Dearing Report* assumed that there are generic skills which can be isolated and taught not in the process of teaching something else, but as skills in their own right. Accordingly, the *Report* recommends (R 31) that postgraduate training shall include 'in addition to understanding of a range of research methods and training in appropriate technical skills, the development of professional skills, such as communication, self-management and planning'.

None of this necessarily assists the development of scholarly habits, such as the persistence in an inquiry which may make it necessary to throw planning out of the window while a 'trail' is followed; or the ability so far to lose oneself in the work that one forgets to buy food for supper or to collect one's dry-cleaning.

In higher education 'the teacher's authority has to be won and cannot be presumed'.[11] Does the university have to meet the expectations of students where they are, or is the idea that the students grow to fit the expectations the university has of them? Scholarship involves an independence of mind which starts things and persists with them even where no one else prompts. These are attributes of the adult mind, and it is of the essence of the university that it teaches adults.

The philosophy and rhetoric teachers of the ancient world rehearsed young men getting an education in things of the mind which were deemed a necessary preparation for the affairs of the world. The teacher–pupil relationship of advanced study has usually been between adults, even if between adults of greatly differing ages and levels of knowledge. That the teaching and learning involves adults remains a distinctive feature of 'higher' education. 'A university is a body of *mature* scholars and scientists' [my italics],[12] said Thorstein Veblen at the beginning of the twentieth century, and that very maturity, that adulthood, provides the natural meeting place of teaching and research.

That is something which may be difficult to remember in the real world of a late twentieth-century 'new university', where a lecturer may face 100 students, some with poor entrance qualifications, where the department in which he teaches is rated low for research, and where even the keenest would-be scholar has little time for his own work. Struggling to keep alive a sense of purpose in that world, a lecturer might see what has just been said as idealistic to the point of romanticism. I ask him to bear with me. This is important.

In an environment where learning has room to move, scholars reach a stage where they teach themselves, or learn from one another and no longer stand in a subordinate relationship to their supervisors or their seniors in age. As a young don in early nineteenth-century Oxford, Newman set about reading his way into the Arian controversy of the fourth century and writing a book about it. He would have been put down as an 'active researcher' in twentieth-century Oxford. He had to find his own way and devise his own methods. He took for granted the place of self-education within a university.[13]

Such a presumption of intellectual equality has implications for the kind of teaching a university ought to do and the attitude it ought to seek to evoke in its students, even if they are not, and do not wish to be, prospective research students. It should treat them not as dependants but as intellectual equals who happen to be beginners. The 'mentor' model, having its vogue in the 1990s, has its dangers if it creates leaders and followers and 'schools' of thought. It also tends to foster a tension between the purposes of teaching and the purposes of research to which one author points in alarm: 'A fanatical pursuit of research and scholarship . . . amounts to a withdrawal from the university and is the bane of staff cooperation and attentive teaching.'[14] At the opposite extreme is a teaching-only pattern which 'denies expertise, turns the academic into a school teacher, and pulls him or her virtually out of the discipline and perhaps out of the overall academic profession'.[15] That is why it is important that there should continue to be a presumption, an expectation, of genuine scholarly exchange between 'adult' learners in every corner of higher education teaching.

Newman saw that not all those capable of teaching (and perhaps teaching well) at degree level are also capable of research. He went further. He thought that 'to discover and to teach are distinct functions; they are also distinct gifts, and are not commonly found united in the same person . . . the common sense of mankind has associated the search after truth with seclusion and quiet. The greatest thinkers have been too intent on their subject to admit of interruption.'[16] He clearly had in mind the truly original thinker, but a good deal of research of a perfectly respectable sort requires patience and exactness rather than a high level of innovative thinking, and it is perhaps this sheer habit of work, this taking for granted that one is seeking to find out something new, to which the university teacher ought automatically to expose his students. The tasks are not separate; they have an intimate connection. 'The attitude of mind which develops in a senior scholar out of the experience of authentic scholarship, an attitude that moderates confidence in the results of study with a continuing skepticism about them, does lead to a sense of sharing in the quest, in which the senior can also learn from the junior',[17] argues Pelikan. Thorstein Veblen thought in the early twentieth century that: '[It is research] scientific and scholarly inquiry [which is constitutive for a university].'[18] He even went so far as to say that 'the work of teaching properly belongs in the university only because and in so far as it incites and facilitates the university man's work of inquiry.'[19]

Despite what he says about the natural remoteness of the researcher, Newman was conscious of his debt to his old tutor, Whately, as the person who 'taught me to think correctly, and (strange office for an instructor) to rely upon myself . . . it has been at your kind suggestion, that I have been since led to employ myself in the consideration of several subjects . . . which I cannot doubt have been very beneficial to my mind'.[20] Newman and Whately well understood the law of scholarship that 'the teacher should teach students, not recruit disciples'.[21]

Newman wrote to Richard Whately when Whately's *Logic* was first published to say: 'I cannot tell you the surprise I felt on seeing you that you had thought it worth while to mention my name, as having contributed to the arrangement of its materials. Whatever I then wrote was written, I am conscious, almost as an Undergraduate's exercise, and consequently of little value, except as regards my own improvement in doing it.'[22] Whately replied thus: 'What you wrote was several years ago, when you were but just a graduate . . . I let it stand as you wrote it, because I could not make it any better; but it does not follow that you could not.'[23]

Whately and Newman taught each other although the relationship between them was that of tutor and student. Teachers are also learners on their own account. Whately writes to Newman about his article on Apollonius: 'I was much interested by your article . . . I shall be able to say more when I have gone over it again. I did not observe any unsound arguments; and this tho' [*sic*] a negative merit is an extremely rare one.'[24]

We can see here the scholar's instinct to reread and reflect, to comment on and criticize, but also to use all grist coming to his mill.

All this is the more striking for the way it exemplifies the power of scholarship to flourish in an environment not well calculated to foster it. Oxford in the eighteenth century had been, in many ways, an idle place, with little care taken over the teaching of students. Newman comments wrily on the tendency of his pupils 'whenever they get a new coachman' to 'make an effort to get the reins slack'.[25] His own undergraduate contemporaries were no doubt much the same. But his own zeal for learning was not thereby diminished.

We are, however, left with some difficulties if we seek to apply this matrix of assumptions to a world of mass access to higher education, where not all students will find this level of independence easy to attain and not all their teachers will be experienced scholars with the habit of original work. There have been visible tensions. In the late 1990s only a relatively small proportion of academic staff formed the core of an institution's employees as its full-time staff. A great many were already on short-term contracts, primarily for research, and to do some teaching as it was needed. Such teaching was of immense value to institution and students and many courses could not run without it. Others, equally essential to the running of the system, were teaching as graduate students or research assistants. This casualization of university teaching is not a good thing, either for the often exploited casual labour, or for the students.

If teaching is of the essence of a university so are students. If students are adult learners, they have, arguably, rights to be treated in ways which fit with that. Students stood in a relationship to the mediaeval gild which has persisted into a 'membership' of the modern university. This 'membership' gives them rights which go beyond the contractual rights created by their admission to the university.[26] The student unrest of the 1960s demonstrated the potential power of the student body. The call was for participation and for student representation on committees, and students have been on committees ever since. However, alongside that, and increasingly so in the last decade, students have been encouraged to see themselves as 'customers' for a 'service' provided by their university. The move of the British Government in 1997 to impose a requirement that students should pay part of their own tuition fees (hitherto born by the public purse) sharpened that consciousness.[27]

The accountability issues here are potentially complex. They are only beginning to be explored at the time of writing, for this theme of the 'adult community' has, as yet, had little airing.

Expertise and professionalism

Nineteenth-century dons were not, strictly, members of a profession. Young men of academic bent were elected to Fellowships of Oxford and Cambridge colleges after taking their first degrees. They remained there until (in many cases) obtaining livings as clergymen. If they married they gave up their Fellowships, which placed a natural age limit on the majority. Only the Master was provided by the College with a house in which he could bring up a family. These were gentlemen amateurs. This does not mean that their scholarship was unremarkable, but it does mean that they were not concerned with questions of career structure within the academic life.

There has since come into being a 'profession', a body of persons who earn their living as academics, who think (in many cases), in terms of 'careers' in higher education and who expect their employers to maintain good practice in the way they treat them.

It is a central theme of this study that there exists a community of scholarship which is, and always has been, independent of the continuance in being of universities and certainly of any given university, and that scholars belong to it by virtue of the work they do, whether or not they are in the employment of a university. Belonging to a scholarly community does not, however, mean that these 'employment' requirements are not important, and that the academic staff of universities ought not to be fairly and decently treated.

It has been argued that knowledge confers status.[28] However, British society has a long-standing distaste for the 'expert'; that was evinced in the tradition of the 'amateur' who did not take money for what he did but could outperform the professional on the sports field. Similarly, the private gentleman scholar might make his contribution to learning from his own home, with his pen and his personal researches. Mr Casaubon in George Eliot's *Middlemarch*, though not in fact the most productive of scholars, might, in principle, have made discoveries to outrank anything achieved in a university. French universities are not always the main centres of French research. The 'professional' scholar who earns his living by teaching students has, historically, been a dim figure – poor, scruffy and not taken seriously in the world. The disinterested pursuit of knowledge is affected when value is not placed upon it. That is equally true whether what is in question is 'approval' or cash value. That does not mean that such work ceases; but it may become work done in a spirit of defiance, by persons disinclined to cooperate with the system.

The patterns of an earlier age are not of merely antiquarian interest. They are the norms of minds engaged in intellectual exploration, and they recur. When we find externally-imposed change seeking to reconstruct such ground rules for reasons which are not in themselves primarily scholarly, we are likely to see resistance, a conflict of interests at a profound level between academia and politics. The question then is who can (or should) call whom to account.

2

Rights and Responsibilities: Academic Freedom and Professional Ethics

Academic freedom

Academic freedom first meant freedom to think in peace, without the distractions of wordly commitments.[1] One of the features of the first universities was the progressive crowding of the syllabus. When Thomas Aquinas set about writing his *Summa Theologiae* in the thirteenth century he bewailed in his preface the hopeless proliferation of topics, the reduplication of effort, the confusion about the order in which things should be done. He put it all into order for systematic study. The problem was being created by the sheer success of the universities, the rush of students, the demand for degrees. In the 1980s something similar was visible in 'the modern "domesticated university" where the scope for sustained, reflective enquiry by the student would appear to be precluded by the continual alterations of subject demanded by timetables, essay requirements and over-full curricula'.[2] There is a case for providing free space for the student to think in, on the ground that this is itself a necessary condition of higher education. Experiments along this line usually prove disappointing in the short-term. 'Study weeks' are used by students to catch up on work neglected rather than to practise thinking like scholars. But that does not mean that there is not value in fostering a culture of 'philosophical leisure', a habit of taking time to take things in.

It has always been obvious to those who did it that serious scholarly writing takes time to mature. Varro in Cicero's *Academica* has a major work on hand (*habeo opus magnum in manibus*); he wants to make it more polished: *politius*. Cicero longs aloud for time and space to study.[3] There is a recognition in both Cicero and Augustine of the need for leisure, *otium*, both for inquiry and also for writing about the results. Augustine fulfilled a long-standing desire then he retired for a time to Cassiciacum with his friends. Newman, too, recognized the need for *otium* so that he could take the time he needed to get not only a proper grasp but also a proper understanding of the subject he was working on. He had to think it over, to reflect at leisure. He wrote to Edward Smedley on 10 February, 1826, of his 'hope of gaining more time for the consideration of the important matter which the history of the early Church contains and of which I have at present but very slender knowledge'.[4]

Time for reflection is not merely a personal luxury; it is a necessary condition of scholarly work. A PhD thesis is, in principle, three years' work, but it may well take longer and a doctoral student must be allowed extra time if he needs it in the interests of completing a better and more finished piece of work. It has become a commonplace complaint that one of the effects of the time constraints imposed by the Research Assessment Exercises was that short-term and hasty work is being published in preference to longer-term and more developed work.

There is, however, another, and perhaps in the end more important, need for space in which to do research, and that is the 'space' to move freely which is provided by the protection of freedom of thought and expression. That freedom is now up against controls some of which are without precedent in universities.

The case for academic freedom of speech is that unless research can be freely conducted as open-ended inquiry, without fear or favour, it cannot serve its proper purpose. It is, in other words, essential to the academic life.

What happens if everyone is allowed to say what he likes in the academic arena? For 'every idea is an incitement'.[5] Oliver Wendell Holmes thought that given free rein, 'free trade in ideas',[6] all ideas have a chance of becoming successful and compelling, and of shaping future attitudes and assumptions. The United States Constitution protects freedom of speech in the First Amendment: 'Congress shall make no law respecting an establishment of religion or abridging the freedom of speech or of the press; or the right of the people peaceably to assemble and to petition the Government for redress of grievances.'

But, however strong the legal protections of free speech, there will be circumstances in which that freedom can have undesirable social consequences, such as incitement to racial hatred. The law has, therefore, developed in ways which balance freedom against necessary limitations on freedom. Academic freedom of speech is defined in the 1988 Act as freedom *within the law*. It is not intended that being an academic employee should confer a freedom (for example) to incite to racial hatred.

Speech which is not formally restrained by rules may, nevertheless, be constrained in subtle ways by its consequences for the speaker's popularity or chances of promotion[7] or the success of his cause. For it is possible to be allowed to speak; but, in circumstances where there may be reprisals, to *prefer to refrain* from doing so. Strong words uttered in common rooms are choked back on committees where their utterance involves being known to have spoken thus by colleagues who may 'use it against you'. Or speech may be constrained by more hard-edged fears of dismissal. The Education Reform Act 1988 recognizes that that is a danger which will present itself on the removal of tenure under the same Act. The academic staff of UK universities have: 'freedom within the law to question and test received wisdom and to put forward new ideas and controversial or unpopular opinions *without placing themselves in jeopardy of losing their jobs'.* [8]

The primary intention of the protection in the 1988 Act would appear to be to prevent interference with freedom of research and inquiry within areas where a member of the academic staff is about his academic business. However, an academic may also wish to speak out about matters connected with the policy or the running of his university. Freedom of speech can thus also be used to *criticize* the running of the university in which the member of staff is employed.[9]

The tension is plain in one contract: Information about the College 'which would embarrass, harm or prejudice the College' may not be disclosed. 'Notwithstanding the above the College affirms that academic staff have freedom within the law to question and test received wisdom . . . etc'.

Here it may be less apparent that this is properly an 'academic' freedom. There has been some testing of this point in law. The leading 'academic freedom of speech' case so far has been in New Zealand: *Rigg v. University of Waikato* [1984] 1 N.Z.L.R. 149. The provisions of the section of the English Education Reform Act 1988 which protects freedom of speech were not, of course, in play. Nevertheless, the case raises key issues for the application of the Act.

In *Rigg* it was held, importantly, that 'the concept of academic freedom applied to University affairs generally and not simply to the discipline in which the academic was engaged'.[10] There is a warning in *Rigg* that if someone has criticized the university in which he is employed any dismissal must be demonstrably 'for reasons of a sufficiently weighty kind to offset any suggestion that he was being dismissed simply because he had dared to criticise'.[11] There is authority here to be weighed against the rule that an employee has a fiduciary duty to be loyal to his employer.[12]

Rigg has the disadvantage as a test case that the claim that freedom of speech must be honoured was weakened by evidence that it had been used irresponsibly. A lecturer, together with a graduate student, published an article which made accusations not only that the University had exposed students to danger of dying of cancer as a result of inadequate supervision of an isotope laboratory, but also that there had been a deliberate atttempt to cover this up and that the University considered students 'dispensable'.

The first allegation could readily be made out to be a proper raising of concerns, although it could be objected that the concern should have been raised internally first, and the University given an opportunity to investigate it. For the second allegation there appeared to be no foundation, and no evidence was brought to support it. That could be considered prima facie an irresponsible use of freedom of speech.

The irresponsibility proved more important here than whether what was said was true or not, for the unnecessary and unjustified vilification threw into question the intention of the authors. Had they meant only or principally to damage the institution? Had they acted in good faith? Rigg, the lecturer, accepted that the article had been 'ill-advised and unjustified' and he apologized. The question the court then had to address was whether the apology was sincere, because upon that hung whether he was likely to repeat the offence or commit one like it in the future. It appeared beyond question that if freedom of speech had been exercized in such a way as to allow something which was untrue as well as damaging to be alleged about the institution, that would not have been a proper exercise of that freedom.

An attempt was also made here to explore the *reasonableness* of the opinions expressed as a test of a proper intention: 'many of the opinions were unreasonable and . . . the emotive wording of the article compounded the lack of accuracy which is apparent in much of the article'.[13]

The concept of academic freedom was usefully taken apart during this case, which tested it hard. It was looked at especially in connection with an idea of a duty of 'responsibility'. It was held by Sir David Beattie, the Visitor of the University of Waikato, that 'freedom involved a responsibility to ensure that criticism was both reasoned and fair'.[14] 'Going hand in hand with . . . academic freedom there is a widely-recognised need for responsibility', said the Commissaries in *Rigg*, citing among other sources the *Association of University Teachers (UK) Bulletin* (1974) (No. 54, p. 8): 'The purposes of higher education cannot be fulfilled unless all those concerned in it are free, independent and critical in their work and pursue it with integrity, scholarship and a sense of responsibility.'

The recent Chris Bland case has provided a similar test in the further arena of comment on public or politically sensitive issues. This lecturer at the University of Edinburgh expressed views many considered to be politically unacceptable in themselves, and which may have been in danger of crossing the boundaries of what he was free to say within the law. The University began by refraining from disciplining him on the grounds that he had the academic's right to freedom of speech. However, he went on to other subjects, and was eventually felt to have crossed a line. Some of the things he said gave offence. For example, to argue that there are innate intellectual differences between races is, to many minds, on the verge of racism, but if it is a statement which its author claims he made on the basis of scientific research, then he is making it as a scholar. An academic may wish to speak freely only about his work as a scholar or teacher, and that is, in itself, a great matter, and essential to doing his job. He may wish to speak on public affairs, and the 'speech' may then be political. However, sometimes, as in this case, the subject matter inescapably makes it both.

In the United States, the First Amendment protects freedom of speech, but it has become the custom for universities to devise codes of permitted speech designed to protect against the giving of offence. With the First Amendment hovering: 'If campus speech restrictions at public universities cover not merely epithets but speech that is part of social deliberation, they might be . . . unconstitutional.'[15]

The most notorious recent examples concern the use of sexually inclusive language and the avoidance of any statement which might be deemed offensive to women or racial minorities or the disabled – that is, to those deemed in some way to be in a weak or disadvantaged position in society. However, to do that is to restrict the freedom of speech of those who wish to make such statements. So are campus speech codes constitutional? A certain amount depends on whether the campus is that of a public or private university.

> To the extent that we are dealing with private universities, the Constitution is not implicated at all, and hence all such restrictions are permissible. Private universities can do whatever they like. They can ban all speech . . . by anyone they want to silence. [But] public universities are subject to the Constitution, and so it is important to try to establish what the First Amendment means for them.[16]

UK universities have gone much less far down this road, but it is now becoming customary for them to produce codes of behaviour in the hope of preventing harassment or bullying or victimization.[17] These inevitably include restrictions on what one person may say to another, even if only in terms of the recipient of the free speech being entitled to object to hearing it.

So freedom to speak as an academic but about matters which overflow the academic's area of expertise, takes us into a grey area, and raises questions as yet only partly resolved.

Trade secrets

Another area where there is potential conflict between an academic's statutory freedom of speech and the privileges or rights of his employer is that of the law governing the confidentiality of trade secrets. Here, 'new university' contracts in the UK frequently appear to create difficulties for the scholar who wishes to share his work freely with other scholars. Here is an example:

1. Duties include:
   - undertaking an agreed number of days per year of research . . . *for the sponsoring organisation*
   - undertaking activities to enhance the reputation of the faculty for research, including . . . the organisation of events to raise the College profile in the academic community
   - promoting and implementing *the corporate policies* of the College
2. The make-up of your duties will be determined . . . by your Dean
3. Your research and scholarly activity will be *principally* self-managed. In addition, these activities . . . will be considered as part of the staff appraisal and development system, under which *objectives for the coming year . . . can be set and achievements over the past year . . . can be assessed.*

4. 'The College will . . . decide [if external work will] compete or conflict with the interests of the College, in which case *the College may at its sole discretion require you not to undertake the work*' (emphasis added).

There is a visible cultural gulf here, between the kinds of management objective these obligations evince, and the reality of the research experience. There is also an assumption that a university as employer owns work it has paid for, as, indeed, in some sense it does. The central difficulty is that intellectual property law was devised for the commercial, not the academic, scene. However, the 'ownership' questions can be complex, for example, in multifunder situations where some persons on a given research project are employees of the University and others of research council or commercial funder. Oxford University in the mid-1990s would offer a contract to academic-related staff which incorporated by reference whatever was laid down from time to time in the Statutes and Ordinances. The University asserted its ownership of patentable and non-patentable inventions, University-commissioned works and works generated by the University's computers; computer software and firmware which 'may reasonably be considered to possess commercial potential'; registered and unregistered designs and topographies. The University did not assert ownership of copyright books, articles, lectures, or other written work apart from that which was commissioned by the University. In the same period the Medical Research Council merely required declaration of any existing commitment to:

> any person or organisation (including commercial concerns, government bodies or former employers) for the development or commercial exploitation of the results of discoveries or inventions, whether patentable or not, or for the provision of information or advice in a consultant capacity or for research collaboration which might lead to commercial exploitation by another body.

The concern in both cases is clearly with commercial exploitation, and nothing is said about any tension with an academic's freedom of speech. But that tension exists, indeed it is acute, especially for many scientists.

If we put the two problem areas together, we can see that a scientist hamstrung by restrictions and at the mercy of patronage for future funding, may well fear to speak out when he sees something which concerns him in the running of a university, or its financing. 'Members of staff often feel, rightly or wrongly, that their own position in the University will be jeopardised if they raise such concerns . . . and sometimes the usual channels may, indeed, be inappropriate . . . Any reprisals against or victimisation of the person reporting the concern will be treated by the University as a serious disciplinary matter', says the Hull University *Policy on the reporting of serious malpractice or abuse* (1997) in an honourable attempt to curb the damaging consequences to an individual of honest whistleblowing.

Professional ethics

The ethics of scholarship

If we are to take a high line about the functions and uses and value of scholarship, we need to give thought to its ethics. First we have to establish that the scholarly task has a moral dimension.

The taking of educational policy-decisions and the detailed carrying out of educational activities, would both seem susceptible to moral evaluation. That is partly because they affect the welfare and the future of those who are taught; therefore of persons in a vulnerable and dependent position.[18] In a civilised society there must at least be a requirement that powers over such persons are not abused. By extension there must be an ethical requirement of protection for the teacher who seeks to defend a student's interests against any pressures which might discourage him from doing so.

The same ethical concern properly belongs to scholarship (understood as research or enquiry), but for different reasons. There the moral context is created by the need for a respect for truth and integrity to be maintained in carrying out the activities of scholarship. For example, it may be held that no scholar ought to distort the truth because his paymaster tells him to; nor ought he to modify what he honestly understands to be the truth, so as to fit current orthodoxies. Nor ought he to teach what he recognizes to be lies to his pupils.

There are other 'oughts'. When a scholar is teaching, he arguably 'ought' to be considering the good of the minds he is addressing, and when he is doing research he arguably 'ought' to be thinking about the truthfulness of what he is doing.

It is this inward ethics of scholarship with which the characters are concerned in Dorothy Sayers' *Gaudy Night*, a novel set in an Oxford women's college in the middle of the twentieth century. They discuss several of the classic issues of scholarly ethics. Should a scholar call a halt to an inquiry if what he finds out is dangerous? 'Establish the facts, no matter what comes of it.'[19] 'If we mayn't establish any conclusion for fear somebody should make an injudicious use of it, we are back in the days of Galileo. There would be an end to discovery.' "Well," said the Dean, "I wish we could stop discovering things like poison gas." '

Are there further constraints of an ethical kind upon the sharing of the results of research, once they are discovered to be 'dangerous knowledge'? ' "There can be no objection to the making of discoveries," said Miss Hillyard, "but is it always expedient to publish them? In the case of Galileo, the Church . . ." "You'll never get any scientist to agree there," broke in Miss Edwards. "To suppress a fact is to publish a falsehood." '[20]

Are there proper ethical considerations upon the individual scholar which relate not to the public interest in the results of his work, but to his own sense of its integrity? 'He had grown enamoured of his own theory and couldn't bear to give it up.' "That's the mark of an unsound scholar, I'm afraid," said Miss Lydgate in a mournful tone, as one speaks of incurable cancer.'[21]

Are such considerations of personal conscience of a lower or higher order than considerations of public interest? 'If it ever occurs to people to value the honour of the mind equally with the honour of the body, we shall get a social revolution of a quite unparalleled sort – and very different from the kind that is being made at the moment.'[22]

Is an 'honest' error morally neutral? Does it cease to be morally neutral when its perpetrator knows it to be an error?

> The only ethical principle which has made science possible is that the truth shall be told all the time. If we do not penalise false statements made in error, we open up the way for false statements by intention. And a false statement of fact, made deliberately is the most serious crime a scientist can commit.[23]

Are there circumstances in which conscious scholarly falsehood could be justified? 'A false statement is published, and the man who could correct it lets it go, out of charitable considerations. Would anybody here do that?'[24] In that conversation the participants lean strongly towards a purist ethic of scholarly truth. But much worse things than poison gas have since been let loose on the world by scientific curiosity.

Integrity

'A bad picture by a good painter is a betrayal of truth – his own truth.' "That's only a relative kind of truth," objected Miss Edwards.'[25] The moral imperatives for the scholar begin with the integrity of the person. We need to begin with constraints upon the individual, because minds are ultimately separate, however they may choose to work together or succeed in influencing one another.

The concept of integrity contains both the idea of a lack of contamination by the relevant vices and the notion of a wholeness or 'completeness of possession' of the virtues. John Henry Newman points out that there is no word in English like 'health' for the body or 'virtue' for the moral nature, which can describe 'a good state of mind' in the intellectual or scholarly sense.[26] He means something which embraces the command of the skill; and also the integrity (in both senses) with which it is exercised. The idea is close to that of the mediaeval *habitus*, though it is unlikely that Newman had that in mind. Newman does not emphasize the need to remain free of the opposing vices of incompetence and intellectual dishonesty. But his image of health automatically carries that stipulation, for the possession of virtue implies the exclusion of vice.

The idea of 'formation' which developed in the mediaeval western Christian spiritual tradition is helpful here. This making and maturing of a mind belonged originally in a context of the moral and religious expectation of the way intellectual powers will be used. 'A habit of mind is formed which lasts through life, of which the attributes are, freedom, equitableness, calmness, moderation, and wisdom.'[27] Newman, who evidently did have a sense of this, also thought the 'formed' mind would have certain skills. He speaks of 'the formation, and consequent grasp, of the intellect'.[28]

It may be that scholarly skills and qualities exist of which it might perhaps be asserted that they have no moral coloration or content, except that of seeking to be true to themselves, in some such sense as that of meeting certain standards in their exercise. Newman gives a lively account of the behaviour of minds which lack the qualities with which he holds that a university education ought to have imbued them. Some 'have no difficulty in contradicting themselves in successive sentences, without being conscious of it . . . others can never look straight before them, never see the point . . . others are hopelessly obstinate and prejudiced, and, after they have been driven from their opinions, return to them the next moment without even an attempt to explain why'.[29] Clarity, sound reasoning, freedom from prejudice are generally recognized as desirable attributes or skills of a trained mind. 'Our desideratum is . . . the force, the steadiness, the comprehensiveness and the versatility of intellect, the command over our own powers, the instinctive just estimate of things as they pass before us.'[30] Out of a professional distaste the possessor of these intellectual skills ought to find it hard to be 'muddled', though that does not in itself hold him back from the use of his skills for devious purposes. There needs to be relevance, a skill in pinpointing the issue and dealing with it purposefully. There needs to be clarity, both in the framing of the problem and in the proposing of solutions. All these are aspects of the rationality Aristotle would speak of in this context.[31] But there are other virtues, more apparent on the modern scene.

'The "law of studies" does link free inquiry inseparably with intellectual honesty', [32] argues Pelikan. He is making a point about the need for a series of relationships between and among the attributes of the scholarly calling, which provide it with its internal checks and balances. The guiding restraint of honesty embraces a respect for things as they are discovered to be, by the best means of enquiry available, open-mindedly arrived at, all hypotheses discarded if they prove unsound on the evidence. Honesty submits to the truth and admits error if it later finds it has been wrong. It speaks the truth even when there is no chance of being found out in a fabrication of the evidence. 'Research in any field of knowledge is still predicated on the assumption that it could be authenticated through repetition by any other trained investigator with access to the same data.'[33] That is the normative restraint. However, there are circumstances in which it may not operate (the experience cannot be duplicated; the manuscript is destroyed in a fire), and then the only restraint is an internal and moral one, a 'duty to truth'.

There needs to be order, for although discoveries may well be fortuitous, it has to be possible to duplicate the experiment or explain what has been found. (That is a different thing from rationalizing after the event in order to make the facts fit a desired outcome. That is something all exercises of discretion, not excluding professional judgements, are subejct to. Examiners and promotions committees and appointments committees can operate to preferred outcomes consciously or unconsciously.)

All this implies a set of standards about methods of enquiry in which there is a check of integrity. Freedom to write what one wishes could allow room for plagiarism if there was not a consciousness of a duty to acknowledge sources. Plagiarism, or at least accusation of plagiarism, is a swelling problem in higher education. At one level it is a simple matter of understanding the rules. Students not taught to footnote what they borrow may not realize that they are plagiarizing. But if the borrowing is from unpublished work, matters are more complex. That can go in either direction, with a research student using ideas or knowledge got from conversation with a supervisor about the supervisor's own research. Or a supervisor – especially in the sciences – may use a student's discoveries without acknowledgement or take credit for them. There are real difficulties here, in relation to the patterns of ownership of ideas and outcomes in teamwork in scientific laboratories which we shall come to later.

Honesty without freedom is impotent, or at best struggles to manifest itself; there can be constraints upon freedom of expression, which prevent the revealing of truths.

Intellectual virtues may need to be tough, because intellectual honesty can be professionallly costly. What is it a duty to resist? In what circumstances is 'a declaration of educational independence called for'?

Professional misconduct

In *R. v. Visitors to Lincoln's Inn, ex parte Calder* and *Same v. Same, ex parte Persaud* [1992] W.L.R. 994 two barristers sought judicial review of the decisions of visitors in cases where they had been found guilty of professional misconduct by a disciplinary tribunal of the Council of the Inns of Court, and had subsequently appealed to the visitors. These cases, which are important principally in relation to questions of visitorial jurisdiction, are also useful in connection with the concept of *professional* misconduct. This is a familiar notion in the arena of medicine and law but is not usually employed with reference to academics.

However, if there is a concept of a 'professional academic judgement' so peculiar to academe that universities cannot properly be interfered with in their exercise of it,[34] there must logically also be a concept of academic '*professional* conduct'. There must be an element of 'good conduct' in being any sort of professional if it is possible to talk of appropriate or proper or adequate discharge of professional tasks and the making of reliable professional judgements.

One of the questions it may certainly be appropriate to ask on the admission of a qualified person to professional practice is whether he is a 'fit and proper' person. *Re Justices of the Court of Common Pleas at Antigua* (1830) I Knapp 267 shows that where no formal arrangements existed, it was found to be essential for judges to be able to determine who were fit and proper persons to practise law. Lord Wynford said (at 268) that 'it is essential for the due administration of justice that some persons should have authority to determine, who are fit persons to practise as advocates and attornies there'.[35] This is deemed to be inalienably a judicial duty. The benchers of the Inns of Court are only 'the agents of the judges in calling to the Bar'.[36] The expression 'fit and proper persons' was used again much more recently in *R v. Benchers of Gray's Inn*, I Doug 353 at 354 [1970] I Q.B. 160 (at 170, *per* Paull J.): 'The professions generally still insist that their members and student members should be "fit and proper" persons.'[37]

The question remains whether this fitness and propriety necessarily involves moral considerations, or whether it simply has to do with professional standards of skill. On the showing of doctors, good professional conduct may properly be deemed to include things other than the relevant technical skills.

The General Medical Council provides doctors with a code of conduct which is exemplary in its clarity and brevity.

Duties of a doctor

- make the care of your patient your first concern;
- treat every patient politely and considerately;
- respect patients' dignity and privacy;
- listen to patients and respect their views;
- give patients information in a way they can understand;
- respect the rights of patients to be fully involved in decisions about their care;
- keep your professional knowledge and skills up to date;
- recognize the limits of your professional competence;
- be honest and trustworthy
- respect and protect confidential information
- make sure that your personal beliefs do not prejudice your patients' care;
- act quickly to protect patients from risk if you have good reason to believe that you or a colleague may not be fit to practise;
- avoid abusing your position as a doctor; and
- work with colleagues in the ways that best serve patients' interests.

In all these matters, you must never discriminate unfairly against your patients or colleagues. And you must always be prepared to justify your actions to them.[38]

Both a doctor and an academic have duties towards people who depend upon their integrity and their maintenance of professional standards. If we substitute 'student' for 'patient' and 'lecturer' for 'doctor' in the code we get quite a close fit. But there are additional dimensions in the work of a lecturer, to do with the responsibility to communicate knowledge and to equip the student to become a 'professional' in the same scholarly profession himself. That requires:

- a concern not only for the person but also for truth;
- a respect for the rights of others to independence of thought;
- a respect for others;
- control of their own work;
- scrupulousness in acknowledging others' work when using it in one's own;
- courage in defending one's own freedom of expression;
- concern to protect freedom of expression for others;
- generosity in sharing knowledge;
- conscientiousness in the preparation of the content of taught courses;
- critical receptiveness to new ideas.

Misconduct and gross misconduct

The forms of 'professional misconduct' recently under discussion in academic life in actual cases are not, as a rule, of the sort which involves abuse of professional position – with the exception of cases of harassment or racial or sexual discrimination. Several things appear to be happening beyond that range which is covered by statutory protections.

Under the Education Reform Act 1988, s. 202, which removes tenure from members of academic staff of universities whose contracts begin after 1987, there is provision for dismissal on the grounds of redundancy, or 'good cause' (defined as 'a reason which is related to his conduct or his capability or qualifications for performing work of the kind which he was appointed or employed to do'). 'Capability . . . means capability assessed by reference to skill, aptitude, health or any other physical or mental quality; and qualification . . . means any degree, diploma or other academic, technical or professional qualification relevant to the office or position held by him.'

There are problems in both these areas, especially in that of health. The institution which has allowed an employee to be bullied into breakdown may then be able to dismiss him on ill-health grounds, although it was itself the cause of the ill-health. A lecturer who, in those circumstances, seeks to get a medical report confirming that he is suffering from stress or breakdown, may find that evidence turned against him and not against his employer.[39]

By far the most important area of difficulty, however, lies in the definition of 'misconduct'. For a lecturer can be disciplined and ultimately dismissed for misconduct and gross misconduct. These offences are imperfectly defined within institutions, and such definitions as do exist vary from institution to institution. In practice, the 'misconduct' may involve no more than questioning the view of the instructions of a 'line manager' or seeking to raise concerns. There is clearly some way to go to achieve a comparability which can lay a groundwork for fairness and consistency in the treatment of lecturers accused of misconduct or gross misconduct.

Here is one code:

8.5 Examples of Behaviour Constituting Gross Misconduct

This list is not intended to be exclusive or exhaustive and offences of a similar gravity will receive the same treatment.

8.5.1 Dishonesty associated with the place of work or job being undertaken.

8.5.2 Deliberate refusal to carry out reasonable lawful and safe instructions of [*sic*] the normal agreed duties of the job.

8.5.3 Gross negligence in failing to attend to, or carry out, the normal agreed duties of the job.

8.5.4 Serious infringements of safety rules or other negligent actions which seriously place the health and safety of other persons in danger.

8.5.5 Wilful unauthorised disclosure of information classified as strictly confidential which could be harmful to the University, its students or employees by other employees who in the course of duty have access to such information, e.g. personal information on employees, students, etc.

The latter is clearly subject to proper constraints, since it can never be acceptable to expose individuals in that way. However, information classified as confidential to the University might include misappropriation or misuse of funds, or something otherwise embarrassing to its management, and to discipline or dismiss an employee who seeks to bring something of that sort to light would be an act of reprisal against a conscientious whistleblower of a kind which the Nolan Committee frowns on in its *Second Report* and the Public Interest (Disclosure) Act of 1998 outlaws.

8.5.6 Acts of violence or vandalism in the course of employment.

8.5.7 Sexual or racial harassment or misconduct at work.

8.5.8 Relevant off-duty misconduct including bringing the University into disrepute.

8.6 Examples of Behaviour Constituting Misconduct

8.6.1 Absenteeism and Lateness.

8.6.2 Dishonesty.

8.6.3 Off-duty misconduct that results in loss of credibility.

8.6.4 Neglect of duty.

8.6.5 Abusive behaviour and/or offensive language at the workplace which is directed at Governors, senior officers, colleagues, students or members of the public.

Behaviour patterns may vary in different work settings and thus an act of discourtesy within one workplace may not be regarded as such in another.

The distinction of ranks is striking here, if it implies that there is one law for the junior and one for the senior.

8.6.6 Victimisation of other employees in the course of duty.
8.6.7 Unlawful discrimination against other employees in the course of duty.
8.6.8 Unlawful discrimination against other employees or members of the public in the course of duty.
8.6.9 Undertaking without prior approval, additional employment outside normal working hours which is detrimental to the work performed as an employee of the University.[40]

No one could quarrel with the definition of a number of these things as misconduct (not doing one's job, victimization or discrimination). But 'loss of credibility' seems a dangerously vague concept. Part of the problem seem to lie in a failure to be clear about the nature of these various 'conduct' offences, and to think them through.

Not doing the job properly: the ethics of the behaviour of the employee of a university

The relationship between unlawful conduct and misconduct (a private, contractual offence) is a grey area in disciplinary codes in higher education. In most disciplinary codes in universities there is some provision as to what is to be done by the institution if an employee commits a criminal offence of which he is found guilty in a court. But there is a wide band of possible behaviour which might not be actionable thus or in tort, but for which the university may seek to discipline the individual.

There is, not infrequently, a movement from disciplining an employee for misconduct to seeking to show that he is ill or incapable and to dismissing him on that ground, or vice versa. There might be a genuine overlap, between not being able to do the job properly because of illness (to which no fault would be attached) and a lack of capability arising from imperfect qualification or other lack of the skills needed. Illness leading to incapability can be self-inflicted – for example, chronic alcoholism. It would then be less clear that there was no blame and so less clear that the route to be taken was 'medical' not 'disciplinary'. A clinically depressed person might, on the other hand, in circumstances for which he was not to blame, be repeatedly absent or late or fail to keep up with his work. Mental disturbance could lead to misconduct. Physical illness could lead to incompetence.

The question would seem to be whether there is blameworthiness. On that would turn whether the appropriate response was punitive or compassionate. This can be crucial to the procedure to be adopted in dealing with the case. For if there is an allegation of misconduct the matter becomes disciplinary. It would presumably in any case be necessary in such a case for the charges to be specified at least sufficiently far to make it possible to say whether the accusation was one of misconduct or of incompetence, and for the accused to be given a chance to reply in case it should turn out that the matter was to be taken as disciplinary. This kind of fudging – often unconscious and arising from failure on the part of administrators to see clearly – has allowed procedurally misconducted hearings under discipline and grievance and appeal procedures to take place throughout higher education in the 1990s.[41] It has been surprisingly difficult to call those responsible to account.

Institutional ethics and misconduct of the employer in the person of a senior officer

Institutions do not 'behave' well or badly; that takes people. When an 'institution' misconducts itself what has actually happened is that a person or persons in senior positions have abused powers which go with their seniority. That is misconduct, and serious misconduct. In practice, it is much less likely that complaints of misconduct or gross misconduct will be made of a senior, while a senior may well level them as charges against a junior.

However, seniors as well as juniors are employees, and a first and very important question is whether seniority should protect from the consequences of misconduct. Similarly, if breakdown of working relations is alleged, the junior is far more likely to be the employee dismissed. Yet, breakdown of relations is a two-way happening, and it is unjust for a situation which may have been created by bullying by a senior to result in dismissal of a junior.

It is clearly important that it should, in principle, be possible to call any officer of a university to account, and some provision is usually notionally present. But it tends to be of the top-down sort – for instance a vice-chancellor may be called to account by a chairman of the board of governors or a chancellor. It can be impossible in practice for a junior to call a senior to account; it took a good deal of time and media pressure to bring about the removal of chief executives as happened at Bournemouth, Portsmouth, Southampton Institute and Huddersfield in the 1990s, and other heads rolled in the process.

Mutual trust between doctors and patients and between doctors in their treatment of one another as colleagues is much stressed throughout the General Medical Council's guidance on *Duties of a doctor*. A lecturer ought to be able to expect to treat and be treated by his institution on a similar 'collegial' basis of mutual respect. That requires at least:

1. that the 'master–servant' relationship, inseparable from the contract of employment, should be modified by the requirement that those who act on behalf of the employer should also behave collegially in their treatment of their fellow lecturers by treating them as equals;
2. that line management structures will not be used as a means of control but only for purposes of efficient administration;

3. that there should be means of direct access to those in the most senior positions by their juniors when someone has a concern to express, with protection against reprisal for the subordinate or those in insecure positions;
4. that the institution will keep its own rules in the implementation of discipline and grievance procedures and other codes of practice it adopts.

Bringing the institution into disrepute

Another aspect of the question of professional conduct in connection with an institution concerns 'bringing the institution into disrepute'.[42] The 'person' being protected from defamation cannot be a municipal corporation.[43] It is not clear whether that means that defamation cannot be claimed when it is contended that a lecturer had brought an institution in which he works 'into disrepute'; but that is an allegation on the basis of which disciplinary procedures are commonly invoked.

There is a question whether, if an institution deserves to be brought into disrepute, it should be able to protect itself against that being made plain in a public forum. The Nolan Committee emphasizes in its *second report* that protecting itself from embarrassment is not a legitimate reason for a university to apply a gag.

For it to be an offence to bring a university into disrepute there must be some assumption that its reputation is of value to it. Reputation has to do with the opinion of others, and in the case of a university that must be above all public opinion, and the good opinion of the community of scholarship. The ethical questions which arise here concern an academic's duty to act according to conscience in any matter where he has standing, for that may arguably extend to the protection of the deeper good of the university – its fulfilment of its scholarly, educational, academic purpose. He may have a duty to ask awkward questions, if he believes it is failing there, even if he causes it embarrassment and even damage in the short-term.

3

Value for Money

Scientific research can rarely be done without expense. It needs laboratories and, increasingly, the support of powerful computing facilities. The necessary funding comes less and less from the public purse and, even where it does, someone has to choose which projects to fund. Funding from commercial or charitable sponsors also has to be competed for. This chapter is concerned with the power games that can result, for there may be a wish to ensure desirable outcomes and a contest for control of the profits.

Freedom of inquiry

Statutory protection of freedom of speech within the law is provided (in England and Wales only) by section 43(1) of the Education (No. 2) Act 1986. This is designed primarily to provide a means of striking a balance between liberty and order when student unions and organizations behave obstructively or riotously, for example, in protesting against a visiting speaker because they disapprove of his views. However, it provides that 'every individual and body of persons concerned in the government of any . . . [university or college] . . . shall take such steps as are reasonably practicable to ensure that freedom of speech with the law is secured for members, students and employees of the establishment and for visiting speakers'. This would appear to extend the protection afforded under the Education Reform Act 1988 to academic and certain academic-related staff, to include students and all employees.[1]

The Education Reform Act 1988 gives 'freedom of speech within the law' specifically (and only?) to academic staff, for the purpose of 'questioning received wisdom'. Such freedom is clearly central to the purposes of their employment if they are to undertake research. That implies that academic staff are taken to need at least that freedom of speech which goes with their professional role. If there is a special 'academic' freedom of speech, scholarship must enjoy a certain privilege here.

Freedom to teach is a consideration in its own right in this arena. It raises special and additional difficulties, since the taught are, by definition, in a vulnerable position because they cannot have the knowledge which would allow them to test for themselves the 'wisdom' which is being imparted to them or challenged by their teachers as 'received'. And there are further problems to do with the attempts to prescribe the syllabus; to impose 'politically correct' usage; and with the ethics of refraining from attempts at indoctrination.

Our main concern in this section, though, is with a freedom of expression which academics may wish to claim in speaking about their own original work. Freedom of speech and freedom of inquiry would both seem to be covered by the 1988 Act's wording about freedom to question and test received wisdom.[2] If freedom of inquiry is a form of freedom of speech, it has another justification than that which is enshrined in the US First Amendment. There the main concern (for historical reasons) is with freedom of *conscience.*

The two were often coupled in the mediaeval disputes about freedom of speech in universities, because those mainly concerned allegations of the teaching of heresy, to which the dissident would rejoin that his conscience required him to question the Church's teaching in the interests of what he saw to be the true faith. Whatever the rights or wrongs of the views being put forward, such courageous stands were not always successful. In 1381 a committee of 12 persons set up in the University of Oxford to look into the teachings of Wyclif came to its conclusions. The Chancellor, William Barton and Robert Rygge, the next Chancellor (from 1382), were both members. A messenger was sent to interrupt Wyclif as he lectured on one of the very subjects on which they had condemned his opinions. Wyclif resisted, arguing that the committee had not been unanimous, but had voted against him only 7:5.[3] Gradually, however, he withdrew from the University.[4]

Freedom of inquiry is freedom to speak to oneself about what one is doing. Self-education within a university[5] includes freedom to equip oneself with any sort of existing knowledge as well as freedom to find out something new. If a scholar wants to learn something, he goes and finds out. He makes his own map for study. He may read, do experiments, talk to experts in the field, or go to conferences to discover what others are doing.

That process of exploration can be curbed by denying access to books or to other living minds, for example, by instructing other scholars and teachers not to communicate with the inquirer. That was the method of censorship in earlier centuries. In the late twentieth-century West, restriction of inquiry takes other and less overt and frank forms. Inquiry can also be curbed by financial sanctions and by the use or abuse of patent-rights and the intellectual property-rights of copyright control.

In practice, researchers in the humanities enjoy a greater freedom here than scientists. A scientist needs more than access to libraries, a pen and paper. He is dependent on substantial funding to do a series of properly set-up experiments. Scientific equipment can be hugely expensive, especially in the molecularly based sciences,[6] so that denial of funding can end-stop a piece of research.

Further, although scholars in both the arts and the sciences have contracts under which a University may exercise its ownership of the copyright of their work,[7] the writer of a book on an arts subject is likely to be free to enjoy his royalties and treat the copyright in his work as if it were his own. The scientist may not, for a complex of reasons we shall come to in a moment, but prominent among these reasons is the scale of the financial investment in him needed if he is to do the work at all.

There has, again, been a consciousness of change in the last decade or so. In 1989, a Reader in the University of Cambridge sent this letter to the Secretary General of the Faculties there:

> A University officer, however senior, is no longer to be regarded primarily as a partner in a joint endeavour but more as an employee who has to render account to some supposedly superior body . . .
>
> I much regret this change, which I find inimical to the kind of academic work I most admire and have tried to emulate . . . The trouble is that whereas formerly it would not have occurred to me to separate my academic activities into those which are the business of the University and those which are not, such a separation now becomes inevitable. In other words, there are aspects of my scientific life which in the new climate of opinion are simply not the business of the University *qua* my employer.
>
> Let me give you an example . . . One of the best-known and most fundamental diagrams in my subject is the famous three-ring Venn Diagram for three sets, first used by John Venn of Caius College in 1880; For over a hundred years no one had seen how this diagram could be generalised to depict an arbitrary number of sets. Four or five could be managed, but more than that seemed impossible.
>
> On the morning of Wednesday, 31st August 1988, which is about as deep into the Long Vacation as one can get, sitting in the living-room of my own house I discovered the general solution . . . Any other contribution I may have made during 1987–8, or for several years previously for that matter, will probably pale into insignificance beside this one, but the point I wish to make is that insofar as I can see, under the new relationship the discovery is no business of the University. It was not made at the behest of any University body as part of any programme of research, it was not made on University premises or using University equipment. Even my background knowledge of the topic is drawn from my own library.
>
> I should never have had these thoughts ten years ago, but now they are forced upon me by an increasingly hostile environment. You mention that other Professors and Readers have included in their reports work for learned societies and participation in conferences. But the University does not pay my subscriptions to learned societies, which I

attend in my own right, or, for the most part, my travel and conference expenses.[8]

To the labourer in the humanities working in his own home or in libraries to which he has access (in Oxford and Cambridge), by a lifetime right which does not depend upon his continuing employment in one of those universities, dependent upon no grant to enable him to finish a series of experiments, it must seem that his work is intimately his own. He may reflect that he would be doing it anyway, for the love of it, employed or not. Even the bread and butter he eats is likely to be partly paid for by fees and royalties which he earns by himself, on the merits of his published work and his skills and expertise as a consultant. He may wish to be free to give his time and work freely and unpaid on committees which write documents and reports, without having to charge a fee which he can pass on to his employer. (Doing it for free has two senses: not only doing it out of generosity and sheer interest in the task in hand; but also doing it unconstrained, that is, not under orders. Doing it for fun is important to that, as is doing it out of dedication.)

A series of assumptions many scholars would, up until now, have made without reflection, had simply not been brought up against hard testing. The hard testing has arrived, as scholars discover what happens when they seek to get on with work which strong vested interests wish to curb; when they want to speak out in protest at changes they deem to be educationally ill-advised; when they seek to defend others whom they see being crushed in the machine.

Freedom to publish: intellectual property, copyright and patents

Scholars work in a community, which has among its attributes an expectation that knowledge will be shared. Is there a: 'moral obligation to convey the results of research to others, an imperative of communicating that corresponds to the indicative of knowing'? Both the results of university research and the data on which it is based should be public,[9] insists Jaroslav Pelikan.

That is to argue, again, that the individual scholar has not ownership of knowledge, but stewardship. It is further to hold that such stewardship cannot be, either at institutional or at individual level, merely a function of custodianship. This is not just a question of holding on to knowledge. [Knowledge] 'must not be passively received, but actually and actively entered into, embraced, mastered'.[10] It must also be disseminated. 'By its insistence on the communication of the results of research, the university likewise proclaims the intellectual virtue of affirming the continuity of the intellectual and scholarly life, upon which each generation builds and to which it contributes in turn.'[11]

So much for the ideal. It sits uncomfortably with the provisions of the law. In 1990, Betty J. Dong, a researcher at the University of California Medical Center in San Francisco, reported the results of a study which appeared to show that several generic levothyroxine preparations were bioequivalent to the more expensive one, Synthyroid, marketed by Boots Pharmaceuticals. Boots, who were acquired by Knoll Pharmaceutical in 1995, set about discrediting the results, and Knoll followed suit. Dong was not able to publish her results until April 1997 (in the *Journal of the American Medical Association*).

The attack was not merely upon the methods used and the scientific credibility of the work; it also took the form of trying to damage Dong professionally by writing to the Vice-Chancellor and Heads of Department of her University. The University of California San Francisco conducted inquiries and found that the research had been 'rigorously conducted'. The attempt to discredit the work therefore failed.

The would-be controllers of its publication tried another tack, using the law of confidentiality.[12] The paper was submitted for publication and accepted in 1994, but had to be withdrawn because Boots threatened legal action on the basis of Dong's signature of a restrictive covenant: 'Data obtained by the investigator while carrying out this study is also considered confidential and is not to be published or otherwise released without written consent.'

In the end, the President of Knoll wrote to the journal's editor to say that the company had decided to allow publication:

> first because we gained a better understanding of the importance of supporting academic freedom and the peer review process; and second, we were concerned that intense media speculation about the study's findings and conclusions was being regarded as fact. Clearly the manuscript needed to be published so the study and our concerns about it could be evaluated in the proper context.[13]

The publishing journal's editor commented: 'When industry get in bed with academia, their agendas and their backgrounds are so different that you'd better be damn careful that you don't end up with suppression of unfavourable results or – worse – dangerous results.'

In a survey in the *Journal of the American Medical Association* (16 April 1997), David Blumenthal found that of the academic life scientists who replied to his questionnaire a high proportion admitted delaying publication of data for more than six months. Their motives were various, from the pragmatic need to give themselves time to prepare patent applications to wanting to keep ahead of competitors and holding back results which were not what they had hoped.[14] Of these motivations, the most striking for our purposes is the perception of the need to preserve a competitive edge, to get ahead of other researchers in the same field. Scientific discovery can move with a rapidity which makes such delays deleterious to the progress of the subject as a whole.

An important further lesson of all this is that an employer or sponsor cannot own someone's mind, and expertise consists in something more than the possession of a knowledge of the latest outcomes.

The law on intellectual property in the UK is much concerned with copyright.[15] The rights of the 'owner' of copyright chiefly consist in deciding whether or not copies may be made and on what terms,[16] but they include making 'an adaptation of the work' or preventing its being made.[17] Copyright protection also applies to unfinished works. This is designed to protect the rights of those who commission work and who have a commercial interest in the results. It was not primarily designed for an academic context, although it may fit that context better where commercial interests have become involved.

Commercial sponsors can protect their financial interests, by patent. Patenting has to be done country by country, except in Europe where a European patent can be obtained. To protect an invention throughout the world it is necessary to take out patents in every country separately, or through the filing of an international patent application. All this takes time and while a patent is pending, work can be frozen.

The would-be patentee has to be careful to preserve his unique or special knowledge of that which he seeks to patent. To publish an article or a letter in a journal, to give a paper at a conference, to place information on the Internet before filing a patent application, is to prejudice the chances of its being granted.

Patents are primarily designed to protect inventions and discoveries from commercial exploitation by those who did not make them. They therefore have a financial value, because the right to use something patented may be granted by the patentee for a fee. A patent does not confer a right to make, use or sell, but a right to exclude others from making, using or selling.

Patent law must take a view on what can be considered to be new. 'Novel' is taken to refer to lack of previous publication or use anywhere in the world. An 'inventive step' is one not obvious to a person skilled in the art. To be patentable, an idea has to be not only new, but also capable of industrial application. That excludes methods of medical or surgical treatment, but not devices or drugs for use in such treatment, which can be manufactured.[18] Then there is the question to what types of activity or discovery or invention patents may apply. Computer programs cannot be patented.[19] However, in some applications for scientific patents a computer program is part of a complex of elements including machines and processes, and in such cases it may be possible to embed the computer program in the application. Biotechnology can be patentable, and that has led to the patenting of DNA or protein sequences and the methods for their preparation and use. It is being found to be necessary to have 'a significant experimental-use exemption'.[20]

A patent does not last forever. In most countries it has to be renewed annually, for a fee, and does not in any case extend beyond 20 years. In the USA it lasts for 17 years from the date of issue. There is a difference between copyright and patent in that a copyright protects the expression of an idea only, and not the idea itself.[21] The idea can be patented, even if it is merely as yet a hypothesis. In recent cases in the US, patents have tended to be respected. However, in cases seeking to challenge the refusal of access to computer software where the protection is by copyright things are not so clear-cut.[22]

How far does this state of affairs amount to an unacceptable limitation on scholarly freedom of inquiry? It certainly constitutes a *practical* restriction, since while a patent is pending everything is in limbo, and after it has been granted, the holder can decide who can continue with the inquiry and for what fee. But in fact it is usual for some 'experimental use' to be allowed even when a patent has been granted, before the patent is deemed to be infringed.[23] This is a necessity where what has been patented is an idea with research potential as yet undeveloped. The most notable recent example of this situation concerns the patenting of basic DNA recombinant technology. The owner of the patent, Stanford University, was willing to license its use at a reasonable fee and as a result the technology had a wide distribution and was able to be used in biotechnological development. The University could have acted differently and thereby impeded research.

In the USA, there is a tension between the discretion of the owners of intellectual property to license its use and the antitrust laws, which constrain the use of property (which includes intellectual property) by a firm which has power to affect the market, and thus restrict the exercise of that discretion.[24] The areas included or affected are price-fixing, the exclusion of competitors, monopoly, mergers and acquisition and patents.

The antitrust laws derive from 'a deep-rooted political tradition against concentrations of power'.[25] However, from their inception it was plain that power to affect the market is not a straightforward matter. Some types of constraint on the use of ideas and discoveries may actually be helpful to competition in one direction while preventing it in another,[26] for example, by eliminating one or more modes of use. 'The true test of legality is whether the restraint imposed is such as merely regulates and perhaps thereby promotes competition', commented Mr Justice Brandeis in 1918 in *Chicago Board of Trade v. United States* (Supreme Court).[27] It was found to be necessary to be flexible. 'The Sherman Act, as a charter of freedom, has a generality and adaptability comparable to that found to be desirable in constitutional provisions.'[28] The recent trend is to seek to distinguish between restraints which are marginal, and those which significantly affect competition.[29]

The US antitrust laws distinguish 'essential facilities', without which work cannot proceed in a given area, and which are classified as remaining accessible to general use even if someone owns the intellectual property in them and wishes to 'refuse to deal'. The 'essential facilities doctrine' . . . 'may impose a duty upon firms controlling and "essential facility" to make that facility available to their rivals'.[30]

The legal principle involved is close to that of monopoly in the UK. 'Under the antitrust laws, conduct by a firm with market power may be illegal if the effect of that conduct is to tend to create or sustain a monopoly'; the firm will be allowed to set its own price, but it will have to sell.[31] Nevertheless, 'every patent is a grant of monopoly power by the state and, as such, is necessarily immune from the prohibitions of antitrust'.[32]

On 31 March 1996, the published work of all active researchers in universities in the UK was attributed to the university which employed them on that date. This was for the purpose of having it counted to that university's credit in the Research Assessment Exercise, so that the university might obtain as large a slice as possible of the financial cake available.[33]

The begetter or creator of this valuable material could not object to his work being 'used' in this way. If he wished to have his work credited to the institution which had nurtured him and paid his salary for many years, he could not insist on that if he was now employed elsewhere. Similarly, if a researcher felt that it was despite, rather than because of, his present institution that he had achieved what he had and did not wish it to profit from his endeavour, he could not prevent its doing so.

A researcher who taught for more than one department might find his work being credited to one rather than the other, without anyone consulting him and even against his wishes. The application of the law here seems largely untested.[34]

Two legal principles seem pertinent. According to the Education Reform Act 1988 (II.124) among 'the powers of a higher education corporation are . . . c). to carry out research and to publish the results of the research or any other material arising out of or in connection with it in such manner as the corporation think fit'.

Of course, a corporate body does not itself do research. Again, that takes people. But the law on intellectual property uses the term 'ownership' to describe the rights of that corporate body over the copyright work of the employee. 'Where a literary . . . work is made by an employee in the course of his employment, his employer is the first owner of any copyright in the work subject to any agreement to the contrary.'[35]

The law on intellectual property was designed for situations rather different from those in which academics have hitherto tended to find themselves, unless they become television dons or set up publishing companies or otherwise become commercial entrepreneurs. So the business of 'ownership' is important. In negotiation of the new contract imposed on lecturers in the former polytechnics and colleges of higher education a distinction was explored between copyright in scholarly work produced in furtherance of an individual's professional career (which remains with the employee) and copyright in such documents as those pertaining to the finance and administration of the university and course materials (which is kept by the employer). It is thus recognized not to be easy to decide what properly belongs to the employer and what to the actual inventor or writer or discoverer.

The contract just cited draws nervously back from the brink of saying that an employer owns all the children of the researcher's mind in whatever circumstances they were produced since he became employed. Normally, a lecturer in the humanities is allowed to keep the royalties from his books. That is surely a tangible recognition of his proprietorial rights in them. Perhaps the employer should have the royalties if it really owns the work? There are employers in the higher education sector who would say it could. 'Intellectual property developed by staff in the course of their duties becomes the property of the University' says University College London. If his contractual 'duties' include research, as they normally will in the case of a university lecturer, he may have no property-rights in the results. The University of Keele says that it 'waives its rights to the ownership of intellectual property relating to the publication of books and articles written by employees', but one can waive only that right which one has. Again (Keele) 'the University *chooses* not . . . to exploit the intellectual property'. At Bristol 'the University will not in normal circumstances seek to benefit from any rights it may have as employer in the academic publications of members of the academic staff'.[36]

It seems anomalous that work whose copyright was 'owned' by the employer with whom it was done could be transferred, without his consent, to another employer on 31 March 1996. Presumably the attribution then involved did not, and could not, transfer to the new institution a legal right to the copyright. Nor could it transfer authorial rights. It does, however, seem to have transferred some sort of right to profit from the publication of the work. Presumably the old employer went on controlling the public use of material which the new employer got the benefit of in terms of government funding, allocated on the basis of the level of achievement in the Research Assessment Exercise.

However, there is a whole new dimension of difficulty, which arises in the situation where not only a university's employees but a university itself become involved in collaborative ventures in which an individual may well face conflict of interest.

Much science now involves contract research for big companies. Consulting contracts are likely to be worth many thousands of pounds a year. It is becoming usual to set up a company composed of the scientists in a university engaged in such work. None of the university's employees can be executive directors, but they can be non-executive directors. The value generated by public equity in the flotation of such a company may be very considerable. The founding scientists may come to be worth millions in their own right, while remaining employees of the university. Oxford University takes equity in these companies itself. It had, on one estimate in the mid-1990s, £60m of equity in these accounts.

Whose is the resulting intellectual property? Does a scientist who has a bright idea in conversation with colleagues over a coffee break in the university's laboratory take it to the new company or give it to the university? A company's director might be under constraint not to say anything connected with a company in which he has equity, when he speaks as a scientist from his university at an international conference. That is, he cannot 'advertise the company's wares'. But the university's interest may be served by the free dissemination of that knowledge, because that raises its reputation in the scientific community.

There are also scientists in the academic community who have entered business on their own account, sometimes while still in the employ of universities, sometimes leaving them for the purpose. In 1995, Alan Kingsman, while remaining Professor of Biochemistry at Oxford, set up Biomedica, a gene therapy company which exploits commercially technology developed in the course of research within the University. David Rhones left the University of Leeds to set up a group of electronics companies. This presents us with another related danger.

Conflicts of interest arise among the authors of multi-author scientific papers, and the editors of scientific journals are not of one mind about their handling. The *New England Journal of Medicine* requires full disclosure of the financial interests of authors. *Epidemiology* and *The Lancet* make no such stipulation and have only limited requirements of self-disclosure.

A key distinction is made in a written statement by the editors of the *New England Journal of Medicine*: 'Because editorials involve interpretation and opinion we require that authors be free of financial associations . . . with a company that stands to gain from the use of a product (or its competitor) discussed in the editorial.'[37]

The implication is that it is possible to separate the reporting of scientific findings from the discussion of their implications in such a way as to allow even those with a clear interest to report, provided they declare it. Were they disqualified from doing so, no study funded by commercial sponsors could be deemed to have scientific credibility.

> Holding all authors fully responsible for all aspects of a scientific paper would inappropriately increase the risks associated with collaboration, both within and between laboratories. This is particularly evident when a collaboration brings together scientists in different specialties, for they cannot be expected to assess each other's work in depth . . . Even for scientists in the same field it will not always be possible for a co-worker with expertise and good intentions to uncover clever fabrications before publication.[38]

There are numerous accountability questions here. There is arguably a duty of accountability on a variety of different grounds – to those who have the ideas, to those who do the work, to those who pay the salaries, to those who contribute the funding, to those who have a duty to prevent suppression or distortion of results – and all these can be in conflict with one another. There is legal accountability which can be established under the headings of moral rights, patent and copyright. The individual scholar and the individual university may well stand bewildered in the midst.

Getting the credit

The researcher's personal rights

Rights have a corollary in responsibilities. The balance of the one against the other is precarious. Where an employer owns the copyright, where patents can be held by commercial partners, or where an author has the moral rights, the intellectual property is carved up by agreements of various possible kinds. 'Authorship equals responsibility.'[39] It is, however, a responsibility much worked upon and turned in various potentially conflicting directions by rights which do not necessarily remain with the author.

There are moral rights in law. These are personal. 'The author of a copyright literary, dramatic, musical or artistic work, and the director of a copyright film, has the right to be identified as the author or director of the work.'[40] This also applies to 'any substantial part of the work'.[41] The author has a right to be identified whenever there is commercial publication, and in a number of other circumstances which involve making it public in some way (such as broadcasting). That 'right does not apply to anything done by or with the authority of the copyright owner where copyright in the work [is] originally vested . . . in the author's employer by virtue of section xi.2'.[42]

There is, therefore, a separation in law between 'ownership', which gives rights about copying ('copyright'), and authorial rights, with the ownership rights overriding those of the author as creator of the work.

Nevertheless, the moral rights I have ought to mean that no one can interfere as he pleases with my work. There is a moral right for the author to object to derogatory treatment of his work, that is, 'addition to, deletion from or alteration to or adaptation of the work', other than translation or musical arrangement involving no more than a change of key. Distortion or mutilation of the work 'prejudicial to the honour or reputation of the author' is also derogatory.[43] But it may again be qualified in the case of works 'in which copyright [was] originally vested in the author's employee by virtue of section xi.2'.[44] And, it is hard to know how that can cover having an idea in conversation during a coffee break which is then borrowed, developed or adapted by others without acknowledgement. Authorial rights seem to subsist only in finished works.

The 'moral rights' of authors are a grey area. A person has a right to be identified as joint author in the case of a work of joint authorship, and to give consent with other joint authors or to object with other joint authors to the use of the material under the various provisions of the Act. This right is infringed 'by any false statement as to the authorship of any work of joint authorship'.[45] This portion of the law would seem especially pertinent in the scientific community, where the muddle about rights is increasingly alarming, for the reasons we have been looking at, and where the individual with the bright idea may well find it extremely difficult to ensure that he gets credit for it.

The individual scientist carries something inalienably his own about with him. While he is working in a laboratory on a piece of research he will have ideas which he may follow up in his own time or using his own resources. He may find the germ of a future project while working with one team, which he may follow through in another laboratory in future years under another contract with a different employer and with a different team.

Arts and sciences produce, characteristically though not exclusively, individual and teamwork respectively. In the scientific community, work remains the property of the laboratory in which it was carried out, because that was where the funding which paid for it belonged, and where the employer was providing the facilities, and so on. It is also the case that because research is normally to a greater or lesser degree a team effort, it may be difficult to say who is the author in the sense of being the creator or inventor or discoverer. It will be easier to say who is or are the author(s) of a published scientific paper in the sense that he or they drafted the actual sentences. It is, however, normal practice for scientific papers to go out under joint authorship, with all contributors to the research listed, even if some of them had nothing to do with the actual writing.

One may work in a team as a PhD student, and thus in a junior capacity and under close direction. Or, the work may be done post-doctorally. Or, it may be done at a relatively senior stage, but not as the head of the laboratory. Work done some years earlier may be 'held' by the head of a laboratory, who can then publish it in a form dictated by himself, and even if he consults with the now much more senior joint author, he may not – and this has happened – bow to that individual's wishes about the use to which the material is to be put. These are complex 'ownership' problems. Things run on usage and are made workable partly by a firm 'head of laboratory' hand, and threats and promises about access to funding. There is a can of leviathan-sized worms here.[46]

That takes us back to one of the fundamentals: the *shared* character of scholarly endeavour. Sharing requires freedom to choose to participate or not to participate on the part of those who contribute to what is shared, on the understanding that what they contribute is inherently theirs to give. Thus, I may choose to share my knowledge with you, but not yet, because I want time to rewrite my text until I am satisfied with it. In the humanities, this is a position understood and respected. And indeed most humanities researchers are ready enough to share their knowledge when it is ready to be shared, because they do not then risk having it stolen. Occasionally, there is a dispute about plagiarism, when the author of one book accuses another of purloining his ideas or even his sentences.

However, if we move to a model in which the emphasis is on the researcher's personal rights and responsibilities, there can be a conflict between one person's freedom to control his work, and that of another.

Fair rewards ought to include the giving of credit where it is due. These are particularly sharp difficulties in the sciences, where work is usually done in teams or groups and the research published under several names. One institute of higher education put in for its Research Assessment Exercise work to which a member of its staff made redundant before 31 March 1996 had contributed as the main author, under the name of another member of staff appearing on the list of co-authors but not himself a main author. The problem of multiple authorship of scientific works submitted in the RAE is far from straightforward. In a sense they all have rights in the piece. Normally, the leading name is the name of the person whose work has made the largest contribution. However, other names may appear whose owners have done none of the work, but merely obtained the funding.

The RAE panels appear to have had no fully thought out method of allocating credit for scientific work where several authors were involved. Where the authors were all in a single department and formed a research team, this was no great matter, since it was the department which was being assessed. However, in the multi-author work which involves individuals from different disciplines and different universities this is a proper consideration.

Control by patronage

Allocating funds to research students is, in the sciences, in some measure an act of patronage in the hands of a head of department or head of laboratory:

> The Research Training Support Grant is paid to departments in institutions as a contribution towards the incidental costs incurred in the training of Research Council supported research students the orientation of whose research is entirely at the discretion of the student, the supervisor and, *where relevant, any industrial or other partner.* As the grant follows the student it provides a well-focused form of funding.[47]

For the individual researcher, long-term planning is difficult under short-term contracts and the renewal of a contract may be at the disposal of a head of department or head of laboratory. It is true that scientists may be needed to complete a specific piece of research, and that no one can know until they finish it whether it will lead on to another, and if it does, whether that new piece of research will require the same team. Nevertheless, it is wasteful to place so substantial a proportion of scientists in a position where they must spend a high proportion of their time seeking fresh or continuing funding; it is also wasteful to have individuals leave a team early because they cannot afford to turn down the opportunity of another contract elsewhere, when the specific expertise of such individuals may be crucial to the completion of the project.

The tradition in the 'ancient' and old universities used to be that scientists had continuing contracts as teachers, which got them over the need for these episodic and uncertain renewals. Now there is increasingly, a separation into two categories, of staff in scientific departments in universities who are expected to teach and those who are expected only to do research. Tensions arise. In Cambridge at the end of 1996 there was a protest call for a vote by scientists who did not want to see those who only had to do research carrying off all the promotions, while those who also had to teach were disadvantaged by having to spend time on teaching which they could not, therefore, give to their research. In another university, a scientist on a short-term contract, but one who had a long history with the department in question, was penalized because he was doing too much teaching and given a renewal of contract for only six months when everyone else on his team was given a year's contract.

Taking responsibility

Getting credit for work is also taking responsibility for it. That is a fundamental principle of the moral rights of authorship. His employer probably cannot force upon an academic something with which he does not want his name associated. A person has a right 'not to have a literary, dramatic, musical or artistic work falsely attributed to him as author'.[48] 'If you haven't done the work, don't put your name on the paper. If you put your name on the paper, then you are stuck with it',[49] says a recent letter in *Science.* However, another letter in the same sequence of correspondence, points out that those whose names are attached to a publication may not have been consulted.

> To put one's name on a paper is an assurance to the scientific community that one has contributed to the work and that one stands behind the work reported. However, one aspect of the co-authorship problem that I have not seen discussed in this forum is that of finding one's name as a co-author on a publication of which one has no knowledge. This recently happened to a colleague and me when we found a paper in a journal listing our names as co-authors, although neither of us had ever contributed to the work, seen the manuscript, or been notified of its submission or publication.[50]
>
> 'Quoting another paper should be a sign that one has examined its findings critically.' Otherwise, as one scientist points out, findings may go unchallenged and become the foundation-stones for later work as though they were incontrovertible.[51]

One solution proposed is to tidy up the requirements of learned journals in this respect: 'Publication of an article should require the mandatory submission of a form signed by all authors verifying that they have read the complete manuscript and take equal responsibility for its contents . . . If scientists do not feel that they can vouch for the integrity of a paper, then they should not assume co-authorship.'[52] The concern of this and other letters in this sequence was with fraudulent misrepresentation of authorship and its relationship to responsibility. But there is also the question of *apportionment* of credit. That is touched on in one letter, suggesting that a statement should be included with every published article, allocating credit:

> The information would be widely useful in judging work submitted for doctoral theses, making hiring and tenure decisions, and evaluating grant applications. To encourage the fair allocation of credit, other useful practices could also be adopted. For example, in cases where two authors have contributed equally to a paper . . . their names might be separated . . . with [an] equal sign.[53]

It is not uncommon for heads of laboratories to be included among the authors of a scientific paper when they have had no part in the work, or even in the discussion of the work. Such 'co-authors' have sometimes subsequently withdrawn their names after fraud has been shown.[54] Had they truly known about the work for which they were claiming part credit, however, they had a responsibility to be aware of its weak points.

There are looming and potentially expensive dangers here. A former research student of the University of Alabama, Birmingham, went to court, claiming that the University had wrongly taken credit for her work in making applications for government grants. A federal jury in Baltimore found in her favour in 1995. The University appealed on the grounds that the precedent would encourage similar lawsuits and that would undermine the internal procedures of universities for dealing with scientific misconduct, leading to their having to find resources to defend against lawsuits which could have been avoided by using the internal route.[55]

Big science, multiple funding and power in too few hands

It has become a commonplace to point to the contrast between 'blue skies' research, pursued for love and out of curiosity but having no obvious immediate practical application, and the 'marketability' of projects of the Technology Foresight kind. It is not difficult to find examples of discoveries of the first type which have turned out, by chance, subsequently to be real money spinners. The argument for risk-taking in funding, *even if it is intended that funding should in principle only go to applicable discoveries*, seems inescapable. That is, even on a business model, it makes business sense to put money into research fired solely by curiosity. Veblen saw that in early twentieth-century America:

> Any system of knowledge may confidently be run back, in the main, to the initiative and bias afforded by two certain impulsive traits of human nature: an Idle Curiosity, and the Instinct of Workmanship . . . 'idle' in the sense that a knowledge of things is sought, apart from any ulterior use of the knowledge so gained. This, of course, does not imply that the knowledge so gained will not be turned to practical account . . .

the instinct of workmanship will unavoidably incline men to turn to account . . . whatever knowledge so becomes available.[56]

Veblen describes with affected cynicism, 'the formal professions of disinterested zeal for the cause of learning that [the executive head of a university] is by tradition required to make from time to time'.[57] One must call it an affected cynicism because elsewhere he writes idealistically, if inconsistently, first that: 'It is incumbent upon . . . [the] executive head of a university . . . to govern the academic personnel and equipment with an eye single to the pursuit of knowledge, and so to conduct its affairs as will most effectually encompass that end',[58] then that: 'The university is to make good both as a corporation of learning and as a business concern dealing with standardised erudition, and the executive head necessarily assumes the responsibility of making it count wholly and unreservedly in each of these divergent, if not incompatible lines.'[59]

Scientists usually work in teams, and the teams now tend to become connected in the larger networks of 'big science'. This is a trend which is being actively fostered. Chris Higgins, Professor of Clinical Biochemistry at Oxford, chaired a 1997 review by the Biotechnology and Biological Sciences Research Council which formulated a new policy. 'Much of biology is changing; it is becoming a "big science" which needs state-of-the-art equipment and can no longer be effectively carried out by small isolated teams', he commented.[60]

The problems of apportionment of credit multiply where a project requires input from scientists working in more than one discipline. In 1997 the Biology and Biological Sciences Research Council in the UK made a policy decision to fund multidisciplinary centres.[61]

There is a cognate problem, that if multidisciplinary work is *ipso facto* 'bigger' in scale, in the number of scientists and the range of equipment it needs, it needs correspondingly more substantial funding. That encourages resort to funding from multiple sources, by, for example, a university, the Wellcome Trust (a charity) and the Medical Research Council (a Government funding body apportioning public funds). Each of these will have an interest in seeing that its money is used as it wishes. It may have policy objectives of its own. These may be incompatible and the funded centre or project may, then, be caught between powerful interests. The funders may want a more or less detailed say in the running of things. There may be lengthy correspondence about the use of tea-making facilities in such an institute.

The multidisciplinary centres planned by the BBSRC have the further intention of avoiding duplication. 'We want to avoid every university setting up structural biology departments.'[62] But that could, in principle, lead to a dangerous concentration of the direction of research in comparatively few hands. Scientific departments and laboratories tend to be run hierarchically. Teams depend upon the direction of a head of laboratory or head of department, who can have a decisive say in the appointment of researchers on short-term contracts, the renewal or non-renewal of those contracts and the allocation of publicly-funded research studentships to individuals. To fall foul of such a powerful individual can be the end of a career, and the more easily so if, in effect, that individual controls the whole of that area of science in the UK.

The habit of withholding reasons for decisions purportedly based on academic judgement makes it difficult to insist on accountability for decisions about publication or appointment or the award of grants. Peer review by anonymous referees where there is no requirement for reasons to be given is a dubious procedure at best. It becomes more so when 'they may be competing at the time of application or in the future with the applicants for the same funds'. Sometimes they are members of the very committees which are considering their applications.[63]

In addition to such conflicts of interest there is the problem of the pressure to conform. A committee may be self-perpetuating, with current members choosing those who are to serve with them next. It may well take a view on the approach which is to be preferred to the solution of a given problem, and then favour applicants proposing work along those lines. Both these practices may prove inimical to the chances of individuals or projects which may overturn orthodoxies.[64] Established academics find it relatively easy to get into print. They will find themselves on editorial boards, or on especially friendly terms with an editor. Conversely, journals can, on the advice of the same established academics, reject submissions. In neither case need reasons be given. 'Professor Hans Krebs – the Nobel Laureate in biochemistry – wrote to me that he thought a journal had the right to refuse to publish a paper if the referees thought that there was something wrong with it, but could not identify the error.'[65] At conferences, a vote can decide which papers will be published, again without reasons having to be given. One scientist was told by his director 'that the Medical Research Council did not like my research'. He asked to be allowed to discuss the reasons for this with those members of the MRC who had expressed this opinion. He was not told their names and no meeting was arranged.[66]

It does not need to be underlined that the larger the arena the more difficult it will be to call anyone to account for the decisions. In a landmark case which established that the Parliamentary Commissioner, and thus other statutory ombudsmen, are subject to judicial review, it was remarked by Simon Brown, L.J. that 'the [ombudsman's] report . . . time and time again . . . criticised the department for maladministration and in particular the local office for mishandling various aspects of the applicant's benefit claims'.[67] However, even where it is plain that something has gone badly wrong, it remains relatively easy for those in charge to find someone else to hide behind or to pass the buck to. Exploratory telephone calls will frequently result in a passing from hand to hand, extension to extension, and protestations of a duty of confidentiality. The owners of the 'too few hands' in which the powers really lie will not easily be identified and still less easily pinned down for comment or forced to act.

Funding and policy control

As long as universities retain legal autonomy, the available sanctions to be used to ensure compliance with the wishes of government or society remain chiefly financial. Indeed, Dearing links the two. The *Report* recommends that the Funding Bodies make a review of the effectiveness of governance 'with appropriate external assistance and benchmarks' a condition of public funding (RR 57, 59). The logical problem with this is that the Funding Bodies are not by remit the proper bodies to make the academic judgement.

There is need, too, for careful further reflection on the ethics of the implication in the *Dearing Report* that funding may also be used for social engineering (RR 2, 3, 4) that is, to encourage funding bodies to reward attempts to open access wider and encourage students from disadvantaged backgrounds to enter higher education. Not all 'social' objectives are equally clearly 'goods', and this looks like the thin end of a dangerous 'wedge'.

There is a suggestion in the *Report*, which is designed to encourage private funding while retaining some public control of it (R 34), that 'an Industrial Partnership Development Fund' be established 'immediately to attract matching funds from industry, and to contribute to regional and economic development'. R 39 speaks of: 'technology incubator units' to provide a place to develop an idea's commercial potential 'within which start-up companies can be fostered for a limited period until they are able to stand alone'. There are also optimistic words on entrepreneurship, over which many universities are already in difficulties and losing out to something resembling exploitation: 'We recommend to higher education institutions that they consider the scope for encouraging entrepreneurship through innovative approaches to programme design and through specialist postgraduate programmes' (R 40).

Here there is no exploration of the problems which can arise from commercial links. Those are starkly apparent in the USA. Loyola University, New Orleans, identifies itself as a 'social justice institution'. Members of the Faculty sign a statement establishing their commitment to ideals of social justice which include the principle that 'education should be wisdom not technical competence'; that education 'must motivate us to a concern for our city, our state, our nation, our planet'. Loyola University's commercial funders get the benefit of 'greenwashing'. Their products achieve a stamp of political correctness by their association with the University.[68] The University may have reservations about this, but there can be no realistic expectation that commercial funders will often want to give serious money to universities out of a disinterested love of learning. They want the association, and they want it to be known. Where the university is dependent on such financing because governments do not give them adequate support, that creates an imbalance of power in terms of who calls the tune.[69]

Commercial investment in universities wants other things, too. It may very well want to control outcomes of scientific research in areas where there is a commercial application of that research, and to discourage research which will not lead directly to such outcomes. At Loyola University, Freeport McMoRan funds an 'environmental communication' chair. That means that it does not need to hire a public relations firm to do that job.[70] Its own environmental record is murky.[71] However, even if it were not especially an offender in this respect there would be a question to be asked about 'buying' such a chair.

In British universities, being able to get grants or other major funding can be a stepping-stone towards promotion. In the United States, too, 'being "politically correct" in academia . . . means having an endowed chair or a lucrative consulting contract'.[73]

Late mediaeval Oxford was as anxious as any modern University to woo potential benefactors. Numerous begging letters survive. The University of Oxford wanted money for a new divinity school at the end of the fifteenth century and it wrote begging letters to potential benefactors promising immortality of memory for their names.[72] The ethics of benefaction have been much in the news in the 1990s, when at both Oxford (the Flick Chair) and Cambridge (a Chair funded by a tobacco company, BAT Industries) there was heated debate about accepting the money, on the grounds that it was morally contaminated – 'dirty' money. There was also, during the same decade, concern over the ethics of the deployment of money, however 'clean' to begin with.

It is, perhaps, natural for commercial interests to want to get control of universities or research departments or projects. Governments should expect that, and seek to build in safeguards to protect the pursuit of truth from distortion or exploitation by commercial funders. But if statutory bodies, as government agencies, co-fund with commerce, those protections may easily be compromised, and with them the machinery of accountability.

4

The Public Interest

The nature of the public interest

'The State is, in my opinion, not competent to direct the work of education and disinterested research which is carried on by Universities, and the responsibility for its conduct must rest solely with their Governing Bodies and teachers',[1] said H. A. L. Fisher in 1922, seeing the danger ahead of his time.

In the sixth century, Boethius died under political house arrest in the days of the ultimate collapse of the Roman Empire. He had seen that a change was coming which threatened the preservation of the culture of the ancient world, and he had begun a project of translating the works of Plato and Aristotle into Latin, so that they would remain accessible as the knowledge of Greek died away in the West. He died before he could finish, but he achieved enough to set the syllabus of academic study in some fields for the next 600 years. He died thinking on a grand scale about the task of the scholar, and with an oppressive sense that political realities were against him.

A modern university has two kinds of duty which may be at odds with one another in a similar way in the late twentieth century. The first is to think in a large way, to be idealistic about the pursuit of truth. But beside any claim to be needed in the public interest on intellectual or spiritual or cultural grounds, there has now to be set an increasingly hard and solid claim to be cost-effective. For universities are expensive things to run. Even on a minimalist provision of secretarial services and room to teach in, they require a vast support-net as institutions. It may be difficult to set the cost tidily beside the effect. A new graduate is not a finished product. In the humanities, a scholar may not reach his peak until his 50s and 60s. If the money is invested on trust, and there are no visible fruits for some time, perhaps none at all, it may be hard to justify going on putting money in.

The argument is heard that universities do not 'deserve' public money unless they 'increase' their output of research or of graduates. The Dearing

Committee's *Report* of 1997 stuck strictly to its remit as the 'national' committee of inquiry into higher education and although the 'vision' of the international scene was kept in view, it was mainly as a trading arena for British higher education that it featured. This essentially 'local-minded' and 'short-term' or ephemeral character of the duty to give value for money begs the question of what 'value' consists in in higher education.

But it can be an insistent consideration. If there is an imperative of intellectual integrity under which all scholars have to be prepared to stick by their honest opinions independently in the service of truth, then independence of mind is the defining characteristic of the scholar. Yet, pressure to inflate degree grades put upon examiners who do not conscientiously believe the higher grades are merited can be strong.[2]

Cicero places at the centre of the justification of scholarly endeavour a 'public interest' conceived more broadly than in terms of money. The legitimate financial interest of the public in the conduct of an institution which is being at least partly funded from the public purse is not in dispute. It is easily assumed, but should not go unquestioned, that public interest arises from and depends upon the degree of public investment on some quantitative and largely financial calculation. But it is less uncontroversial what (if any) other kinds of interest the public may legitimately have in such an institution. If, by its activities, an institution can affect the public arena morally, intellectually or in other ways, does that create a presumption that there is a public interest in its activities? If it does, the higher-level duty of a university to scholarship becomes in itself a matter of public interest, and the discharging of purposes of financial accountability becomes only one of the proper considerations.

The highest education in the ancient world, especially the Roman world, was designed to fit the citizen for public life. That meant he had to be an effective public speaker who could marshal literary and historical examples and knew his way about the schools of philosophy, especially insofar as they concerned themselves with the moral purposes of life. Right living for individuals who were also citizens was a matter of sustained interest. In both the ancient Greek and the ancient Roman worlds,[3] there are notions of the 'educator as statesman' colouring what we should now call the 'public interest' question. It was for the common good that there should be persons fitted by education to lead in society.[4] That idea is still alive; indeed, it informs the *Dearing Report.* Now, however, it is coupled with the assumption that public interest arises from and depends upon the scale of public investment, in a way which was not a relevant consideration in the ancient world.

The 'public interest' of the highest levels of education was differently, but still consciously perceived in the Middle Ages. In the Middle Ages a whole class of persons lived solely to pray, and these members of religious orders were supported by the community – willingly enough, to judge by gifts of land to monasteries. The well-connected and socially important faithful who made these gifts took the view that they were doing something useful for the whole community. Other people were too busy to do it; the monks kept a watching brief for a humanity generally too much occupied with staying alive. This is not out of line with Elizabethan thinking. 'That there may not lack a supply of persons . . .' is a sentiment of prayers at University sermons in Oxford and Cambridge.

Universities have a purpose in the modern world with which all this affords parallels. Trained professionals and well-stocked minds are still socially necessary. However, it remains true that scholars, like monks, feel the need of leisure and freedom from distraction in which to do something of its nature reflective, even rather uncertain, in its ultimate unfolding. Society has to make an act of trust that the results will be worth it, and be prepared to write off a few instances where they are not, for the sake of the unpredictable, but great, results which may from time to time come of the act of trust.

Is a university an organ of the State?

Universities which award degrees which are recognized by EU member countries, are in their turn recognized by the European Commission to be carrying out a public function on behalf of the State.[5] That may imply that universities are part of the State and, if it does, that would properly give the State some degree of control. It would make universities in some respects accountable to the State.

Foster v. British Gas plc [1990] 3 All E.R. 897, raised a number of questions about what constitutes part of the State in the context of the UK legal system. In EEC Commission Directive (EEC) 80/723, there is a distinction between 'public authorities', defined as 'the state and regional or local authorities', and 'public undertakings', which are defined as 'any undertaking over which the public authorities may exercise directly or indirectly a dominant influence by virtue of their ownership of it, their financial partnership therein, or the rules which govern it'.[6] Even this second category envisages the State having a degree of control.

In *Foster v. British Gas plc* (at 912) the question is raised whether 'the concepts "state" and "individual"' are 'together exhaustive or is there, in between them, a third category of persons or bodies . . . If the existence of such a category is accepted, the question arises whether with regard to the possible direct effect of provisions or directives it must be put on the same footing as the category "state" or the category "individuals".' This discussion is set in the context of EEC law, where, as it is pointed out (at 913), since it is easier to be clear 'in everyday language' what an individual is, the tendency will be to place bodies in a category with the State and to regard them as part of the State; it could be argued that 'a public undertaking . . . must not benefit from the default of its member state and in that sense must be brought under the concept of "the state".'

General power of control of this sort could exist separately from powers to determine in detail what happens inside an institution. In the case of the

British Gas Corporation it was held that the Secretary of State had powers of control over it, but 'no power to interfere in the ordinary business management of the corporation'.[7] In *Turpie v. University of Glasgow* (19 September 1986, unreported)[8] an industrial tribunal held that the University was not an organ of the State even though 80 per cent of its funding came from the State. 'The industrial tribunal based its decision on the considerable freedom enjoyed by universities in the organisation of their teaching and research and in their long tradition of independent thought.' The underlying issue is whether there can be a public interest in a body, part of whose definition is its independence, so that its autonomy is constitutive; and, if so, how far that interest is an interest in running it.

In what interest?

Lord Haldane, in the *Report of the Machinery of Government Committees* of 1918, argued that governments should not seek to exercise control over research, applied or pure. That assumption has gone. 'Separation of the power of the state from the direction of research as carried on in the universities and, to a lesser extent, in the research councils' own institutes' began to disappear in the late 1980s.[9] In 1986, the *Second Joint Report of the Chairmen of the Advisory Council for Applied Research and Development and the Advisory Board for the Research Councils* said: 'It is becoming increasingly urgent to ensure that the investment made in the science base contributes more effectively to wealth creation. To achieve this . . . links between the science base and industry need to be strengthened and extended.' It was already being argued then that universities should 'generate a volume and quality of research proposals sufficient to allow the agencies, particularly the research councils, to select those which meet their criteria and are likely to further their scientific policies',[10] as though it was beyond question that it was proper for them to have policies and to enforce them by selecting in their favour.

That implies that funding can properly be used as a means of directing policy. It can be withheld, making certain projects impossible. There can be a threat to withhold it, unless there is compliance with policy directives. There can be promises that if policy directives are complied with, then extra funding will follow.

'Much effective surveillance of the academic work is exercise through the board's control of the budget', observed Thorstein Veblen shrewdly in early twentieth-century USA.[11]

> The academic head is vested with somewhat autocratic powers, within the lines effectually laid down in the budget; he is in effect responsible to the governing body alone, and his responsibility in that direction chiefly touches his observance of the pecuniary specifications of the budget.[12]

> The modern civilised community is reluctant to trust its serious interests to others than men of pecuniary substance, who have proved their fitness for the direction of academic affairs by acquiring, or by otherwise being possessed of, considerable wealth.[13]

But he knew that businessmen can have the idea that 'what is of no use in business is not worthwhile'.[14] *A fortiori*, governments may do the same.

In the UK, the Research Councils are a major funding source for universities. They now have a lengthy history. The *Report* of the Machinery of Government Committee (the *Haldane Report*),[15] recommended that the funding of external government scientific research should follow the model of the Department of Scientific and Industrial Research (DSIR) established in 1916.[16] The original idea, indeed the guiding principle, was that the Research Councils should have an independent membership '(both scientific and laymen), full-time scientifically qualified secretaries and direct negotiation of funding from the Treasury'. On this 'Haldane principle' the Medical Research Council (MRC) was set up in 1920, the Agricultural Research Council (ARC) in 1931 and the Nature Conservancy (NC) in 1949.[17] The key principle seems to have been that the Research Councils should act as a buffer state between the universities and the Government.

That has, or ought to have, implications for the way the Government proceeds. Arguably, it ought to keep its hands off direct allocation. But it will naturally be difficult for any government to resist the temptation to intrude upon the processes of allocation in order to ensure that policies are implemented. After the Education Reform Act 1988 came into force a representative of the Secretary of State was entitled to take part in any deliberations (though not decisions) at meetings of the Universities Funding Council (UFC) or any of its committees. The Secretary of State was entitled to receive copies of any documents distributed to members of the UFC or any of its committees.[18] In 1997 the Higher Education Quality Council (a body under the control of the Committee of Vice-Chancellors and Principals (CVCP) and therefore of the universities themselves) was replaced by a new Quality Assurance Agency. This is a company limited by guarantee. The members ('shareholders') are the representative bodies, but four of the 14 directors are nominated by the Higher Education Funding Councils. The same Funding Councils, together with the representative bodies, fund the Agency on the basis of a service level agreement. The agency is, therefore, in a sense 'owned' by the statutory bodies as well as by representatives of the universities. Thus, there is a grey area in terms of the degree to which government oversight can become government intrusion, and at a detailed level of decisionmaking about which research projects are to be funded.

However, it is a fact of life that there is a limited amount of money which can come to universities from the public purse; and that the size of this pot depends a good deal on policy and priority decisions by governments; and that that is influenced partly by political perceptions of what will go down well with voters. UK governments now increasingly appeal to the 'national interest' or the 'public interest' as justification for taking an active and even *dirigiste* interest in the deployment of research funding.

The 'national interest' is, on the face of it, the interest of the citizens whose money is being spent. It does not follow, though, that it is in their wider or 'public' interest that it should be spent on projects favoured by the national government. The question whether there is a 'national interest' distinct from the 'public interest' is sharp in arenas of scientific work, such as the medical and pharmaceutical, where the public interest clearly extends beyond national boundaries,[19] and the citizens of the UK may benefit from discoveries made elsewhere.

Even where that is not obviously so, short-sighted political planning can create a conflict between a national and a wider interest. In the European Union, academic scientists apply to Brussels to get access to support which was assigned under national budgets. However, decision-making takes place at European level about where it is to go, and commercial developers and researchers may win funds in preference to academic scientists. The decisions may be taken on the basis of policy preferences ('applied' rather than 'basic' research, for example); there are results of a different sort (funding of 'commercial' rather than 'academic' projects). This may have long-term consequences which the contributing countries may not have intended, in which national interest can, in the end, not be well served, and even the larger public interest may be lost sight of.[20]

Within a State, government-driven preferences or the preferences of Funding Councils or their equivalent may change radically and unpredictably, and that can have a stop-go effect. In 1981, the UGC had two leading ideas: that every institution should have 'some things' it was 'good at', and that students should be encouraged to move to the sciences 'in the national economic interest'.[21] However, a broad encouragement to invest in science and to persuade institutions to especially hard effort in at least some areas, has shifted its emphasis. There is now talk of preferential research funding for the high performers. 'Research funding should be invested wherever the highest quality research is being done.'[22] There has been a further significant shift towards industrially relevant projects: 'The Government remains committed to its policy for science, engineering and technology as set out in the 1993 White Paper *Realising Our Potential* which is to promote high quality basic, strategic and applied research, and related postgraduate training, thereby enhancing the United Kingdom's industrial competitiveness and quality of life.'[23]

There is, at the time of writing in 1997, currently a strong bias towards initiatives of a technological sort. 'Consideration is being given to brigading under the Foresight banner a number of Department of Trade and Industry schemes.'[24] The Higher Education Funding Council for England (HEFCE) circular of February 1997, *Joint Research Equipment Initiative: HEFCE and DENI Awards* describes how institutions were invited to submit applications on certain assumptions about the objectives of this 'initiative': 'to enable high-quality research that is relevant to the Technology Foresight

Programme generic science and technology priorities to be conducted'.[25] So the 'national interest' has been identified not just with science but with certain types of science.

Government funding is not given without strings. The strings may be of the simple sort, which requires only a respectable financial return. But increasingly – and the quotations above could be multiplied almost endlessly – they involved the manipulation of research according to policy, and increasingly this policy speaks of 'national need' and defines that need in terms of applied science:

> The Council also wishes to look forward and to be able to *shape the distribution* of funds, ensuring that the overall balance of distribution fulfils its *objectives and responds to national priorities.* It therefore wishes to include a *policy* factor in setting the quanta which will allow it to influence the distribution between subjects, based on national needs and international standing . . . In future the Council proposes to look first at whether the institutions themselves are *responding to national needs.* However, it may also wish to reinforce institutional decisions or to anticipate areas of need (emphasis added).[26]

Even where funding is private, it can exert policy control if governments allow or encourage it to do so. Conflict of interest arising when someone has loyalties both to a university and to a commercial funder or firm of his own, can result not only in *prescribing* the content and direction of research, but in *proscribing* the publication of outcomes, or even preventing the preliminary discussion of findings at conferences if questions are asked which might require the researcher to 'give away' information from which he or a commercial sponsor hope to make a profit. Here the verb 'give' is load-bearing, for this confidentiality is of a trade-secrets type and it is designed to protect commercial interests. That runs directly counter to the principle of the free exchange of information within the community of scholarship on which scientists, in general, proceeded until recent years.

In a recent USA study,[27] the notion is floated that we are entering a period not of 'public' but of 'quasi-public' interest and funding. There are 'joint ventures with business, lifelong learning programmes, community relations, and research centres and institutes'. And 'increasing private giving is a strategic priority of most public colleges and universities'.[28] A similar 'quasi-public' character is being given to private funding in the UK by Government approval. A HEFCE circular of February 1997 seeks 'to promote partnerships between Higher Education Institutions and external sponsors of research'.[29] The only model on which private funding can hope to remain free of this sort of direction is endowment; and real independence there depends on the giver of the funds refraining from building in terms which will deny that independence. That requires an unusual giver, for usually, and naturally enough, there is a wish to have one's name associated with an act of generosity and to have a say in the use of the money.

There is a deeper coloration, almost an 'infiltration' of patterns of thought from industry and commerce, which cannot be held off even by decisively separating the money from the funder before it is used. Kurland quotes the phrase 'R and D portfolio', with the comment: 'the thesis seems to be that by invoking the mighty concept of the "portfolio", the traditionally thorny problem of balancing allocations to different sorts of research programs will simply vanish'.[30]

The problem is that if management language of 'tendering' and 'delivering' and 'customer' is consistently used, it ceases to be a striking image and becomes a reality. It ceases to be a metaphor and becomes a literal usage. This can directly affect the claim of 'research' judgements to be purely expert judgements in the relevant field, uncontaminated by non-academic considerations. Among the Electors (appointing committee) for the Professorship of Respiratory Medicine in Cambridge in 1997 were six academics, from various universities, a Consultant Cardio-Thoracic Surgeon from Papworth NHS Trust Hospital, and the Chief Executive of Addenbrooke's NHS Trust Hospital. The last represented the NHS management and was, therefore, unable to contribute an academic judgement. However, if among the requirements for the new Professor was that he should be acceptable to the hospital management, he might have been able to contribute a relevant *professional* judgement. On the other hand, if it was conceded that someone must be able to make that assessment, his presence as a sole representative of that type of judgement might be out of balance. It would be appropriate to consider what the balance of Electors ought to be.

There has been a climate change in this area too. In 1986 Dr Reece, senior member of the Advisory Council for Applied Research and Development, in evidence to the House of Lords Select Committee on Science and Technology, conceded it was not appropriate for governments to interfere with the essentially academic professional judgement of those who set up the actual research process: 'Changing research is a difficult and expensive process so you can only do it on rare occasions but we do not do it at all in this country. We are but margin tinkerers.'[31] This contrasting statement from a HEFCE circular raised few eyebrows in 1997: 'Applications . . . were peer reviewed by the relevant Research Council. Applications were assessed against the objectives of the initiative and judged on their value for money, including the level of matching funding achieved.'[32] But it mixes academic criteria with criteria which are not academic but financial.

A hands-off policy (on the basis that only experts can make expert judgements) has become a hands-on policy (on the basis that managers have a managerial expertise which is itself a professional judgement and which it is a proper one for them to seek to make in the fields of other professionals).

If managerial judgement has authority over professional judgement, that inculcates a subordinate attitude of mind. Academics need a degree of arrogance in their fields if they are to be pioneers and they need to find that arrogance checked by their peers – if they out-argue them fair and square. It is profoundly damaging to academic integrity and therefore, ultimately, to the quality of the work, to have to bow to masters with other priorities in order to be able to get the work done at all. Kurland again: 'a bottom-up planned, peer-reviewed resource allocation system is slowly replacing the command systems of some former Soviet client states'.[33] The pattern or resource-allocation for funding in the rest of the world appears to be moving the other way.

Kurland suggests a response of lobbying, 'for laws that regulate and limit the permissible activities of industry on university campuses'. He points to the principle that in 'no country' does 'private industry have a natural right to exploit public resources for its own ends'.[34] Whether or not the legislative route would prove helpful – and if the problem is also cultural, it is not clear that it would in itself be sufficient – this proposal points up the dilemma that if states seek to save public money by encouraging private funding they may in the end not serve the public, or even the national interest, because they will open a hornets' nest of consequences, whose occupants may be hard to entice back to the nest once freed.

We come now to the question, what sorts of public interest are involved in the control of the ways funding is to be deployed. In *The Guardian* of 18 February 1997, it was hinted that there was dispute in Whitehall as to whether a research team or individual winning a grant should retain control of it. The Research Councils[35] steer a proportion of the £1.3 billion annual science budget to individual researchers by means of separate project grants. However, the infrastructure has to be kept up. The three Higher Education Funding Councils give a comparable figure of about £1 billion of research funds to institutions in the form of block grants designed to maintain it. The HEFCE circular of February 1997 (*Joint Research Equipment Initiative: HEFCE and DENI Awards*) says that they set out 'to contribute generally to the physical research infrastructure in Higher Education Institutions'.[36]

The internal deployment of these funds is at the disposal of individual universities. It is therefore of importance how internal allocations policy is decided, for in a university where, in practice, the decision is at the discretion of the Vice-Chancellor, or an oligarchy surrounding the Vice-Chancellor, a great deal of public money is disposed of by relatively few persons, in ways for which they may not easily be accountable.[37] The débâcle of 1994–6 at Lancaster shows how easily huge sums of money may be moved around in a university's budget without sufficient monitoring.[38]

'It is far cheaper to grant partial operating costs to an established research unit than it is to create one from scratch and maintain it at an industrial site that is wholly self-financed.'[39] So the grant-winning individual or team may depend upon the provision of at least an infrastructure of laboratory space and the basic facilities to do the work for which the grant was made. It appears inescapable that there will be a continuing need in every institution both to sustain an infrastructure, which is a long-term commitment, and to provide funds for specific pieces of work, some short-term, some taking longer, but all in principle disconnectable from the continuing provision of the basic facilities for 'doing science'. That universal duality of the requirements for doing scientific research sets up in every case a pattern of divergent and perhaps conflicting interest. The interest of the institution providing the house-room will only coincide with that of those involved with the specific project so long as it gets the benefits. Those may be financial, or to do with prestige and fame, or to do with the very retention of control.

The persons doing the research have an interest in those things. So may others, the outside funders, public and commercial, who are sustaining either arm of this dual funding. They may attach strings to their funding, to ensure that they retain a right to the benefits. In one sense, such funders are seeking to call to account those they are funding. On the other hand, they themselves need to be called to account if there is not to be a danger that they will pull the strings to their own advantage.

A high proportion of the submissions to the Dearing Committee in 1996–7 were concerned with the degree of selectivity in future funding for research and the problems of establishing criteria for such selection if all universities could not have bigger and better funds from a public purse which was not bottomless. There was a party which wanted to see the creation of a 'superleague' of universities, that is, a recognition that some universities as a whole deserve better funding. There was a cognate view which said that funding should be targeted selectively, but towards strong departments. The *CVCP Submission to HEFCE on Funding Method for Teaching from 1998–9* acknowledges that 'there are difficulties in determining an appropriate link between funding and quality. Some would argue', it comments:

> that poor quality should receive additional funding to bring it up to scratch. Others would argue that high quality should be rewarded with additional funding or additional student numbers. One problem with the latter is that, if a high quality rating has already been achieved with a particular level of resource what additional benefit would be gained from providing more money? Another problem with the latter is that additional student numbers may not be wanted and having them may lead to a diminution in quality. CVCP would prefer to see a threshold system operate in which low quality, as defined by a cut off point for quality assessment ratings (or equivalent under the Single Quality Agency), would make that subject ineligible for additional student numbers.

Is it, then, the right thing to direct funding to those who need it because they are *not* doing well, or to those who *are* doing well, as a reward, so that they can do better?

The perfectly correct contention that diversity of provision is a good thing should not be confused with an endorsement of the naturally occurring hierarchy of privilege and advantage as a good thing. To call for preferential financial treatment for those who are already strong (in department or university) is to be seen to take that line. Teaching students of limited ability in a hostile environment also deserves a high level of resourcing and is indubitably in the public interest.

However, if the argument is that there is simply not enough money to do both, then the public interest question shifts, and we have to ask whether it is more important that the best research should happen, even if at a high cost to the run-of-the-mill, or those merely approaching the starting blocks as researchers. Principles of selection have then to be devised. But no given principle derives necessarily from the sheer shortage of funds.

There is a rough division in policy planning between basic, strategic and applied research. It is customary to pay at least lip-service to the importance of the first two categories, because the last will more easily look after itself by generating a profit. 'All of the HE Funding Councils' research funds and over 90 per cent of the research funding provided by the Research Councils is spent in support of basic and strategic research',[40] said the Office of Science and Technology in 1997. But there is an irony in using the public policy tool to direct opportunities for research funding towards individuals whose defining characteristic is that their work is their own idea. 'The Realising our Potential Awards scheme was launched in February 1994 with the dual aims of first, enhancing collaboration between the science and engineering base and industry and second, providing funds to researchers, who are already interacting with industry, to carry out research in an area of their own choice.'[41]

The public interest in saving public money by encouraging private funding is clear enough. There may be a further benefit, in allowing scope for independently-conceived projects to be helped in ways Research Councils' money may not be free to do. 'To qualify a researcher needs to be funded by industry for strategic research and his/her proposal, which should *not* be in collaboration with industry, must meet simple tests of originality and practicality . . . the nature of ROPA should not be misunderstood; it is a responsive mode award which funds work defined solely by the researcher.'[42]

But there are drawbacks. The first is that there is not necessarily a tidy link between the project generated by an individual's own ideas and 'basic' or 'strategic' research. The second is that the same piece of research may prove to be of all three types. Out of a project conceived as applied may come basic principles or a long-term strategic project. Or, something which begins as basic or strategic research may turn out to be no such thing, but have one small practical outcome in a commercially exploitable discovery.

The humanities researcher and the scientist alike are, if they are university researchers, engaged in a task which defines itself as they go along. Even if the research project they begin on is tightly defined, they may have ideas while they are doing it which cannot be kept within those bounds, which may lead on elsewhere; they may also have insights which undermine the whole rationale of the experiment.

The first rule of research is that it would not be research if it was clear at the outset where it would lead. It is neglect of that rule which leads pharmaceutical companies to react with hostile surprise when research into which they have put funds fails to endorse the superiority of their product over others, as it did in the *Dong* case.[43]

Another rule of research, recognized, as we have seen, from the classical period, is that it is impossible accurately to foretell how long it will take; indeed some mental space, leisure, *otium*, is needed to provide time for standing back and thinking about where it is going. But the present quantitatively-based funding system works on the assumption that since there is not enough money to go round, it must be apportioned in the most modest units of resource possible, and those doing research must be able to say fairly accurately at the outset how long it will take.

What are described as 'people-related programmes' are defined in the 1997 paper on *Allocation of the Science Budget* under the heads of the various schemes for funding research studentships at various levels, including the University Research Fellowship schemes, designed for 'the highest quality post-doctoral fellows, who have usually had one or more fixed-term post-doctoral appointments'.[44] However, their continuing to work at all as scientists, and especially their obtaining permanent contracts with a university which will allow them to go on working as scientists until retiring age, then depends dangerously on the patronage of heads of department and appointing committees. It must, at least sometimes, happen that those who keep their noses clean feel the benefit. And that may itself not be in the public interest if, arguably, that interest lies in academic fearlessness, a terrible, sometimes ruthless honesty, which can break through barriers.

But does it? The great dilemma of accountability for funding is that governments and commercial and charitable funders alike are bound to want their money put to 'good' use. None of the three is likely to be willing to 'waste' it. But each will define 'waste' in a different way, in accordance with its own priorities. Above all, historically, each will want the academic interest to be subordinated to something else, and fearless honesty and pursuit of the truth will often be embarrassing to that something else.

The funder can withdraw funding as a token of disapproval which is also a tool of control. For the scholar to withdraw the work of an independent mind seems a feeble riposte, though it brings the project to a halt.

Conclusion

What are the common factors in the areas of accountability to a wider world we have been looking at? Let us postulate the existence of communities in which an intellectual endeavour is going forward, which can realize its purposes only if it can work without constraints other than those naturally and properly arising from the nature of the task. The traditional checks on this endeavour are those of truth and honesty and rigour, and they are prompts to the work as well as curbs upon it. There are, as we shall see in the next section, practical problems with this idea within these university communities. But in the interface between universities and the world there are factors working upon it which affect it materially.

One is certainly the problem of interference by financial considerations, and particularly by persons or bodies or governments using money as a means of control for their own benefit.

A second is interference by patronage for selfish or otherwise vested interests.

So, one of our chief 'accountability' problems in this study is the need to call such interference to order; to create and maintain space for the academic task; and to see that protectiveness as working to the public interest, not least in producing a cost-effectiveness and efficiency geared to a more profound set of values for the money than are easily quantified by headcounts and outputs.

Part 2

Calling to Account within Universities

Introduction

A university is a complex human community with structures which are naturally both hierarchical and collegial. It has employees and members. Some individuals – the academic staff – are both members and employees. It has teachers and students. It has contractual relationships of employment and contractual relationships to provide courses for students. It handles vast sums of public money. Calling it, or its constituent elements or officers, to account for its behaviour and performance is not an easy matter. We must now try to take the machine apart to see how it works.

5

Structure and Purpose

The leading modern English case to discuss the nature of a university in an attempt to define it in law is *St David's College, Lampeter v. Ministry of Education, S.I. 1948, No. 1655.* This set out the following considerations:

- What does the 'ordinary man' understand a university to be?
- What was the intention of the founder?
- Is the institution of an appropriate size?
- Does the institution provide an appropriate range of subjects?

The determining point was held by Vaizey J. to be that a university has to be incorporated and that has to be done with the intention to create a university.[1]

This places 'intention' high on the agenda for the making of a university. But that in turn begs the question of definition, for if it is not beyond question what a university is, it is impossible to be sure that what it was intended to create in one case is the same as what it was intended to create in another.

We do not seem to have proceeded much further with this since. A *Memorandum of General Principles governing the grant of charters* in the 1970s suggests a framework of questions to be asked before it is decided whether an institution ought to be given a royal charter.

1. Are the objects of the institution such as might suitably be *recognised* by the grant of a Charter?
2. Has it been established sufficiently long to prove its stability and utility?
3. Is its financial position sound?
4. Is it fully representative of the interests it purports to serve, and is its status in its own sphere generally *recognised*?
5. Does its standing or circumstances differentiate it from other organisations with somewhat similar objects.[2]

It has become easy to lose sight of the fact that universities are communities of *people*, among whom the advancement of knowledge goes on and teaching is carried out. The question is how those communities are to be kept together and sustained in activities in which there is sufficient coherence for it to be possible to argue that they are defined by a common and continuing purpose. When we have an idea of how this holding-together works, we can begin to see whether there is a purpose to it which we can call 'the purpose of a university'.

We are now facing sharply the problem that an original mind has in every sense to be 'fed'. In the late twentieth century, certain kinds of inquiry require expensive equipment and collaborative effort. But advanced intellectual activity, conducted on substantially the same underlying assumption that it takes place within a community of scholarship, and experienced by those who describe it in strikingly similar terms century by century, has not always felt the same need for structural or institutional 'support'. There is, historically, no necessary connection between a particular university structure and the fostering of the work of scholarship and teaching, though some structures may arguably impede it.

Therefore we have to look hard at the institutional frameworks within which communities of scholars have had their being. It is possible to point to ways in which scholarly requirements have, at certain times, had a shaping effect on institutions. There was no *institutional* continuity between the ancient Greek schools and those of the Western Middle Ages, and in most places it would also be hard to argue for a real continuity within the Western half of the old Roman Empire. The fall of the Roman Empire ended the ancient educational system in its structural forms. The mediaeval schools are largely a fresh creation. They arose in attachment to cathedrals, to meet the needs of the cathedrals for educated canons, and in monasteries, to meet the requirement for monks who could sing the offices and engage in *lectio divina* to their soul's health. The former became the seed of the early universities, for they served a need for educated persons who could work in the world.[3] But something else acted as a catalyst, and that was student demand coupled with, and perhaps generating, a supply of masters.

Thus, teaching rather than research created universities. The first universities formed themselves from the wandering scholars who taught, at the fringes of the cathedral schools of the late eleventh and twelfth centuries, and the students who followed them. In their early patterns of teaching and learning we can see an inner life, indeed an innate *vitality*, informing and shaping teaching methods and ultimately deciding the form of the universities themselves. For the students literally followed these latter-day 'peripatetic' masters if they moved on. The institutionally solid cathedral schools provided places where a student community could be 'found' and, perhaps, seduced to move across to the free-standing 'schools' which were to grow into universities.

Peter Abelard achieved fame by teaching in that way at Laon and Paris. He became, he says, 'a conscious imitator of the Peripatetics of the ancient world',[4] as he went about 'disputing'.[5] Already, disputation was a skill Abelard discovered that he could use to make his name and win himself a place as a master. He soon found himself in controversial arguments with William of Champeaux, whom he describes as his *praeceptor* at Paris. 'I seemed to win the argument sometimes', he says complacently.[6]

Students would follow a popular master, and records of the early lectures show that there were interruptions and challenges and loud comparisons made by students between what their lecturer was saying and what another master was saying. This disputatiousness of the early mediaeval academic scene grew more formal, but at this date it does not seem to have been wholly different in character from the more freely-structured debates of Socratic dialogue. Socrates taught by discourse. In Plato's accounts of his dialogues the teacher is always several steps ahead of the students. It is not apparent that he himself learns from the dialogue. In Augustine's dialogues, though Augustine is the leader, there is a meeting of minds between fellow explorers, and the teacher acknowledges that he himself learns. Abelard's early experience of disputation was not incompatible with an 'Augustinian' real sharing of ideas; and, in the mediaeval university disputation as it evolves after his time there continued to be a true *litis contestatio* of opinions and a challenge of mind by mind.

Arguments pro and con in mediaeval university disputations involve citations of authorities. Here are nascent structural principles of 'higher' education as involving the communication of knowledge, by teachers live and dead, *antiqui* and *moderni* acting in disputatious concert.

It was not until nearly a century later than Abelard's youth that there were (even in northern Europe) sufficient teachers who continued as teachers in one place, for it to become appropriate for them to organize themselves into gilds or *universitates* for their mutual protection, to set up structures for teaching and examining which made students formally a kind of 'apprentices', and bachelors of arts 'journeymen'. In these first formal structures, the 'masters' are the lords of the gild, peers and collaborators in its governance. The model was that of all the trade or craft gilds of mediaeval northern Europe. This was a corporate body, whose full members, the masters, shared equally in its running, and whose apprentices and journeymen could qualify for that membership.[7]

It remains important that a university is a community. A strand in the definition of a university which has been of consistent importance is the notion that it is a corporation. The informal structure of the mediaeval gild attained a formality in the later Middle Ages in England through the system of granting royal charters; these recognized a legal status. There was also incorporation in the forming in 1992 of the 'new' UK universities, but there the corporators are the Board of Governors not the whole academic community. The difference is fundamental, because in these latter-day structures collegiality has ceased to be of the essence. It has been replaced by hierarchy.

The corporate structure not only expressed a relationship of equality among its members, it was also concerned with the maintenance of standards. Like any other craft association, a mediaeval university was a gild whose members kept a tight control of admission, permission to teach and examining.

Institutional *structures* are not inimical to the work of scholarship, both teaching and inquiry. They may indeed be helpful to the teacher. They save the individual teacher having to make independent arrangements to collect students together, and having to seek to hold onto them in competition with others. They can provide an assurance which will help to ensure that there are students offering themselves in the future, that what is taught meets an acceptable standard and that any mark of mastery of the subject, such as a degree or *gradus*,[8] conferred on the student at the end of a period of study, has some meaning.

Structures also make it possible for a good level of academic competence to persist in periods when no truly outstanding original minds are available to provide a natural leadership of thought and inquiry in order to set standards directly. The patient routine teaching of what is already known to the next generation is of value. It can be argued that this maintenance of a decent competence in academic disciplines, this role of stewardship, however unexciting, is a proper role for a university, and should always form a substratum of its work.

This brings us to one of the crucial points at which the outwardness of structures is coupled with consequences for the 'inwardness' of what a university does.[9] It has been remarked in a modern USA context that the selection of individuals to teach in universities does not always result in the best but sometimes the second best holding posts.[10] Originality is not necessarily rebellion; but requiring conformity either discourages it or (because it is not easy to discourage original thought in those to whom it comes), keeps it outside the system and tends to deny it recognition.

Cornford's warning

Structures can be helpful or unhelpful to scholarship and teaching in the way they distribute *powers*. F.M. Cornford's *Microcosmographia Academica*, first published in 1908, describes a world in which the academic 'politicians' of an ancient university conduct a series of moves upon a chess board.[11] He is both cynical and idealistic. There is, he stresses at the beginning and the end of his manual, for those who would win power in their university, a place of quiet within it where the real work is done, which is where even the academic politicians really live, and to which the ambitious young politician will in due course discover that he wants to betake himself too. That is the world of scholarship. 'There is another world within this microcosm – a silent, reasonable world . . . Some day you may go back to it; and you will enjoy its calm the more for your excursion in the world of unreason.'[12]

There are enduring truths at the heart of the entertainment in the *Microcosmographia*, and they are worth a look. Cornford knew that academics are, on the whole, pusillanimous souls:

> The Political Motive in the academic breast is . . . *Fear* – genuine, perpetual, heartfelt timorousness . . . The proper objects of Fear . . . are (in order of importance):
>
> Giving yourself away;
> Females;
> What Dr ——— will say;
> The Public Washing of Linen;
> Socialism, otherwise Atheism;
> The Great World; etc., etc., etc.[13]
>
> Conviction has never yet been produced by an appeal to reason, which only makes people uncomfortable. If you want to move them, you must address your arguments to prejudice and the political motive.[14]

He knew, too, that the fear goes with caution and that the outcome with which academics are happiest is frequently no outcome at all:

> There is only one argument for doing something. The rest are arguments for doing nothing.
>
> The argument for doing something is that it is the right thing to do. But then, of course, comes the difficulty of making sure that it is right . . . the only justifiable attitude of mind is suspense of judgement; and this attitude, besides being peculiarly congenial to the academic temperament, has the advantage of being comparatively easy to attain. There remains the duty of persuading others to be equally judicious, and to refrain from plunging into reckless courses which might lead them heaven knows whither . . . It is obvious that inaction can have no consequences at all.[15]

There are refinements of this principle. It goes with an anxiety to avoid embarrassing publicity and to keep everything under wraps even within the university.

There are various devices for ensuring that nothing is done, and that it is not done as quietly as possible, which modern academics will still recognize:

> The *Principle of the Wedge* is that you should not act justly now for fear of raising expectations that you may act still more justly in the future – expectations which you are afraid you will not have the courage to satisfy. A little reflection will make it evident that the Wedge argument implies the admission that the persons who use it cannot prove that the action is not just. If they could, that would be the sole and sufficient reason for not doing it, and this argument would be superfluous.[16]

> The *Principle of the Dangerous Precedent* is that you should not now do an admittedly right action for fear you, or your equally timid successors, should not have the courage to do right in some future case . . . It follows that nothing should ever be done for the first time.[17]

> Another argument is that '*the machinery for effecting the proposed objects already exists*'. This should be urged in cases where the existing machinery has never worked, and is now so rusty that there is no chance of its being set in motion.[18]
>
> The *Alternative Proposal*... is a form of Red Herring. As soon as three or more alternatives are in the field, there is pretty sure to be a majority against any one of them, and nothing will be done.[19]
>
> The method of *Prevarication* is based upon a very characteristic trait of the academic mind... The principle is, that a few bad reasons for doing something neutralise all the good reasons for doing it. Since this is devoutly believed, it is often the best policy to argue weakly against the side you favour.[20]
>
> *Wild Cat* is an epithet applicable to persons who bring forward a scheme unanimously agreed upon by experts after exhaustive consideration of thirty-five or more alternative proposals. In its wider use it applies to all ideas which were not familiar in 1881.[21]
>
> The argument '*that you remember exactly the same proposal being rejected in 1867*', is a very strong one in itself.[22]

There are devices which depend upon skill with thought and word:

> Talk slowly and indistinctly at a little distance from the point.[23]
>
> Once start a comma and the whole pack will be off, full cry, especially if they have had a literary training. (Adullamites affect to despise commas, and even their respect for syntax is often not above suspicion.) But comma-hunting is so exciting as to be a little dangerous. When attention is entirely concentrated on punctuation, there is some fear that the conduct of business may suffer, and a proposal get through without being properly obstructed on its demerits.[24]

This was not a world in which the business motive was unknown or the financial incentive absent. There was a figure known as The Good Business Man:

> He is one whose mind has not been warped and narrowed by merely intellectual interests, and who, at the same time, has not those odious pushing qualities which are unhappily required for making a figure in buisness anywhere else. He has had his finger on the pulse of the Great World – a distant and rather terrifying region, which it is very necessary to keep in touch with, though it must not be allowed on any account to touch you.[25]

But the Good Business Man is no longer a risible amateur in a university. He, or his professional counterpart, is now likely to be in a position of great influence. He is especially important to the scientific community, which depends on the allocation of sizeable funds to be able to do any work at all. Cornford despises the scientists of the Cambridge of his day as barbarians, but he recognizes this distinctive feature of their conscious needs:

> The Adullamites are dangerous, because they know what they want; and that is, all the money there is going. They inhabit a series of caves near Downing Street. They say to one another, 'If you will scratch my back, I will scratch yours; and if you won't, I will scratch your face.' It will be seen that these cave-dwellers are not refined, like classical men. That is why they succeed in getting all the money there is going.[26]

Something else has changed, though not in Oxford and Cambridge themselves. That is the power held by academics individually within their own universities. Cornford writes for his young academic politician on the assumption that if he chooses to engage in the affairs of his university he can do so, on a level footing with everyone else, that the power to be had is that of influence: 'It is clear that twenty independent persons, each of whom has a different reason for not doing a certain thing, and no one of whom will compromise with any other, constitutes a most effective check upon the rashness of individuals.'[27] But that is true only if the 20 independent persons are in a position to refuse to compromise. Only then can they engage in the kind of trading of favours Cornford describes with such relish: 'My Jobs are public-spirited proposals, which happen (much to my regret) to involve the advancement of a personal friend, or (still more to my regret) of myself. Your Jobs are insidious intrigues for the advancement of yourself and your friends, speciously disguised as public-spirited proposals.'[28] His Cambridge was full of such horse-trading:

> Squaring can be carried on at lunch, but it is better that we should meet casually . . . When we have succeeded in meeting accidentally, it is etiquette to talk about indifferent matters for ten minutes and then part. After walking five paces in the opposite direction, you should call me back, and begin with the words, 'Oh, by the way, if you should happen . . .' The nature of Your Job must then be vaguely indicated, without mentioning names; and it should be treated by both parties as a matter of very small importance. You should hint that I am a very influential person, and that the whole thing is a secret between us. Then we shall part as before, and I shall call you back and introduce the subject of My Job, in the same formula. By observing this procedure we shall emphasise the fact that there is *no connection whatsoever* between my supporting your Job and your supporting mine. This absence of connection is the essential feature of squaring.[29]

No one would want to argue that Cornford's academic world is ideal. It manifests the worst features of academic conduct; beyond weakness and cowardice lie spite and pettiness. But the checks and balances within it were strong. No single individual could acquire a power which enabled him to dictate without challenge the policy of the institution or the futures of those who worked in it, though he might well succeed in damaging irretrievably the lives and careers of a few of those who opposed him.

Some of the inherent features of Cornford's Cambridge remain those of any academic community, because they derive from the inalienable nature of the community of scholarship. In the 1980s things looked like this to one observer:

> The factory floor in higher education is cluttered with bundles of knowledge that are attended by professionals. The professionals push and pull on their respective bundles. If they are doing research, they are trying to increase the size of the bundle and even to reconstitute it. If engaged in scholarship other than research, they are conserving, criticising, and reworking it. If teaching, they are trying to pass some of it on to the flow-through clientèle we call students, encouraging them to think about its nature, how it may be used, and perhaps take up a career devoted to it.[30]

There are features of academic governance which are peculiar to it, and arise out of this unavoidable ownership of his own expertise by its possessor. These persist even where management patterns change, so as to entrust authority to professional managers:

> Academic departments consist in part of autocrats who individually run certain operations, even dictatorially, and then come together as equals and part-equals to decide collectively on large matters, thereby operating in a way not readily duplicated in other sectors of society. The other sectors are different in that they are not simultaneously discipline-based and discipline-diversified. They are not extensively composed as a matrix of disciplines and enterprises.[31]

Burton Clark's principle is that there remains a residuum of such personally localized expertise which makes it impossible for any system of governance of an academic community to be susceptible to a complete takeover by any imposed organizational structure:

> Scholarly expertise confers a crucial and distinctive kind of authority. One aspect of that authority is personal: individual [lecturers] exercise extensive supervision over the work of students, and senior [lecturers] often do so over the work of junior faculty, with their decisions typically not closely circumscribed by bureaucratic rules or by collegial norms that foreclose individual discretion.[32]

He likens the personal authority of the scholar to that of the master in the mediaeval gild. For collegial authority is based on a presumption of the equality of the persons making a decision, in which each has an equal vote because each is, as a scholar, also his own master.

The question is whether that is sufficiently important to override the drawback of apparent delay and inefficiency in decision-making. There are, arguably, strong reasons why it is. The first is the need for checks and balances. The second has to do with the definition of efficiency. We must now look at both.

6

Institutional Autonomy: Academics and Managers

In Cornford's Cambridge a cat could look at a king and tell him what he thought of him. The young academic politician was disadvantaged only by his youth and naivety, not by any lack of personal position. He was held back only by the consideration of the harm he might do to himself in the power game if he spoke out too freely or in the wrong company. Ability could win its way. But if a chief executive or a line manager is obeyed because of his office and not respected because of the personal ability he shows in discharging it, incompetence or bad judgement may not be checked. And conversely, his personal views may become the official views, again without check. The distinction of person and office is easily blurred.

Where the power resides: the collegial structure

The chancellor of the ancient universities of England embodied the university in its dealings with the town, in such pecuniary matters as the letting of halls and the engagement of servants by scholars; and in such disciplinary matters as the banishment or imprisonment of loose women, keeping the peace and the morals of the university in general. He had archidiaconal powers at least from 1214 in Oxford, when the bishop instituted a Chancellor on whom he conferred the powers of an archdeacon. But these apparently giant powers are not in many respects as great as those of professional life and death now held by the chief executive of a 'new' university over his academic staff. He may be able to make policy and deploy huge financial resources and hire and fire, with very little check upon him.

'The government of a competitive university is necessarily of an autocratic character.'[1] That seemed to Thorstein Veblen to follow from the business and commercial imperatives of competition which were making themselves felt in American universities at the beginning of the twentieth century. It is a theme much in evidence again in the latter part of the twentieth century in British university governance. The governance structures of British universities fall into broad categories, depending roughly upon the period of their coming into being. The ancient universities of Oxford and Cambridge retain patterns of governance in which a mediaeval collegiality persists. Academic democracy with checks and balances was in evidence not only in the sixteenth century,[2] but strikingly in the 1689 case when Cambridge sought to resist the wishes of the King and to assert its right to give or withhold its degrees at its own choice.[3]

In Oxford and Cambridge the vast majority of members of the academic staff are still automatically members of what remains the governing body of the University. In the case of Oxford this governing body is called 'Congregation'. In the case of Cambridge, 'the Regent House'. The thousands of members never actually meet; neither the Senate House in Cambridge nor the Sheldonian Theatre in Oxford would be big enough to contain them. But they do have frequent *opportunities* to do so, as many as choose, in formal live debates on issues of concern to the University; they can always call a ballot by getting the necessary signatures if they see the need; and no major decisions can be taken without an expression of their collective will.

In Oxford in 1996[4] an attempt was made to limit membership of those entitled to speak in Congregation by altering the age limit. The age limit for membership of the equivalent forum in Cambridge, the Senate, which includes all MAs, not only those who form the academic staff of the University, had been altered to 70 in Cambridge some years before, without undue controversy. The Oxford move was made by fiat of its Council. There was a mention in the Oxford University *Gazette*. No one noticed the implications until a matter arose on which the University needed to debate and vote. Then a huge row broke out, as it was contended on the one part that beyond a certain age individuals would inevitably become out of touch with University affairs and so should no longer have a decisive say in them; and on the other, that elder statesmen are of inestimable value to a mature democracy, that such elder statesmen regularly served the University on committees and that they would be a loss from the governing community. The elder statesmen themselves had views on that.

As a rule, the governing bodies of Oxford and Cambridge are slumbrous, and many Reports to the University of Cambridge are put up for Discussion with no takers. But if anything seems to be being slipped past them they, too, wake to lively action. In the summer of 1996 plans were laid to build an Institute of Management Studies on a piece of land which had been given to the University of Oxford by Merton College on the understanding that it would be kept green as a playing field. There were four things wrong with that in the view of members of Congregation. First, the Council slipped the decision through in such a way that it was published in the middle of the Long Vacation while most members of the University were not about. Secondly, it overrode an agreement which Merton College had intended to be binding and thus called into question the value of promises made by the University or its Colleges. Thirdly, it accepted money for the endowment from a source which some were prepared to question, or on terms they thought in themselves unacceptable. Fourthly, many in Oxford were of the opinion that Management Studies was not a proper discipline for that ancient University, not 'rigorous enough'. They were, perhaps, reinforced in that opinion by the awareness that Cambridge had got ahead with its Judge Institute of Management Studies so that any such Institute subsequently set up in Oxford would look like an imitation.

Each of these is a substantive question. The debate showed academe at its best and at its worst: sharp, stylish, stimulating fresh insights, evincing prejudices, scoring points, settling old scores – the *Microcosmographia* in action. The question is whether for all its human failings such a system is better than rule by managerial fiat or the will of a chief executive, where the personal prejudices are those of a single individual, not those of numerous individuals keeping one another in balance.

It has already been conceded that the substantive objection to such full academic democracy is that it can make decision-making slow. But speedy decisions are not always sound decisions and the stage where it seems too late to go back now is quickly reached.[5] That may be so even if there is no question about the desirability of the end in view. Hasty legislation almost always turns out to have failed to allow for something important.

Democracy does not always get things right. It can also reflect donnish pettiness and academic self-interest. Nevertheless, it will be a central thesis of this study that it remains better than the alternatives.

Oxford and Cambridge have both been examining their structures. In the 1990s, Oxford set up a North Commission, chaired by the then Vice-Chancellor, Peter North, to look into its structures of governance.[6] It called in Coopers and Lybrand to take a look and make a report. This report was the work of two relatively young consultants, who put it together by talking to members and representatives of the University's committees and faculties and colleges and other structures. There was a general invitation to everyone to send in comments.

It was found to be impossible for any outsider to penetrate far into the old dark recesses of the system. However, a few outline comments came sharply to prominence. It was, for example, the view of the team that there was room to improve efficiency of decision-making.

In Cambridge a few years earlier there had been a similar review of structures by the Wass Syndicate, also intended to improve efficiency without loss of accountability. This did not touch the powers of the Regent House, but it sought to transfer more authority in the day-to-day running of affairs to the Council, elected directly by the Regent House and still accountable to it. Fail-safe mechanisms were put in place, to prevent power being concentrated in too few hands. A Board of Scrutiny was set up to monitor the financial affairs of the University, to look into the Annual Reports of the Council and the General Board, and to have right of access to any papers of committees it asked for in that connection.

In Cambridge, there is a system of checks and balances within the central structures themselves. The General Board of the Faculties has responsibility for the educational and academic work of the University, but it is subject to the powers of the Council, which is the executive and policy-making body. And the Council represents the Regent House, which is the governing body of the University.[7]

If the General Board or the Council wishes to 'do' anything, it publishes a Report. That is opened a week or two later to a Discussion in the Senate House, at which any member of the Regent House may speak. All speeches are published verbatim. The Council then has a right to respond to what has been said. The action or change of policy is finally made by the publishing and passing of a Grace. If no one objects to the published Grace, the Grace is deemed to come into effect at a stated date and time. If objection is made requiring an amendment, which can be done by getting ten signatures, there has to be a ballot. Flysheets are circulated by way of 'campaigning speeches'.

A clear distinction remains in principle between administrative officers, who are 'civil servants', and 'academic' officers, the scholars of the University, the heirs of the Masters of Arts of the mediaeval *universitas.* As in Oxford, that is somewhat blurred by the fact that the senior administrative officers are also members of Congregation or the Regent House, if they have degrees of the University. However, there is no question of their having authority of any sort over academic staff.

On the whole, this sophisticated process works in the mature democracy of ancient and very confident universities. It is a notable feature of disputes that strong things can be said, with broad smiles on the faces of those who disagree with, but appreciate, a well-put point.

Checks and balances: hierarchy and line management

The contrast with the governance of the 'new' (post-1992) universities is enormous. They have a corporation to govern them, too, but it does not consist of all the university's academic officers. Indeed, such officers may have only the slightest toe-hold in the system of governance: 'For each higher education corporation established on or after the appointed day there shall be an instrument (to be known as the instrument of government) providing for the constitution of the corporation and making such other provision as is required under this section.'[8] This instrument of government must comply with Schedule 7 to the Act: 'In relation to a higher education corporation for which an instrument of government has effect the members of the corporation for the time being shall be known as the board of governors of the institution conducted by the corporation.'[9]

New universities in England are thus governed by a 'board' of between 12 and 24 members, of whom the vice-chancellor is one, unless he declines to be a member. Up to 13 members must be 'independent'. That is, they must be drawn from persons with experience in industry, employment, commerce or a profession. These must form the majority. Up to two further governors may be teachers and up to two students. The remainder may be coopted, and at least one of them must have experience in educational provision.

The governance structure of the old universities is much more variable. Their founding charters or Acts of Parliament create or permit a multiplicity of systems. It is usual for their Councils or Senates to have a substantial proportion of academic staff. There is usually also a Court, which is a mainly representative body with nominal ultimate authority over the university. In Scotland the 'governing body' may be called a 'board of management', but there is still nothing resembling full academic democracy.

The inclusion of the vice-chancellor *ex officio* on the governing body of new universities has led to difficulties when an institution has been managed in such a way that it became necessary to seek to get rid of the chief executive. The Board of Governors has that responsibility; but the person whose conduct is being brought into question is a member of that Board. Politics, personal factors and sheer embarrassment, tend to allow him to stay.[10]

Other difficulties attend the provisions that 'up to thirteen [the 'independent members'] of the corporation shall be members appearing to the appointing authority to have experience of, and to have shown capacity in, industrial, commercial or employment matters of the practice of any profession'. These are intended to bring perspectives from public life and to help the institution serve public needs. However, those whose backgrounds are in business will bring assumptions which, because they tie in directly with financial aspects of management of the institutions, may create an imbalance. Further, there is no explicit provision for a membership drawn from the arts or religious communities, representing, in short, the full span of the 'interests' of the community. It is significant that the concept of the 'parent governor' is altogether missing. There is no international voice.

Of the industrial and commercial and business and professional members between one and four may be nominated 'by the members of the corporation who are either independent members or initial nominee members and the principal of the institution (if he is a member)'. These 'initial nominee members' breed their successors. A structure which begins with nominations and becomes self-perpetuating is inherently dangerous.

The academic community is conspicuously under-represented in the provisions for achieving a balance of interests on the Board of Governors of such an institution. So the academic staff on whose professional expertise much of the ancient justification for the autonomy of universities rests, no longer make up the membership of the body corporate except at Oxford and Cambridge. The dangers of that are only beginning to be fully visible.

The *Dearing Report* (R 54) separated 'the ultimate decision-making body', and 'a wider representative role, to inform decision-making but not to take decisions'. This recommendation comes under the heading of 'enabling governance to become more effective' (Chapter 15.32 ff.), and its thrust would appear to be a separation of 'decisions by a few' from 'advice from the many'. Because academic staff have limited representation on the governing bodies of 'new' (post-1992) universities in the UK, their interests and concerns can easily be suppressed or denied a full hearing. Apart from the central question of the acceptability of non-professional decisionmakers making decisions about professional matters (an absurdity obvious enough in the case of businessmen telling doctors their medical business), there is the fact that non-academic considerations can easily be allowed to outweigh numerically, or in force, those of the academic community, when persons who are not scholars seek to run things. The persons who sit on boards of Governors representing the local community and other interests are acting only in a very 'part-time' capacity. In practice, therefore, they often have no profound sense of the institution they govern and little contact with its workings.

The separation of powers

The Nolan Committee noticed, in preparing its *Second Report*,[11] that one college of further education had a 'formal system by which nominations' to the governing body 'were sought from companies which had large numbers of employees as students'. Is this a good or a bad thing? Such companies have a real interest in such a college. But then again, it is a vested interest.

There are dangers in the blurring of the distinctions which underlie the doctrine of the separation of powers. The Nolan Committee in its *Second Report* concentrated on governance at the top levels of institutions, with special reference to preventing vested interest or other sorts of 'sleaze' from corrupting their management. In practice, though, it is the running of things at lower levels which most commonly gives cause for concern, and where things much more often go wrong.

It has been held that the separation of powers rests not on a legal principle but on a political one.[12] Nevertheless, at its root must lie the rule of natural justice that no one may be judge in his own case. If there is no such rule, there is a danger that vested interest can make a law and apply it; and ensure that it is enforced, with no check upon it to prevent unfair disadvantage to those subject to it. There has to be, for safety's sake, a rule which insists upon the separation of powers and makes sure that different persons exercise the separated powers.

There are practical difficulties in finding enough senior persons to discharge separate duties separately, even in an organization as large as a university. Thus, a head of department may decide the promotion prospects of the members of his department and give them to understand that he will be willing to help if they will toe the line. A dean or vice-chancellor will frequently be both accuser and judge in a discipline process.

All structures which entrust authority to some over others will have a tendency to move in the direction of the oppression of the others by the some. Therefore, there must be checks and balances in the system, and since they will not work unless there is some means of making them work, that must also be provided for.

The checks and balances available vary greatly from institution to institution, both in their form and in their effect. That means that the respect paid to the key principle, that prejudice to fair outcome can be prevented only by separation of powers, is everywhere set at risk. This is particularly a problem with line management systems, where a problem can normally be taken only to an immediate senior, who can only in exceptional circumstances and with difficulty be bypassed so that someone else may be consulted. If a head of department can apportion teaching loads, put up for promotion and institute disciplinary proceedings, that means he can exercise a variety of constraints on the professional lives of members of his department.

There is a tendency for powers to concentrate in a few hands, here as in the grant awarding area.[13] The same names appear on committees, and get to have a say in who arrives on other committees. Appointments to committees are often made on the say-so of an individual who suggests a name. Others are glad to be relieved of the task of thinking of suggestions themselves. There may be some cursory inquiry into the suitability of the suggestion. The person with whom it originates is reassuring. The appointment is made. There is thus an almost invisible danger, and that is degeneration towards rule by a hidden oligarchy of the same few sitting on too many of the university's committees.[14] That is a pattern exacerbated by the practice of creating committees by secret nomination processes. There need be no sinister intent in this, for it is more likely to be a result of too few persons coming forward to share the work. It does, however, create a class of those who 'count' in the running of the university, and that is dangerous.

Once committees are up and running there is a tendency to let them get on with it. The function of all supervisory bodies is to call the chief executive and subordinate officers to account in their framing and implementation of internal rules. However, it is shrewdly pointed out by Caldwell that, in universities, decisions are effectively taken by subordinate committees and are 'rarely disturbed by the highest governing body'.[15] That means that even if it is possible to give an answer to the question 'to whom is the decision-maker accountable?' in terms of the constitution or structure of the university, that internal accountability may be no more than nominal. And in many instances that effectively denies a remedy where there has been injustice or mismanagement or even simply mistake or misjudgement within a university's decision-making.

Each new university has a clerk or secretary to its governing body, who has a duty to oversee 'the legal propriety of the university's actions' and to advise the governing body if there is cause for concern. The Nolan Committee notes (without undue concern) that this officer will also usually 'report for management purposes to the Chief Executive' on whom he may be offering critical comment to the governing body.[16] There can even sometimes be 'improper collusion between a small group of lay members and the Chief Executive' on a new university's governing body.[17] That can make it almost impossible to call the chief executive or other senior officers to account if there is abuse.

Regulation is not readily achieved at a higher level either. The Secretary of State was responsible for the legislation which set up the new universities and he made the first appointments to their boards, but they are now self-perpetuating bodies, which makes them also largely *de facto* self-regulating bodies. There is no authority in the executive (in the person of the Secretary of State) to place individuals on governing bodies or to remove them. The governing body of each institution is self-regulating in that it alone can dismiss its members, though changes to the rules of governance of the old universities must be approved by the Privy Council, on the advice of the Department for Education and Employment.[18]

It is not wholly clear whether the intention of the legislation which established a pattern of inclusion of independent members on the governing bodies of the new universities was to ensure that academic self-interest was checked by a proper concern for 'the public interest' in these publicly funded bodies; or to ensure that machinery existed for checking abuses of powers by the administrators of the university. The latter is one of the principal functions of the traditional visitor, and it remains an area in which accountability is important.

The Commissioners were, under the Education Reform Act 1988, Sched. 11, to have: 'power to do anything which appears to them necessary or expedient for the purpose of or in connection with the discharge of their functions, including in particular power to require any officer of a qualifying institution to furnish any information, or to produce any documents, relating to the institution or its instruments or government'. But the Commissioners are now disbanded, their work of devising the Model Statute done, with no provision for its amendment.

Defensive strategies of institutions include resisting amendments required by the courts. Even if a case goes to court and the court decides in favour of the applicant, it may not be easy to shift the decision in another direction. 'Recognised techniques exist for the circumvention of court orders'.[19] These include delay, taking the same decision again; or – on the part of governments – the making of new legislation to nullify the effects of the judgement. It is unlikely that the minds of the administrators will be won or changed so that there will be a genuine rethinking of policy: 'Administrative law judgements . . . may sometimes be seen as a tedious but unavoidable detour on a previously mapped-out route . . . they entail no genuine reconsideration of policy.'[20]

In the case of industrial tribunal findings, too, the institution may seek simply to ignore the order, as London Guildhall University did in the case of Amir Majid.[21]

So, we come back to the question whether legislative, executive and judicial are types of power which need to be separated in the running of a university. The making of regulations in universities; the running of things according to those regulations; and the adjudication of discipline and grievance processes fall tidily into those categories.

Senior persons in universities rarely set out to be tyrants. The Director of the Southampton Institute who took 'early retirement' in 1997 was a natural entrepreneur. He did a great deal for his institution by taking it ambitiously forward into franchising ventures overseas, creating foreign campuses in Athens and Alicante and elsewhere, and trying to raise its profile and status so that it could become a university. But he needed money for the ventures, so he started making staff redundant on the home campus. He sacked one research scientist in the middle of the academic year. His students protested. The scientist went to an industrial tribunal and won his case.[22] Other staff made redundant did the same. The Higher Education Quality Council, the watchdog of the Committee of Vice-Chancellors and Principals, made adverse reports. The Director sought to sue it. The Higher Education Funding Council for England (HEFCE) raised serious questions about the funding and standards of an overseas campus of the institution. It did an audit; it was not satisfied and it did another audit. The Director told staff that he took this as a compliment. He headed a delegation to go and tell the Chief Executive of the HEFCE that there was a conspiracy among the staff to discredit the institution. He threatened to sue the press, local and national, over reports in their pages. He put out an official newsletter designed to tell staff and students at the institution that all would be well if it were not for conspiracy against the Director and his senior staff. He hired an ex-detective superintendent to conduct inquiries into the activities of members of staff who were producing a satirical magazine to counter this official *Newsletter.* The issue of 20 March 1997 contains the following:

> *Dunghill launches investigation*
> A very serious spoof has come to the attention of the Dunghill editorial (contented lecturers section). This takes the form of a letter, circulated to all staff, purportedly in the name of a Professor David Leyland. We do not believe it has done much damage, because any fool can see that it is a transparent forgery. There are a number of easy-to-detect factors which lead to this conclusion:
>
> 1. Not many people in the Institute (or outside it) know of the existence of *The Dunghill.* Only an idiot would circulate a letter to staff announcing its existence.
> 2. The letter includes the amusing notion that people will be scared to express their views in case a *Dunghill* reporter rushes off and prints it. This is a jolly conceit but no normal person would hold such views.
> 3. The purported 'denial' that phone tapping and computer hacking has taken place seems designed to spread the idea around that these things have in fact taken place. No serious manager would commit such a schoolboy mistake in communications with staff.

A 'Staff communication review' at Southampton Institute was conducted by Geoffrey Hall at the request of the Chairman of the Board of Governors in November 1996. This independent report underlined the problem that a large number of staff from most senior to the most junior could not speak out in criticism 'for fear of the consequences'.[23] There was anxiety 'as to how Professor Hall would be able to operate freely within the Institute and at the same time ensure that strict confidentiality would prevail until his report was submitted'.[24] The staff were certainly found to be feeling concerns. 'The recent intention to restructure the faculties again and reduce their number from nine to six has led to widespread confusion, worry and deep concern.'[25]

The report expressed, though not in exactly this terminology, the conflict which can arise between a presumption that academic staff have a right to hold and express views as professionals and members of an institution of higher education (collegiality), and the assumption that there are things which must be decided at the top of an institution and simply passed on to those in subordinate positions (hierarchy). 'The lack of serious academic debate is referred to and the importance of attaining academic maturity through rigorous open debate is emphasised.'[26]

Nottingham Trent, the 'new' university which was validating the degrees of the institution, began to look into the running of courses on another overseas campus. It produced a report highly critical of the institution's lack of vigilance. 'The university is at a loss to understand the reasons for . . . the failures of the institute to assure itself that appropriate arrangements were in place for the effective delivery of its academic programmes.'[27]

Because the Board of Governors had the Director among its members, it found it difficult to call him to account and the balance of power and interest among the Governors was complicated by the surprise and uncertainty some of them felt at being in a situation they could not have envisaged. The problem of ordinary people simply not knowing what to do is not uncommon, and it is embarrassing to sit round a table with a man whose behaviour is being called into question.

The most difficult thing to achieve is a rigorous objectivity, the capacity of senior persons to distance themselves from their actions and admit fault. That is the ultimate separation of powers. It is important that 'staff development' is not taken to apply only to those in junior positions. The *Dearing Report* of 1997 says nothing of this, merely that the vice-chancellor must 'command' the 'confidence' of 'the governing body and the Academic Board or Senate'. It looks for 'Provision of [a] clear framework of authority and accountability' as a 'duty of a governing body' (15.48). It does not, however, grasp a nettle which threatens to become a rampant weed in higher education.

What is efficiency?

On the face of it 'efficiency' appears a clear good, but much depends on what it is taken to mean. Forming a consensus takes time. Lord Annan commented to the Franks Commission that Oxford moved at the pace of its most recalcitrant members.[28] However, taking time may, as Cornford warns, be a means of persuading the problem to go away or allowing sufficient time to elapse for everyone to have forgotten what it was.

So, although considered decisions must be better, the problem is to ensure that decisions are made by the people who see most clearly and who are free of interest which may distort their judgement, while ensuring that there remain means of changing the decision if even a paragon among decision-makers gets it wrong. That is the heart of efficiency.

Lord Curzon of Kedleston was Chancellor of Oxford at the time of the *Report of the Hebdomadal Council on Principles and Methods of University Reform* (1910). He presided at many of the 105 meetings of committees of the Council and the 23 special sittings of the Council. There was a driving intellect, but no powers to take the decisions out of the hands of the proper decision-makers.[29] In 1910, there were no such things as professional managers in the universities of Britain. So at that date it was impossible to pose the problem which now presents itself, with increasing urgency, of the difference it makes for a university to be run by persons with powers to give orders and persons with only a duty to give advice. It is quite clear in the Oxford and Cambridge Statutes that administrative officers are civil servants. They 'service' committees as their secretaries. They are not members of those committees. But H. E. D. Blakiston, who had been Vice-Chancellor of Oxford, perceived in the 1920s that it was possible for permanent officials to usurp an authority they were denied under the statutes.[30] By simply being there continuously, having the ears of those on and chairing committees, having control of the paper work, a 'civil servant' may in reality become the maker of policy. That remains the case.

> The post of secretary means that its holder is not a member of the committee and has no voting rights . . . The statutes are designed to make the distinction between those who belong to the committees and those who service them. Officials will offer their advice if requested and some would offer it in any case if they felt the need to intervene. Naturally the weight their advice carries will depend on the strength of the personalities involved and their experience.[31]

Nor was the dilemma of the need to preserve collegiality and the need to get things done so sharp in 1910 as it has since become: 'The University of Cambridge must conduct its business efficiently, and it must be prompt and decisive in its dealings with outside bodies. It must also remain, as it is now, a self-governing community of scholars. Our recommendations, which are to be seen as an integrated whole, are designed to satisfy these two fundamental requirements',[32] said the Wass Syndicate in its 1989 proposals for constitutional reform in Cambridge.

However, one of the prompters to the reforms was the growing feeling within the University of Cambridge that 'the democratic rights of members of the Regent House had been eroded over the years by the encroachment of the central bodies and that this process ought to be reversed'.[33] There can be a gap between constitutional provisions and political realities.[34] The Regent House at Cambridge and Congregation in Oxford are the rulers only if they rouse themselves. It has been shrewdly noted that 'what constrains the real controllers of executive authority is the *potential* power of Congregation and the Regent House. It is wise to tread warily to avoid unleashing a storm'.[35]

The problem the Wass Syndicate reforms in Cambridge failed to resolve – and that has become evident as the reform has 'settled down' – has been that of the balance of power. The Regent House remains the governing body and it can still put a stop to policy decisions taken by the central bodies by a ballot. However, that is a cumbersome and unpredictable mechanism. It would be far better if the central bodies consulted the Regent House at an early stage; and if they did so with a genuine openness to listen. The pattern has increasingly been for a Report to be published, a Discussion of the Senate to be duly held, any remarks answered in a subsequent Notice by *setting aside* the points made in the Discussion or by *failing to answer at all* those which prove hard to set aside, before the central bodies go ahead regardless with what they had planned to do. At that stage, it is only by calling for an amendment to the Grace that the Regent House can put a stop to things. This is no way to do business. It is confrontational and divides the community very publicly, for these events enter the public domain as they are recorded in the *University Reporter*. The University of Cambridge has repeatedly perceived the need for devolvement of powers: 'One of the most likely ways in which to bring about an improvement will be by greater use of delegated powers.'[36] What was envisaged there, however, was delegation to committees, and it is not nearly so easy to see how to devolve practical decision-making to the whole community.

Civil service and management

'Among . . . the higher administrative officials . . . it is fairly indispensable to include one or more adroit parliamentarians, competent to procure the necessary modicum of sanction for all arbitrary acts of the executive from a distrustful faculty convened as a deliberative body. These men must be at least partially in the confidence of the executive head.'[37] Cabals and secrecy, politics and levers, are to be glimpsed here, as in Cornford's Cambridge.[38] In Veblen's North American context of the early twentieth century, there was already recognized to be a place, indeed a need, for managerial dominance; a natural enmity between the academic staff and their would-be rulers replaces the rivalries of academic equals. Entrusting to 'managers' powers to direct the work of academics crucially alters the balance of power in a university. The Cornford games change.

Another Veblen remark has a startlingly modern ring in its assumption that academics cannot set their own scholarly purposes and accomplish them, but that someone must be 'empowered to act' to bring them to heel.

> It is . . . of the essence of this scheme of academic control that the captain of erudition should freely exercise the power of academic life and death over the members of his staff, to reward the good and faithful servant and to abase the recalcitrant. Otherwise discipline would be a difficult matter, and the formally requisite 'advice and consent' could be procured only tardily and grudgingly.[39]

That is a dangerous doctrine and Veblen knew it. The problem created by placing managers over academic professionals is clear at once if we look at it in the context of medical provision:

> Health management is an increasingly broadly-based profession, containing people from an increasingly wide variety of professional backgrounds and health service managers, unlike the clinical professions, have no regulation by statute and no professional disciplinary machinery. If a nurse or doctor practises in a manner considered dangerous to the public, the practitioner can be deregistered and will not get employment elsewhere. This is not the case for health managers, who in theory could foul up a job on a grand scale only to re-emerge in another post in another organisation, with no sanctions beyond those involving employment law.[40]

There is thus a potential discrepancy of some seriousness between the ethical restrictions on one category and those on the other, which reflects a disjunction between the recognized relevant expertise required in the one and the general managerial skills expected in the other. If, however, the manager makes a decision which affects patient safety, as he well may, he is not accountable in the same way as the doctors and nurses he manages.

There are at least two problems, plain from NHS experience. First, managers are not likely to be as competent to judge such things as those who are professional academics. Second, there can be a discrepancy of interest: managers may be more interested in making the choice which will save or make money.

Nevil Johnson asks in an article in the *Oxford Magazine*:

> whether management is an appropriate category to apply to a university. If the answer turns out to be 'only to a very limited extent', then universities might have a better chance of resisting the temptation to take over forms of organisation and the values accompanying them that are likely to distort their activities and even to corrupt them in the performance of those essential tasks to which most of us think they are committed . . . In the public services . . . 'administration' is out, whilst 'management' is in . . . A university managed like an industrial enterprise . . . would . . . no longer be a university . . . We cannot 'manage' people into successful teaching, nor can we ensure by good management that people do high quality research or write original books.[41]

It is nowadays argued that that task of administration itself requires a professional skill; that management is a professional skill in its own right. It would follow that managers do not necessarily need to know anything about the professional arena over which they are to exercise managerial powers. There have been recent CAFAS cases sharpening this point, in which an academic still within the probationary period after appointment, has been set 'aims and objectives' by a manager who is not an academic, who has then terminated the academic's contract on the basis of his decision that the aims and objectives have not been attained.

The *Dearing Report* made a distinction between 'deciding overall policy, guidance and review' and 'executive management or operational delivery' (15.32). Management is a means to the end of a university's achieving its purpose. 'Management' is not specific to the university enterprise. Indeed, if 'managing' is a professional activity it is *ipso facto* not a professional act which can only, or best, be carried out in a university. So arguably, if there was a conflict of judgement, the academic ought to dominate. The policy ought to be made by those who have the expertise needed to serve the university's purpose.

It is sometimes objected that only a management able to see ahead and plan clear-headedly, even if it means taking 'tough decisions', is able to do what is ultimately for the good of the university. However, that view makes a number of assumptions. 'One good reason for managerial intervention would be if managers knew more about quality than most of the professional service deliverers.'[42] But if they do not, that justification disappears.

Again, an 'argument for managerial intervention is that the managers represent the collective interest of the organisation, and in particular the interests of its chief stakeholders . . . thus management claims a special custodianship for the "public interest"'.[43] But the 'collective interest' may be otherwise defined, in terms of the community of scholarship or the collegial wish of the corporate body, and that must certainly be true in the Oxford and Cambridge systems of governance. The 'stakeholders' will presumably include those employed in the institution and the students, as well as the wider community of scholarship. Managers cannot, unless they are academics, determine the best interests of these persons. The 'stakeholders' are, in the comment just quoted, taken to be the public and that, in practice, means the public as holders of purse strings. That is a limited vision.

Managerial powers, however benignly exercised – and it should be emphasized that the good intention is usually there in the running of universities – involve, by definition, subordination of the managed. Nevil Johnson again points in particular to 'the idea of getting certain things done by controlling or guiding the behaviour of those involved'.[44] The 'tough decisions' argument is *ipso facto* the 'unpopular decisions' argument. Decisions do not need to be forced through if they are what everyone wants anyway.

This scene, with its inherent problems, is most sharply defined where managers and academics form two distinct communities in a university.

Often in the 'old' universities in the UK the pattern is rather different, with a proportion of senior administrative offices being held by heads of department, who are themselves academics. Such officers are, in fact, holding two offices, which may be in conflict. It might be, for example, that financial constraint required the making of redundancies, but the academic needs of the university required the maintenance of a good staff–student ratio. Which imperative should the head of department obey when asked to name the lecturers who are to go?[45]

The Cambridge *Reporter* of 12 February 1997, carries a list of the duties of heads of department, in connection with a *Report on payments additional to stipend* for these and certain other officers. Many faculties in Cambridge have no departments, merely a rotating Chairmanship of the Faculty Board. So to set up a list of duties which were also powers would create an anomalous situation in which some academic employees would, in effect, have a 'boss' and others would not. Various terms in the Cambridge list evoke managerial control: 'monitoring supervision arrangements'; 'implementing Department policy'; 'promoting a strategic view of research priorities for the Department'; 'reviewing and prioritizing staffing needs'; and 'determining Departmental practice in relation to hours of work, holiday entitlement, promotions, and promotion of unestablished research staff'. Heads of department are, among lots of other like things, to 'monitor the performance of all staff and [deal] with those who are not satisfactorily performing their duties or fulfilling the conditions of their tenure'. It becomes an urgent question: who is checking up on the heads of department.

'Heads of Department also act as representatives of their Departments . . . representing the interests of the Department in the relevant fields outside the University, both nationally and internationally.' One may represent in various ways. MPs are free to vote on behalf of their constituents in any way they like, and the constitutents cannot do anything about it except not vote for the MP next time. Ecclesiologically, a bishop is a representative who (in principle) expresses the common mind of his people, not his own views. Then there are representatives who are tokens or symbols or figureheads. What is the intended remit here? May a head of department really be taken to speak for all the diverse scholars who happen to share his broad subject area and work on the same corridor but who, if they do not have minds of their own, have no business in a university? Is his *persona* to be theirs in the world's theatre?

Heads of department are to communicate 'effectively to members of the Department information on University policy decisions', says the Cambridge text. But members of the Regent House are equals in the running of the University. They have a right to participate directly in the making of policy decisions, which are ultimately theirs to make; though normally the Council will do the job on their behalf they have to be told what it proposes, and they can say no. Any member of the Regent House could quarrel with the Report in a speech when it is discussed in the Senate House, as all Reports must be. Heads of department have no special role in policy-making and should have no information about policy communicated to them which is not announced directly to the whole Regent House in the *Reporter*.

This is all very well, the manager may say. But universities have to be run; there has to be some organization. That is all very well, the academic may say. But we have to be able to do something about it if the organization is misplaced, mistaken and will not listen to reason.

7

Membership, Employment, Office

There are a number of respects in which the relationships between universities and their academic staff and students are peculiarly complicated. Accountability is potentially compromised by the resulting difficulty in establishing where a remedy may lie. The early cases dealing with disputes over Fellowships at Oxford and Cambridge colleges were silent on the subject of contract. What was at issue was office, a 'subsisting, permanent, substantive position which had an existence independent from the person who filled it, which went on and was filled in succession by successive holders'.[1] 'Office' still appears in a university context. In *Thomas v. University of Bradford* [1987] 1 A.C. 795 it was recognized that the plaintiff was both an employee of the university under a contract of service and the holder of an office in the university, as well as being a member of it and a corporator. It has been argued that dismissal from employment is different from dismissal from 'an office where the body employing the man is under some statutory or other restriction as to the kind of contract it can make with its servants, or the grounds on which it can dismiss them'.[2] Arguably, universities may still come into that category, and remedies through employment law may be limited.

In universities some of the employees (normally the academic staff but not porters, kitchen staff, cleaners)[3] and students (at least while they remain its students) and perhaps graduates, are 'members', though not necessarily members with identical privileges.[4] Membership, in a university with a visitor, may require that the matter be dealt with domestically; that means that a member may be denied access to the courts in search of a remedy.

The corporate character of universities remains significant in creating a presumption that they have a *common* purpose and that there is accordingly a *collective* 'good' to be served. That has been held to be important over against the claims of the individual. In *Rigg v. University of Waikato* [1984] 1 N.Z.L.R. 149 (at 153) it was possible to cite 'the overall interests of the University and its members' as a proper determining factor in the decision taken, although it affected a particular individual member adversely. There is an inherent tension of this sort in all situations where a complainant is a member of the body against which he has a complaint. Both these implications of membership may thus compromise accountability.

Membership is collegial and that is at odds with the fundamentally master–servant character of the employment relationship in which a member of the academic staff may also stand to his university.[5] In the case of students the 'membership' relationship also 'crosses' with a hierarchical contractual relationship, this time that of master and pupil or even 'parent' and 'child'.[6]

Student contracts have terms like any other contract. Student contracts are not, of course, employment contracts but agreements that the university will provide courses and teaching and facilities necessary to complete those courses; that it will in due course 'examine' the student and, if he satisfies the university's requirements, award him a degree or diploma at the end of the process. In return for all this he normally pays the university a fee.

A student might sue for breach of an implied term of his contract on the grounds that he was not offered support, feedback, counselling or tuition when he had to resit an examination. Damages might be awarded if it was shown that a student had been negligently taught or examined, that the university had not properly interpreted its rules, that it had not properly followed its rules or that it had not observed the general principles of fairness.

In *Schmidt v. Secretary of State for Home Affairs* [1969] 2 Ch. 149 (at 157, *per* Ungoed-Thomas J.) it was argued that students are in a contractual relationship with the university, which may be far more complex as to what the university gets out of it:

> students are, by definition, persons who study and that studying does not affect or infect anyone but the student – that is, it is a process of taking in and not giving out . . . [But] study does not exclude practising as an element in studying, as, for example, in the case of medical students: nor does it exclude contributing by the very presence of students to the success of the . . . centre in this county where they study.

There is more than a hint here that the contractual relationship, even in the case of students, is tied to the purpose of the university.

Contractual obligations of academic staff are certainly tied to the purpose of the university. Under the Education Reform Act 1988, s. 124 'a higher education corporation shall have power –

(a) to provide higher education;
(b) to provide further education; and
(c) to carry out research and to publish the results of the research or any other material arising out of or connected with it in such manner as the corporation think fit'.

To that end such a corporation shall have power 'to enter into contracts, including in particular

(i) contracts for the employment of teachers and other staff for the purposes of or in connection with carrying on any such activities and
(ii) contracts with respect to the carrying on by the corporation of any such activities'.

It is a commonplace that one cannot imply a term simply because it is reasonable to do so, but only when it is necessary to give 'business efficacy' to the contract. This is the *Moorcock* doctrine (1888) 13 PD 157. This concept of 'business efficacy' could, however, readily be translated into 'purpose' if the contract is with a university.

The strictly contractual relationship of an academic employee and a university may itself be multiplex. Phillips J., in *Throsby v. Imperial College of Science and Technology* [1978] 2 All E.R. 465, said: 'we see no reason in principle why a man should not have two quite separate contracts of employment with the same employer, or why it is not possible to terminate one only'. In this instance an individual was both a 'lecturer' and warden of a hall of residence.

The relationship of contract carries with it the possibility of breach of contract, and therefore of actions for breach of contract. In contract actions there are strict procedural requirements, including witness statements, the requirement that people come to court to explain what they did and full disclosure of documents on both sides. Those would apply to both staff and students alleging breach of contract.

Nevertheless, different remedies are available to staff and to students. A member of staff can claim unfair dismissal, as a student clearly cannot. Employment law will normally exclude judicial review for a member of staff, unless the case raises public law issues or affects a 'category' of staff. A student may have access to judicial review, unless the university has a visitor.

The 'balance of convenience' may be different for a member of staff and a student. That is to say, the balance may work in favour of a student seeking an injunction. It is more inconvenient to the student to be dismissed than for the university to keep him. That balance will not so easily work in favour of a member of staff.

It would be misleading to suggest that the the 'membership' relationship is free from requirements of obedience. Membership does appear, paradoxically, to involve subjection to the statutes, ordinances and regulations of a university, even though it is fundamentally a relationship of a 'collegial' kind, and thus between equals.[7] There is a problem with that if membership is perpetual, as it is in the case of graduates. It could not realistically be held that they remained subject to every one of the university's statutes for the rest of their lives. So a requirement of obedience must be conditional upon the type of membership relationship.

When one person gives orders to another in a university it is not always evident whether any duty of obedience derives from the contractual or employment relationship. A senior member of the academic staff may say to a student, 'If you do not do as I say you will be sent down.' The same senior member of the academic staff might say to a junior member of his department, 'If you do not do as I say you will be disciplined or dismissed.' In the first case the student has a *status* (*status pupillari*). In the second case the junior lecturer is bound by the master–servant character of the employment relationship, and the requirement that he obey all reasonable instructions. But it can be asked in a given situation in exactly what capacity the senior member of staff acts on behalf of the university, and whether he is specifically empowered to speak 'as if he were the university' to the student or 'as if he were the employer' to the junior lecturer.[8]

The duty of obedience has been discussed in a number of cases where the mutual rights and obligations of corporators, members and officers of a corporation have been at issue. In *Ex parte Berkhamsted Free School* (1813) 2 Ves. and B. 134 there was a question whether the Master of a corporation who was a member of that corporation, was bound to reside. In *Attorney-General v. Crook* (1836) I Keen 121 it was asked whether such a Master was under obligation to conduct divine service. But here the obedience in question was clearly obedience to regulations which have the purpose of serving the body's collective good, not obedience to the employer's orders.

The difference is that when a master gives orders to a servant, he is seeking to get his money's worth in return for paying the salary. When a corporate body requires its members to keep the rules of the community it is seeking to preserve the body's integrity. A contract is between an individual and the employer and any duty of obedience relates to the better performance of the contract. Obedience to rules of a corporate body is for the good of all.

The Education Reform Act 1988, s. 206 marks one boundary here. Because it excludes visitorial jurisdiction 'in respect of any dispute relating to a member of the academic staff which concerns his appointment or employment or the termination of his appointment or employment'; a matter under that head could be taken to the courts. A student might go the same way if he could find a route. For instance, in Canada *Wong v. University of Toronto* [1991] 79 D.L.R. (4th) 652 explored a new avenue. A student sued in tort, alleging negligence and breach of the University's duty of care towards him under a proposed new heading of 'educational malpractice'. The court held that there was no such wrong in tort,[9] but other devices are sure to be tried.

No one can be forced to be a member of a corporation and those who object on religious grounds can be exempted from membership if the statutes of a given university allow.[10] This raises an interesting question as to whether a would-be student complainant or a member of the academic staff seeking to take a dispute to court, could obtain such exemption and then, on the basis that he is not a member of the university, claim that the visitor did not have exclusive jurisdiction in his case so as to be free to take it to court.

There is a tangle of conflicting precedent on whether a dispute can remain 'domestic' and therefore properly within the bounds of the corporation's affairs and its visitor's jurisdiction, when the rules, customs, or procedures at issue are among the terms of a contract.[11] In *Wislang* it was held that it could: 'What the authorities show, as I read them, is that matters may well be in breach of a contract of employment, yet within visitorial jurisdiction, if those matters are of an internal domestic character or touch upon the interpretation or execution of private rules and regulations of the university. The source of the obligation on which Miss Thomas relies for her claim is the domestic laws of the university, its statutes and ordinances. It is her case that the university has failed either in the proper interpretation of its statutes or in their proper application. Miss Thomas is not relying on a contractual obligation *other than an obligation by the university to comply with its own domestic laws*'[12] (my italics). That is important for its implications for the jurisdiction under which disputes can be resolved.

It is not difficult to envisage a 'mixed' scenario in which, in the course of an action in an industrial tribunal over alleged breaches of employment law, it might become necessary 'to interpret or adjudicate on the private laws of the foundation'. Smith suggests that if that happened it would be necessary for the proceedings to be adjourned while the visitor carried out that task.[13] *Tubbs v. Auckland University Council* (1908) 27 N.Z.L.R. 149, concerning the summary dismissal of a professor, was decided on contractual grounds. (The visitor's jurisdiction was not discussed.) However, it can also be asked whether a court's decision could be set aside if it were subsequently discovered that the visitor had had jurisdiction but had not been approached so as to be allowed to exercise it.

Thus, a problem distinct from the question whether visitorial jurisdiction is exclusive of that of the courts is whether it covers all aspects of a university's activities, including the fulfilment of the contracts into which it enters with members who are employees. In *Murdoch University v. Bloom* [1980] W.A.R. 193 (at 197) Burt C.J. said that 'it will be difficult to say on what side of the line a particular matter or dispute will fall. Is the matter arising "domestic" or "internal" he asks? If it is, then it is within the jurisdiction of the Visitor. If it is not, it is a matter to be decided by the courts.'[14] The only route open to a lecturer who wishes to challenge a decision about his employment (for example, in connection with the continuance of a contract after a probationary period, or promotion), where there is a visitor is to seek to show that there has been some breach of his rights under employment law, and that the matter is therefore contractual not domestic, affecting him as employee and *not* as a member, and that may be very difficult.

The earliest mention of a contractual claim with a body having a visitor seems to have been *Thomson v. University of London* (1864) 33 L.J. Ch. 625. It was not held there that the existence of a contract *ipso facto* took a dispute outside the jurisdiction of the visitor. But it is not so clear that it may not do so now. 'A dispute or difference of opinion between the parties as to the proper construction of [a] contract [between the defendant and the body corporate] is not . . . an "internal" or "domestic" matter.'[15]

Peter M. Smith distinguishes here between contracts or terms of a contract which require the parties to act *vis-à-vis* one another 'in conformity with the statutes, regulations, customs etc of the foundation', and those which 'are not derived from any statutes, ordinances etc of the foundation but stem from the agreement of the parties, and which involve no interpretation or application of these domestic laws of the foundation' (such as a failure to pay the salary).[16]

This duality can even, perhaps, be deemed to set up parallel or coexisting jurisdictions. 'A contract of employment may contain terms some of which are concerned with private or special rights given as a member of the university and the terms expressed or implied which give purely contractual or statutory rights. In these circumstances the visitorial and industrial jurisdiction coexist . . . but the visitorial jurisdiction is not ousted.'[17] But if a visitor's decision is held to be unreviewable that must imply the existence of parallel jurisdictions in which 'coexistence' does involve mutual exclusion.

There seem to be civil rights issues here, if it can really turn out that a remedy which would be available to another employee (even a non-academic employee of the same university) is denied to a member of the academic staff because he is also a member of the university:

> A member who has a contract of service with a corporation . . . is entitled, if that contract is wrongfully breached or determined by the corporation, to sue in the ordinary courts of the realm for damages or other remedy in respect of the breach. I do not think that the member's common law right to sue in such case is excluded by the visitorial jurisdiction which would exist over him as a member. The latter jurisdiction is based on the member's status as a member of the corporation, and does not . . . remove common law rights based not on that status but on the general law of contract . . . It would not . . . be an acceptable state of the law that, if the member has a contract of employment which the employer has breached, the member should be wholly displaced from his common law remedies simply because he is an employee of a university or other body whose constitution includes visitorial powers.[18]

At the heart of the question whether employment disputes or disputes involving students should be handled in the courts or (at least in the first instance) by universities internally, lies the division we have met again and again in these pages, between matters which it is proper for a university to keep in its own hands and matters which it is not. This all goes to the autonomy of universities and their accountability in the world outside.

Serious questions about employment rights are involved in decisions affecting continuance of a contract and, perhaps, of an upgrading of an employee by promotion, where academic judgements are made under the domestic laws of a university.[19]

In *Vaneck v. Governors of the University of Alberta* [1975] 5 W.W.R. 429, the decision not to grant tenure was challenged.[20] Whether or not it was an 'employment decision', this clearly involved professional academic judgement. The Alberta Faculty Handbook (106.6) makes reference to the requirement that 'a successful candidate for tenure must have exhibited satisfactory performances during his probationary period and should be considered worthy of advancement' and that it is 'the responsibility of a tenure committee to examine all aspects of the appointee's contribution, to assess his probable continued progress and to make a recommendation based thereon'.[21] However, the component of consequence for employment may mean that such a judgement becomes justiciable in the UK of 20 years later.

Decisions at the end of a period of probation are particularly interesting here. The granting of 'tenure' is no longer a possibility in England, though staff with pre-1987 contracts retain their tenure.[22] Nevertheless, at the end of a period of probation a lecturer may still be given an indefinite contract which will normally be expected to continue until retirement age.[23] 'The right to be considered for tenure is one of the terms of employment of members of the teaching staff of the university. It is a contractual right . . . but the consequence of a denial of tenure is the termination of the employment of the disappointed candidate',[24] which ends the contract, so there were questions about the legitimacy of dismissal in one Canadian case.

If someone is promoted in an English university today he is technically being appointed to a new job, and that is deemed by the Education Reform Act 1988 to place him under a new contract. This has the effect of ending his tenure if he previously had a pre-1987 contract:

> A person shall be taken to be promoted . . . if . . . the terms of his contract are varied . . . so that . . . his rate of remuneration is increased to a rate which exceeds the highest point on his former pay scale . . . or . . . he is paid on another scale on which the highest point at the date the variation takes effect exceed the highest point on his former pay scale at that date; or . . . he is paid on a basis which does not provide for a maximum rate of remuneration.[25]

If someone is given a special payment for good work but no new title, he is, apparently, not thus given a new job. However, where promotion involves the payment of a higher *salary* and the creation of a new standing for the teacher in the university, it can be argued that it constitutes the making of a new appointment.[26]

The academic judgement at issue may not, therefore, concern 'regrading' but rather the selection of candidates for new posts. What are the university's duties with regard to setting the number of such posts and advertising them for competition? If a university creates a post it normally advertises it and accepts applications from those not already its employees. It does not usually do this in connection with an internal promotions procedure.

It may be, then, that promotions are not strictly to new posts at all, but merely *changes* of contractual relationship with an employee *amounting to* the making of a new contract. In that case, the basis from which the process begins is the existing contractual relationship and the employee will have some rights, including a 'reasonable expectation' that there will be due reward for achievement. If that could be argued it might affect the university's right as an employer to limit the rewards on offer in such a way that not all those who achieve objectives it has itself defined get the promotion promised in return for that satisfactory performance.

Academic tenure is now an increasingly sharply focused issue. The test case on academic tenure before the Education Reform Act 1988 took tenure away was *Page v. Visitor of Hull University* [1993] 1 All E.R. 97. Under the Education Reform Act 1988, academic staff appointed in UK universities after 20 November 1987 or promoted after that date could be made redundant, but not before it.[27] Page had a contract which somewhat fudged the issue because it both gave him tenure until the retirement age and stated that the contract could be terminated by three months' notice on either side. He was made redundant.

He appealed to the University's Visitor. The Visitor dismissed his appeal. He sought judicial review and the High Court held that it had jurisdiction to grant judicial review of the Visitor's decision. The Visitor and the University appealed to the Court of Appeal on the grounds that on a true construction of its statutes the University had been entitled to terminate the contract and that therefore the Visitor had not misconstrued them. Only if he had done so and thus acted *ultra vires* would the courts have had supervisory jurisdiction. The final appeal to the House of Lords challenged the construction which had been put upon the statutes. It was held that the court had no jurisdiction to determine disputes arising under the domestic law of the University or the proper application of those laws to the applicant under their jurisdiction.[28] So, in the end, the case became a debate about jurisdiction and the redundancy question could not be directly addressed. But a tenured member of staff had been dismissed.

There is likely to be a spate of coming cases on the powers of a university to dismiss by reason of redundancy. The Model Statute requires that the creation of a redundancy involve two decision-making elements. The first is the forming of a policy by the institution's governing body or council. The second is the selection of individuals to be made redundant according to that policy. There is a right of appeal against the selection but not against the policy. So there is intended to be no interference with the policy-making function of the university, which is clearly a legitimate expression of its autonomy, but a single member may apparently query the application of that policy to him, presumably as an employee.

There is an acceptance in the legislation that the forming of an academic judgement about an individual in the selection of candidates for redundancy (is he competent?) is necessary, and may result in his dismissal.

A redundancy may be deemed 'reasonable' if the employer's requirement for the service the employee is providing has diminished or ceased.[29] That might be the case even if there was continuing student demand. So the judgement of the institution could be wholly unrelated to the answer to the question whether an individual is competent, and involve a policy decision only. Again, that would be its own business, but it might blur the distinction between the creation of a policy about redundancy and the selection of persons to be made redundant.

There are many crevices in which a call for accountability can lodge and be lost here, but perhaps the most important of them is the strong fence around a university's domestic affairs which remains despite the new limitation of visitorial jurisdiction under the 1988 Education Reform Act. This presents a dilemma. The apologist who would want to protect academic activity from interference from governments or statutory, charitable, private or commercial funders, would want to emphasize their autonomy. But this is an autonomy in scholarly research and teaching arenas, where professional or academic judgement is being exercised. The apologist who is concerned to discourage tyranny over academic (or other) employees would not want universities to claim an autonomy by reason of their domesticity which would prevent their being called to account through the courts, so that individuals might have a remedy for injustice.

8

Making the Rules: Internal Legislation

What is the proper remit of 'domestic' law in universities?

The courts would not interfere in a child's dispute with its parents over its pocket money. There are two bases on which anybody may make and administer its own rules, regulations or 'laws'. The first is under statutory authority to do so. The second is strictly privately, within a 'domestic' forum, and the UK courts will be reluctant to interfere. But in the UK – the relationships of universities and States are different elsewhere in the world – the authority of universities to make their own rules has now been intruded upon by statute.[1] The discipline and grievance procedures devised by the University Commissioners in the Model Statute under the 1988 Act are legally binding on the old universities (though not on the new). So there appears to have been an intention to make statutorily binding on bodies with a long tradition of having a peculiarly domestic law, rules of conduct they have not made themselves. This opens up new possibilities in terms of the relationship between public and private law. It remains a question whether, if an employee of a university with a visitor were to argue that the university had broken not its own domestic rules but the statutorily binding ones of the Model Statute, he might have recourse to the courts, on the grounds that the laws in question were not private but public.

The UK's Education Reform Act 1988, s. 205 lays down a procedure by which the University Commissioners were to oversee modifications to the statutes of a given university, sending them details and also the then Universities Funding Council and any other persons or bodies it seemed 'appropriate to consult'; after taking into account any representations made in response, the Commissioners were to submit the modifications to the Queen in Council. There can be no sense in which such statutes remain private law if by that is meant law made internally and independently and solely by the university concerned.[2]

A 'new' university in England can still make its own rules, though there appear to be some restrictions. For instance, dismissals in a new university are regulated by its articles of government. There is a degree of regulation by the State here as to the content of such articles.[3]

Normally, the statutes will form the primary internal legislation of an institution and below them its ordinances. Then will come rules and regulations. The old 'local government' charters gave corporations in England powers to make such 'bye-laws'. This is an inherent power. It allows a body to make rules to regulate matters connected with the purposes for which it was brought into being.[4] The intention is that it should be a means by which the *body* can better express its definitive character ('be what it is'); and better achieve the purposes for which it exists ('do its job').[5] In the case of universities, powers to hold property and employ staff are clearly means to the end of fostering learning and research, and so such regulation could properly govern such matters, and the principles on which contracts of employment were to be framed.

However, a university could not, for example, make a rule to stop teaching and doing research, and give itself up to running a fairground, or it would cease to be a university on any ordinary understanding of the term.

The extent of the power exercised by the body concerned also appears to be a factor which determines what its bye-laws may cover. There can be great variation from university to university as to whether, for example, the composition of Faculty Boards is determined by the statutes or left to ordinances.[6] The exact pattern of delegation of authority to make regulations may vary a great deal.

With these provisos, there can be a number of pragmatic reasons for the delegation of legislation. The time of the primary legislative body or legislator is limited. It is unlikely to have all the necessary expertise among its membership to frame rules for the smallest contingencies. Urgent problems may arise at a time when the legislative body is not in session.[7] There is also a danger that political or personal motives may endanger the adequacy of legislative provision, which can thus perhaps be better made by those not governed by such motives.

So there are questions about who is empowered to make regulations, and by what process; how they can be challenged; how they can be amended; what kinds of things they may govern or determine; on whom they may be binding; where at the end of that line a discretion of the decision-maker is created or fettered by such internal rules; whether it has to be stated what is rule and what is an exercise of discretion; whether it has to be clear what relationship exists between the authority to make rules and the authority to exercise discretion (can the same person make a rule which says he has absolute discretion and then exercise his discretion unfettered?); what is the relationship between the advice given by administrative officers and the decisions made by decisionmakers (in a 'civil service' structure, minister and civil servant are clearly differentiated in their powers and responsibilities; in a managerial structure that line is blurred); in an 'old' university where the head of department who is an academic decision-maker is also an administrative officer, there is an overlap of functions. These are important questions for practical reasons in universities. If the same person makes a rule which says he has absolute discretion and then exercises his discretion unfettered the boundary between legislative and judicial functions is blurred.

What, then, governs the making of rules under which acts of, and within, universities can be called to account? A chartered corporation is not subject to the doctrine of *ultra vires*.[8] A body created by or under statutory authority or under companies legislation is. That means it is legally incapable of doing anything which is not within the objects and powers for which it was created or reasonably incidental to them.[9] 'Incidental' has to be close to the original objects and powers.[10] For example, powers to hold property and employ staff are clearly means to the end of fostering learning and research.

A modern university may be created under statutory authority or it may be a chartered corporation. Oxford and Cambridge are corporations by prescription with statutory powers to make their own statutes, so, despite this restriction, the principles established in *Ashbury Railway Carriage Co v. Riche* may apply to them: 'no attempt shall be made to use the corporate life for any other purpose than that which is so specified'.[11] Again, in *Attorney-General v. Great Eastern Railway* (1880) 5 App. Cas. 473 (at 481) Lord Blackburn said: 'those things which are incident to, and may reasonably and properly be done under the main purpose, though they may not be literally within it, would not be prohibited . . . When a Railway Company has been created for public purposes, the Legislature must be held to have prohibited every act of the company which its incorporating statutes do not warrant expressly or by fair implication.'[12]

Rights and responsibilities can be seen as correlative. Those in positions of authority may be held to have a responsibility to protect and secure the rights of those who lack their powers. So fundamental principles might seek to protect fundamental rights or seek to enforce duties correlative with those rights. If there should prove to be such irreducible and irreversible principles, they would apply at every level of legislation, and therefore also at that level where a public or private body makes its own 'internal' regulations, and they would presumably apply whether or not that is done under statute.[13]

The downward flow of powers to make subordinate regulations is matched by an upward flow of accountability to the primary legislator. All orders, rules and regulations made by ministers, departments and other bodies owe their legal force to Acts of Parliament, except where the Crown retains the original prerogative power.[14] Oxford and Cambridge, for example, have powers to enact their own statutes under the Oxford and Cambridge Act 1923. Thus, for example, health service managers are accountable through the hierarchy to the Secretary of State for Health because 'they are there to implement the policies of the government of the day which has been elected to govern the country's affairs'.[15] Nevertheless, there is a danger that managers will come to think of themselves as having a function of government (as distinct from a role to play in internal governance), if they are not constantly made to understand that they do not.

The governing principle determining what should go into regulations, is that they should carry through the intention of the primary legislation under which they are made; or of the founder if the body is a private eleemosynary foundation; or both, in a university which is now partly a public body.

The purpose of a university may be taken to be a settled thing from the moment of foundation or incorporation, and perhaps essentially unchangeable without altering the purpose of the foundation which defines it and justifies its existence and is therefore of its *esse.* But institutions also have policy, which can be altered over time. There must be a limitation on such policy changes, in that they cannot alter the original intention of the founder. That might be so if there is conflict between two sets of 'intentions', purpose and policy; for example, if a university said it ought to foster freedom of scholarly investigation and a government said it ought to give preference to Technology Foresight.[16]

University committees and university bodies may make rules, especially for the conduct of their own affairs, which become, at least for a time, the university's regulations *de facto,* although they may never be published as such.[17] But in practice a committee may well stumble through its business, making or changing its rules as it goes along, and not necessarily keeping note of what they are. There is an obvious danger that in either the procedurally more orderly or the more informal mode of operation, regulations may well contradict the published rules of the institution if there is no awareness among the members of the committee that they must not.

Rule-making may be done by a university's appointing an 'officer' to do it. There are, however, further difficulties with this method, for there is a question here about the need to distinguish the roles of a 'civil service' from those of 'persons with powers' in a given system. These arise with particular sharpness where the 'curia' becomes a 'management', and thus lord not servant of the academic officers of the university. This has increasingly become a problem in the new management structures arising in universities, especially since 1992.

Inevitably, there will be ways in which administrative officers can influence outcomes. But that is different from their having direct authority to act. So it is appropriate to ask what authority either a 'manager' or a 'civil servant' type of administrative officer has to make or interpret the rules made for purposes of arriving at academic judgements when he himself is not, or not for the purposes of that exercise, an academic. In the Research Assessment Exercise of 1996 there was a HEFCE policy distinction between matters which it was proper for a 'civil service' to deal with (such as the decision what information was to be collected, how it was to be amassed, when it was to be sent to the panels), and matters involving the making of academic judgements upon the material, which fell to the panels. However, there was, naturally, a large grey area in which it is hard to say what was an academic and what a managerial decision.

In a 'civil service' structure, minister and civil servant are clearly differentiated in their powers and responsibilities; in a managerial structure that line is blurred. Indeed, managers in a line management structure have powers over those below them in the line, which in new universities frequently do mean the crossing of a line between those who are trained in management and those who are employed to teach and do research.

There may be dangers of another sort in allowing an administrative officer to appoint to committees or boards. There is the problem of ensuring that such appointments are made on merit and ability rather than with consideration for the political affiliation of those appointed (or some other factor not directly academic, such as a willingness to 'work with' managers, or to accept certain priorities). Committees can be packaged in such a way as materially to affect both their rule-making and their decisionmaking.

The most important and powerful officer in most universities is the vice-chancellor. The powers of a vice-chancellor of a new university as chief executive are, in principle, limited to making suggestions to the Board of Governors, but, in practice, the members of the Board of Governors are unlikely to interfere with what will readily become 'his' decisions.

> The Provost [or Vice-Chancellor] shall be responsible *to the Board of Governors*
>
> (i) for making proposals to the Board of Governors about the educational character and objectives of the University and for implementing the decisions of the Board of Governors in this respect;
> (ii) for the organisation, direction and management of the University and leadership of the Staff;
> (iii) for the organisation, appraisal, grading, assignment, discipline, suspension and dismissal of members of Staff appointed under Article 34 (iii);
> (iv) having regard to the educational objectives of the University and subject to the responsibilities of the Academic Council in matters relating to the quality, curriculum content operation and delivery of courses, for the planning and determination of the academic programmes and other activities of the University, after consultation with the Academic Council;
> (v) for the maintenance of Student discipline and (within the Regulations) for the suspension or expulsion of Students on disciplinary grounds and for implementing decisions to expel Students for academic reasons.[18]

For the taking of specifically academic judgements, an expert body ought to be set up. In a new university: 'The Board of Governors shall establish an Academic Council of not more than forty members comprising the Provost and such of the members of the Staff and Students as are determined by the Bye-Laws with the proviso that a majority of the members of the Council shall be holders of posts at head of department or comparable level or above.[19]

Its remit is limited by the requirement to respect the purpose of the University.

> Subject to the responsibilities of the Board of Governors and of the Provost, the Academic Council shall be responsible to the Board for the following matters, having regard at all times to the educational character and objectives of the University as determined by the Board of Governors:
>
> (i) the teaching, courses, scholarship and research of the University, including: criteria for the admission of Students, the appointment and removal of internal and external examiners; policies and procedures for the examination and assessment of the academic performance of Students; the content of the curriculum; the quality of courses including matters relating to validation or accreditation by external bodies; procedures for the award of qualifications and honorary academic titles and procedures for the explusion of Students for academic reasons;
> (ii) considering the development of the academic activities of the University and the resources needed for them and advising the Provost and the Board of Governors thereon;
> (iii) such other matters as the Board of Governors or the Provost may assign to the Academic Council from time to time.

What makes a regulation 'binding' or valid?

'Valid' is linked etymologically with *valens*, having an effect. Regulations will be 'effective' in this sense of being binding on those who are in some way subject to the body or institution, as employees or as members, and if as members, perhaps as members in various classes, which in a university will especially include students and lecturers.[20]

A regulation does not necessarily have less force than primary legislation: 'Every Bye-law or Regulation made by the Board shall have effect as if the same was contained in these Articles save that they may at any time or times be revoked or varied by the Board in like manner as they may be made.'[21]

Among the powers of the London Guildhall Board of Governors at the time of writing is that of delegation: 'The Board of Governors may, subject to the Bye-laws and the Regulations, delegate to any Committee of the Board or to such persons or bodies and on such terms and conditions as it shall from time to time **think fit** all or any of the powers and duties conferred upon it by these Articles or otherwise.'[22] This delegation involves an exercise of discretion, but the discretion to delegate is not unfettered:

> PROVIDED THAT
> (a) the Board shall not be empowered or competent to so delegate all or any of its powers or duties in connection with:

(i) the determination of the educational character and objectives of the University; or
(ii) the approval of the annual estimate of income and expenditure of the University; or
(iii) the approval, amendment or variation of the Bye-Laws;
(iv) the approval of the Regulations other than regulations governing the conduct of individual courses;
(v) the appointment or dismissal of the Provost or the Secretary; and

(b) the Board of Governors shall not delegate to any person who is not a Governor or to any body or committee that does not consist exclusively of the Governors:
(i) the termination of the membership of any Member of the University; or
(ii) any act or thing which under or by virtue of any p. ovision of the Act is required to be done by the Board of Governors; or
(iii) the appraisal, discipline or suspension of the Provost or the Secretary.[23]

Authorization of expenditure can be delegated 'within such limits as the Board of Governors deems reasonably necessary for the proper performance . . . of the functions assigned' to a given person or body.[24]

The running principles determining what may and may not be delegated in this institution are that nothing must alter the purpose of the University or interfere with the overall control exercised by the Board of Governors.

Where bye-laws are made, they too must be in keeping with the primary legislation.

(i) No Bye-law shall have effect if and to the extent that it is inconsistent with the memorandum or Articles of Association of the University and in addition every Regulation shall have effect subject to the Bye-laws;[25]

There is a confusion of principle, however, in the provision that:

(ii) no Bye-Law or Regulations concerning the academic work of the University shall be made until the Academic Council has been given an opportunity to consider and report to the Board of Governors thereon and until any reports made by the Academic Council in response to that opportunity have been considered by the Board of Governors.[26]

This protects the powers of control of the Board of Governors as though they all possessed the expert skills necessary to make an academic judgement and, as a principle of overseeing, it may have its dangers.

In a university decision-making context we must look at a 'fitness for purpose' in the decisionmaking. That could be understood in various ways. It might mean making a choice which will benefit the University. To choose a candidate for admission as a student because his father is able to give a large benefaction would present a dilemma here. A university arguably needs such benefactions if government funding is inadequate, in order to fulfil its purposes. However, a benefaction to establish a Chair is now frequently linked to stipulations about the field of the professorship and that may limit the kind of person who shall hold it. A university must fulfil its purpose better if it has academic staff of the highest possible quality. But a Chair with a restricted field might require the appointment of a less able candidate. So the purpose of acquiring funding so that the institution might continue to flourish might be in conflict with the purpose of ensuring high quality in its work.

The intention of legislation not only may properly embody or express the policy or purpose of an institution; it must. The purpose of a university, presumably, cannot change without its ceasing to be a university. But its policy may. Policy is made on behalf of universities by various routes. In new universities and some 'old' ones it can amount to no more than an act of the will of the chief executive. But policy can change without ever being stated to change when it implicitly informs, for example, funding, with funds being earmarked for purposes which will strengthen the likelihoods of certain outcomes. There is a danger that substantive points of law may be included at the level of what in intention 'stands under' the primary legislation, if the rationale for the making of the primary legislation is not clearly understood. An 'enabling act' (or its internal equivalent) may in principle, if it is not carefully watched, allow for substantial alterations of policy or administration by the executive, without the new questions arising being addressed directly and identified as policy changes by the legislative. If the principles of subordination involved are not wholly clear there is a danger that substantive points of law can get involved, and even become lodged in the crevices of regulations.

Keeping the rules: those subject to them

Over whom do the regulations of a University extend? It seems indisputable that a person who wants a degree places himself under the degree-giving institution's rules for the purpose of obtaining it.

> The holding of examinations and the conferring of degrees being one . . . object of this University, all the regulations, that is, the construction of all the regulations and the carrying into effect of all those regulations as among persons who are either actually members of the University or who come in and subject themselves to be at least *pro hac vice* members of the University – I mean with respect to the degrees which they seek to have conferred upon them – all those are regulations of the domus.[27]

(There has recently been realization that students must be informed of such rules.)

It is less clear how such solely internal rules can properly regulate the *employment* situation. The granting of promotion to academic staff is hard to classify in relation to the rule of 'achieving the objects of the institution'. It could be argued that it will encourage staff to perform better if a carrot is held out to them. However, if there are not enough opportunities or if the selection of those to be promoted is perceived to be unfair, the opposite may happen, and staff may lose goodwill and work less hard for the university. An institution could equally argue that it helps it achieve its objectives if it can 'hire and fire' at will, on any grounds it chooses.

An employment contract cannot lay down every detail of an employee's daily work. So there is a 'managerial prerogative' which allows instructions to be given which add to any obligations laid down in the contract.[28] Employees are thus under obedience to their employers in what continues in English law to be a master–servant employment relationship. It may not be clear to either party in what circumstances a subordinate can refuse the command of his or her superior, unless it is obviously unreasonable, or professionally detrimental to the employee; or seeks to require him to commit some criminal act.[29]

Members of a university, especially student members, may have a duty of obedience as a condition of membership, but that rests on a different principle. A member is subject to domestic laws of the university. A good broad test of what those embrace is what falls under the jurisdiction of the visitor in a university which has one, for the visitor is the interpreter of the domestic laws.[30] Megarry V.-C. said in *Patel v. University of Bradford Senate* [1979] 2 All E.R. 582, C.A. that a visitor's jurisdiction is complete over the withholding of examination results, appointments to university committees, dismissal of students from a university and readmission of students to a university. That was not meant to be an exhaustive list. It was merely that these points arose in the case in question. But the last two, which concern membership, are clearly central, in that a university's regulations must, by definition, have internal reference, and must therefore be capable of deciding who is and who is not 'within' an institution or a body, and thus whether they do or do not refer to him.

Keeping the rules: those who apply them

In certain circumstances, the failure to keep procedural rules which have been established by the decision-making body itself (or *for* the decision-making body by the authority which empowers it to make the decision), may open a university to the courts requiring it to do so.[31] 'A public authority is bound by its undertakings as to the procedure it will follow, provided they do not conflict with its duty',[32] and provided it has not published revisions of those procedures,[33] so that those affected know that the rules have changed. There is thus a requirement that changes to rules be published (*cf. Blackpool Corporation v. Locker* [1948] 1 K.B. 349 (at 369, *per* Scott L.J.): 'it seems to me vital to the whole English theory of the liberty of the subject, that the affected person should be able at any time to ascertain what legislation affecting his rights has been passed under sub-delegated powers').

Bad law and bad drafting

There are several ways in which private laws may be faulty. It may be possible to show that such procedural safeguards as exist to ensure the attainment of fairness are not adequate. Then it may reasonably be asked, 'what additional procedural safeguards are required to ensure the attainment of fairness?'[34] Lord Bridge of Harwich set out certain principles in *Lloyd v. McMahon*: 'It is well-established that when a statute has conferred on any body the power to make decisions affecting individuals, the courts will not only require the procedure prescribed by statute to be followed, but will readily imply so much and no more to be introduced by way of additional procedural safeguards as will ensure the attainment of fairness.'[35]

There is also the possibility of conflict within internal legislation. *Oakes v. Sidney Sussex College, Cambridge* [1988] 1 All E.R. 1005 provides an example of the kinds of anomaly which can arise in the drafting of internal regulations. The statutes of the College constituted a body known as the Master and Fellows (1.s.3d). This body had at the time of the case, powers 'to decide any questions which may arise as to the interpretation or operation of [the] Statutes'. 39.2 of the Statutes adds: 'any question which may arise as to the interpretation or operation of these Statutes shall be decided by the Master and Fellows at a College meeting specially summoned by the Master, who shall give at least six days' notice thereof, provided that the Master or any two Fellows may, within six months, appeal against such decision to the Visitor, whose Judgement thereon shall be final'. So the Master and Fellows, under the Visitor, are the interpreters of the Statutes.

However, there were at least two other 'bodies' which could interpret the rules. The governing body is distinct from the Master and Fellows, in that it consists of senior members with four junior members. This body may make the decision (8.s.2) to remove or suspend a Fellow for 'grave misconduct' or 'neglect of duty'. The Master and Fellows decide what constituted 'gross misconduct' or 'neglect of duty'.

In the case of a student, 'the Master and Tutors in consultation' shall have power to refuse permission to continue in residence to any student (except a Scholar or Exhibitioner) who fails an examination or fails to pay his College bills (9.4). This appears not to be a 'body' of the same sort as the governing body, but a committee. It 'consults' and then its members make a decision. But under 9.5 and 9.6 it is the governing body which has power to remove from the College a member of the College in *statu pupillari* (which would here include a Scholar or Exhibitioner), and in that case, the student has a right to be heard in his own defence. The interpretation falls to a different body of members acting on a different basis.

Badly drafted regulations can thus result in anomaly and contradiction. In the *Sidney Sussex* case, it was noted that:

> on disciplinary charges leading to the suspension or deprivation of Fellows, the appeal goes expressly from the decision of the governing body to the Visitor . . . if Ch 39 is given its wide literal meaning it commits *any* question arising as to the interpretation or operation of the statutes to the master and fellows. That is wholly inconsistent with a decision on that point in the context of Ch 8 being made by the governing body with an appeal direct to the Visitor. A similar position applies on appeals from the removal of officers under Ch 21.[36]

A regulation may be declared void if its application is uncertain.[37]

Again, a regulation will not be upheld by the courts if it is unreasonable.[38] 'If [bye-laws] were found to be partial and unequal in their operation . . . if they were manifestly unjust.'

And finally, validity of regulations may be affected by failure to publish them. This is a common problem in universities where promotions procedures and other rules are not communicated to those whose interests are affected and sometimes not even to those charged with implementing them, and where changes are made and only partially circulated with no real understanding of the implications of such casualness.

'Necessary' or 'convenient' rules

'The courts must . . . formulate their own criteria for determining whether the procedural rules are to be regarded as mandatory, in which case disobedience will render void or voidable what has been done, or as directory, in which case disobedience will be treated as an irregularity not affecting the validity of what has been done.'[40] There are rules which express the intention of primary legislation, and rules which are merely an administrative convenience. The two sets of categories, mandatory/directory, expressing the intention of the legislation and being for administrative convenience, may not be identical, but the problems these distinctions can create are closely related.

The test that 'no substantial prejudice has been suffered by those for whose benefit the requirements were introduced' is important.[41] We may, therefore, ask whether a rule was introduced for the benefit of students or academic staff or the university as a whole or for the convenience of administrators. If it was introduced for the convenience of administrators but was to the prejudice of those whose interests were affected it must be unfair. If it was introduced for the benefit of those whose interests were affected but worked to their disadvantage it was unfair.

Changing the rules

The Interpretation Act 1978, s. 14 lays down that a statutory power to make 'rules, regulations and bye-laws . . . shall be construed as including a power to revoke, amend or re-enact them, subject to the same conditions as applied to the making of them'.

The machinery by which regulations are, in practice, amended in universities is highly variable. It can be as informal as a memo sent round by a member of a department suggesting that in future the weighing of marks on the borderline for candidates hoping to proceed from an MPhil to be registered for a PhD should be differently handled if other members of staff involved agree; to a procedure of the utmost formality, involving the revision going through Parliament or the Privy Council. In either case, there are questions about the standing of any rules whose force is not defined when they are made.

There are questions about the scope rules leave for the exercise of discretion, without the rules themselves having to be changed, or being deemed to have been changed. Rules for adjudicating on an MPhil candidate's application to go on to a PhD are a good case in point. The intention of formulating such rules may be to ensure that no one capable of completing the course and going on to a PhD is prevented from doing so by failure on the part of those running the MPhil course to pick up any difficulties at an early stage. But the result of building in more complex rules may be to make it hard to keep that end in view, so that candidates may be prevented by a technicality from continuing with their courses. For instance, a poor mark in a first 'course essay' may or may not be an indicator that the student is of only modest ability, but a second essay might show that the student was in fact very able. If the poor 'first mark' was turned by a change in the rules into an absolute barrier, it could stop a good student proceeding to the PhD.[42]

So there are many points at which universities might be legally accountable in their rule-making and their operation of their rules. There are still more points at which they ought to be a great deal more conscious what they are doing, and alert to the implications, in the interests of clarity and fairness.

9

The Rights of the Subordinate and the Insubordinate

Suppose the academic employee receives the minutes of a committee meeting or agenda or letter from an administrator headed 'confidential', and the document contains information which he believes it is not in the public interest to keep secret?

There is an 'implied term of fidelity' in a contract of employment, a duty of good faith on the part of the employee towards the employer. That might seem to place a member of the academic staff under an obligation not to speak out in a way which might bring the institution into disrepute and this has indeed been invoked as a ground for discipline or dismissal.

The duty of fidelity is not reciprocal on a basis of equality because the employment relationship, being a master–servant relationship, is unequal. Nevertheless, the employer has some duty to act in good faith towards the employee. That was demonstrated in *Robinson v. Crompton Parkinson Ltd* [1978] I.C.R. 401. An employee successfully appealed against the findings of an industrial tribunal. It was held on appeal that where an employer demonstrated that he lacked trust and confidence in an employee, that could amount to a repudiation of the contract of employment. 'In a contract of employment, and in conditions of employment, there has to be a mutual trust and confidence between master and servant. Although most of the reported cases deal with the master seeking remedy against a servant or former servant for acting in breach of confidence or in breach of trust, that action can only be upon the basis that trust and confidence is mutual.'[1] In another case, where an employee's honesty was impugned, it was held that the employers: 'had indicated in the clearest terms that they no longer had any confidence in him or his honesty and it is not unreasonable that he should consider that by adopting this attitude in a situation for which he was not responsible they had destroyed any basis of confidence that could ever exist between them and him in future'.[2]

What is it acceptable to blow the whistle about?

Whistleblowing does not have to be about anything inherently serious. Serious issues may lie behind superficially small problems. Even if they do not, a small matter to a university may be a large matter to affected individuals. Triviality and vexatiousness are not the same thing as 'raising minor matters'.

Nor does whistleblowing have to be about abuse or malpractice only. There may be circumstances in which the whistle ought to be blown when there has merely been a mistake, but the mistake has not been acknowledged when it is pointed out, the institution's management has closed ranks, sought to cover up the error, blocked and stalled, and dug in its heels about putting it right; where a code of good practice has been ignored and there has been a refusal to return to it when that is pointed out. It is unusual for an institution or its officers to respond with anything other than an attempt to silence a whistleblower, or to diminish or counteract the effect of what he has said. A study of cases involving patient neglect and staff brutality in UK hospitals found that those with an 'investment' in the profession and the hospital will frequently seek to cover up wrongdoing and justify themselves and the activities which are being challenged. A phenomenon which often surprises the principled whistleblower is this willingness of ordinary fellow-professionals to collude with abuse of one sort or another.[3] It is the more marked in the case of those in positions of responsibility who stand to lose face if some error – and it is often error not deliberate wrongdoing – is exposed. It is all rather like heresy. No one is a heretic because he makes a mistake. A heretic is someone who persists in the error when it is pointed out to him.

Whistleblowing certainly does not have to be about financial malpractice only, although much of the emphasis of the Nolan Committee's work in the 1990s was in that area. In universities it ought to be a reason to blow the whistle if examiners are put under pressure to pass candidates they honestly consider to have failed, in order to keep up the numbers; or, if standards are lowered in other ways, such as over the admission of students.

Procedural unfairness is a further proper ground for whistleblowing, for example, over the appointment or promotion of staff.

Reprisal for whistleblowing is, in itself, a proper ground for whistleblowing on the back of a first blowing of the whistle. (Rather on the principle that one may allege victimization as a separate head of complaint if there is reprisal after the bringing of a sex or race discrimination case.) But it may be subtle and hard to prove. In 1981 the BBC made a *Horizon* programme called 'No one will listen to me' where academics argued for views which they said were being blocked by the 'Establishment'. One of the scientists was taken off all undergraduate teaching at the University of Surrey as a result of appearing on the programme. The department in which he served was closed down within two years and he was not placed in another department although all his colleagues were.[4]

The principle that conscientious whistleblowing ought to be in the public interest includes the assumption that the employer's true interest is *also* a public interest; that is, that it is in the employer's interest to behave honourably and to be seen to behave honourably:

> The University, like all other public bodies, has a duty to conduct its affairs in a responsible way . . . The University recognises the need to protect the personal confidentiality of those who work within the University and is committed to the principles of academic freedom embodied in its charter and statutes and enshrined in statute, and therefore to permit staff to speak freely and without being subject to disciplinary sanctions or victimisation, about academic standards and related matters, providing that they do so lawfully, without malice, and in the public interest and in a way which respects proper confidentiality.[5]

The public interest is an interest wider than the personal interest of the whistleblower. But it is not a reasonable requirement that the conscientious whistleblower ought to be required to act only if he himself has not suffered from the practice of which he is complaining. For one thing, that may affect his standing, and the possibility of his having resort to the courts for a remedy for injustice done to him personally. Provided the whistleblowing is done for the benefit of the institution or for others' good as well as that of the whistleblower, it remains conscientious whistleblowing. Injustice in an individual case may show up a wider problem: indeed, that may well be how the matter comes to light.

A whistleblower may draw attention to conduct which 'violates norms'; or he may 'challenge' the norm itself.[6] He may demonstrate that no norms exist in a given system. In any case, he is an unwelcome and uncomfortable presence, especially if he is persistent.

What happens when the whistle is blown?

The Nolan Committee made recommendations in its *Second* and *Fourth Reports* designed to encourage universities, like other public bodies, to rethink their attitudes to whistleblowing, to learn to see it as something which should be encouraged, and the whistleblower as hero not villain (*Fourth Report*, 22). This is in recognition of the fact that there is, inevitably, an imbalance of power between whistleblower and institution, which has to be consciously adjusted by the more powerful 'side', or improprieties will not come to light because employees will be too frightened to speak out.

However, under these broad protections there have to be procedures for investigating what the whistleblower alleges. In most universities these are, as yet, sketchy in the extreme. It may be provided that the vice-chancellor will inquire, but there is no detailed procedure for the making of such an inquiry and the vice-chancellor clearly cannot be the proper officer to inquire if he himself happens to be the subject of the complaint. Going up a management 'line' has obvious disadvantages. There may be nowhere to go outside the institution except the media. Cambridge has a statute (K.5) which enables concerns to be raised, but its implementation proved a tricky business in the 1990s.[7] It is asking a lot of an institution to approach such a complaint with an open mind, and to investigate it fairly and fearless of the consequences if it discovers that there was ground for the complaint.

The state of whistleblower legislation in the UK

There has been a legislative lacuna in UK law for the protection of whistle-blowers.[8] US employment law works on a different set of checks and balances from that of the UK. In the UK, an employee dismissed without good reason can seek redress through the courts. In the US, there has been a less strong requirement that employees should not be dismissed without good reason. Similarly, in UK law the requirement to act in good faith is strong. In the US, it is only comparatively recently that it has become unacceptable not to act in good faith as an employee, and statutory whistleblower protection often exists only for specific groups of employees.[9]

An employee has been able, on occasion, to argue successfully that he was dismissed for some action which was in the public interest. The employer would then be liable in the tort of abusive discharge.[10] However, the connection between an action promoted by conscience in the public interest and the stated grounds for an employee's dismissal may be tortuous, and great damage can be done professionally to an employee in ways for which the law offers no protection in practice. One US employee in a pharmaceutical company refused to conduct certain trials on the grounds that an element in the substance being tested was potentially carcinogenic. Management pressure was applied and other members of the team got on with the trials. The one who refused was accused of being irresponsible and showing bad judgement. She was taken off all work on the trials. She was demoted and restricted from associating with certain colleagues. She resigned, claiming that damage had been done to her professional reputation and her career had been disrupted. The matter went one way and then the other at trial and subsequently on appeal. It was held by the appellate division of the New Jersey Superior Court that only significant matters of clear and well-defined public policy could be brought into play against an employer's right to hire and fire at will.[11]

Even where statute makes the conduct about which the whistleblower is protesting illegal, it will not necessarily follow that the employee who blows the whistle will be held to have been acting in the public interest.[12] In the case just cited, the employee's motives were arguably scientific and scholarly as well as arising from concerns for the public interest.

Two Private Member's Bills attempted to deal with the need for whistleblower protection in the UK during the 1990s. The second of them, the Shepard Private Member's Bill of 1997, placed the onus on the whistleblower to show that he was acting in the public interest, not on the employer to show that he was not. The Public Interest (Disclosure) Act becomes law as this book goes to press.

Protecting the conscientious informer

A tendency to reward conformity seems inevitable in a system concerned with 'development' and the attaining of 'aims' and 'objectives' set by line managers for (even if sometimes also with) those they 'manage'. However, the great advances of scientific and other discovery have often been made by those who were nonconformist in their attitudes and practices and independent in their work. This paradox is particularly sharp in universities. It was striking that when appraisal was first introduced in Cambridge it had to be stressed in order to make it even partly acceptable to scholars accustomed to being their own masters, that appraisers were to have no authority to seek to direct a member of the academic staff in his research. Even there, talk of heads of departments having a duty in that direction began to creep in in 1997. There is an uneasy relationship in some of the new universities between the direction of research and independence of inquiry. The very post of 'Director of Research' is ambiguous. It requires its holder to oversee work by academic staff which is, of its essence, the work of independent minds.

The person of independent mind may, however, apply it in other ways than in the pursuit of his research. He may use it to ask awkward questions about the running of his institution or higher education in general. How much trouble should someone be allowed to make without penalty? On what issues? And by what channels?

Firms in the US now often have codes of ethics and patterns of expectation about conduct in their managements, which all encourage protection of whistleblowers.[13] This is the best route – internal willingness to stand corrected, to take criticism seriously. But failing that, legal protection may help. In the US there have been attempts to encourage whistleblowing with rewards and incentives, but those do not tempt the conscientious whistleblower who is motivated by a sense of indignation at a wrong 'unrighted'. The removal of the danger of reprisal may have more effect.

What protection should there be for whistleblowers and how should it be enforced? It can be extremely difficult to protect against subtle forms of disadvantaging. Whistleblowers encounter a response. There are many intangible and unquantifiable costs of whistleblowing, in the isolation from colleagues and the almost inevitable hostility.[14] There may be intimidation, including threats to career prospects; there may be passivity or disbelief, ignoring their concerns; there may be suspension; managers may put complainants under surveillance; the complainants may be called 'sick' or told that they are unable to cope; complainants may be moved sideways, disciplined, dismissed. There will almost certainly be a closing of ranks against them.[15] Someone can easily become a 'marked' man. He can be denied all sorts of opportunities to 'rise' or to 'act' within an institution. At best, whistleblowers have to be both patient and persistent. There are likely to be periods of delay, during which they may be dismissed and unable to obtain good references, and, if they seek another job, will be unable to show the prospective new employer that the complaint in the previous post has been upheld as valid.[16]

There is of course a real danger that an alleged 'concern' has been raised solely with a purpose of causing trouble, even of 'getting back at' a senior. Conversely, a whistleblower may claim that the protest was carried out on ethical grounds, indeed that a professional ethical code made it necessary.[17] That principle could be important in seeking to distinguish between the troublemaker and the conscientious objector. Yet, there could still be an element of personal hostility, even in a complaint justifiable on conscience grounds.

An employee's whistleblowing conduct may be deemed excessive, even if the subject of the whistleblowing is a legitimate concern. In one US case it was seen to be 'so excessive and so deliberately calculated to inflict needless economic hardship on the employer' as to lose the protection of Title VII Civil Rights Act 1964.[18] The Graham Pink case involved an individual obsessively continuing to raise the same concerns even after they had been met.[19]

> What do you do when you have listened to a complaint, have investigated it, found little or no evidence to support it, explained your feelings to the complainant, advised him what action to take if he finds himself unable to cope with the situation on the ward, and he still goes on writing letters of complaint to everyone from hospital managers to union officials, MPs, the Secretary of State for Health and the Prime Minister? The volume of correspondence was monumentally time-consuming for authority staff, as the people who received letters from Pink wrote in their turn to the authority for an explanation.[20]

The problem with the *Pink* case was that the media listened to what he said but did not on the whole check up on what he said, so that he was believed and the managers were not. It was also an unusual feature of this case that the complaints he was making gave the impression that the ward he worked on was uniquely or especially bad in the respects for which he criticized it, whereas in fact, although there were certainly faults, it was arguably suffering only from the staffing and resource problems which were affecting other similar wards elsewhere.

A very different case was that of Charles Robertson,[21] an accountant who was concerned that he might be being asked to give false information to the Inland Revenue. He asked for reassurance and was told 'never again to attempt to communicate with a non-executive director, other than through proper line-management channels'. He was unable to believe that there could be anything but a fair resolution in the end. 'It seemed inconceivable to me that I could ever suffer because of this affair, given that I was the totally innocent party . . . the prospect of my position being at risk never entered my head.'[22] He came to feel 'beleagured, threatened, isolated'.[23] He was suspended. 'It is felt that your letter of 16 March is defamatory to the Company, and the correspondence is defamatory to senior individuals of the Company.' There was an investigation of his 'conduct', without a hearing, after which he was sent a report. He was eventually sacked.[24]

Standing

Who has standing to blow the whistle? A father who was an employee of the university as a porter might have a son in the physics department, and have serious concerns about the teaching or examining arrangements there. He could blow the whistle, having standing as an employee.

The *Dearing Report* speaks of 'suitable provision in employment contracts for "whistleblowing"' (15.61). There is a strong paragraph (15.67) seeking to insist on protection of individuals (staff) who attempt to expose 'honestly judged malpractice'. Whistleblowing is defined by Dearing, somewhat inexactly, as involving situations 'where an individual member of staff feels so strongly that important matters of legitimate wider concern are going astray within the institution's senior management or governance that he or she decides to bring them to a wider audience' (15.66). It is unclear whether this is meant to refer to 'going public' outside the institution or to seeking to bring concerns to the appropriate authorities inside it. Both are modes of whistleblowing, but whereas the first is clearly a proper action of an employee, where he should be protected from reprisal, the second can be appropriate only where the matter is already in the public domain, or all internal avenues have been exhausted, and in the first instance should involve those who are the proper persons to receive such a complaint, such as MPs or the HEFCE.

The *Dearing Report* envisages a shrinking of the core of permanent academic staff in universities. That has already been taking place, with concomitant dangers to freedom of speech, for those who are on short-term contracts cannot easily risk speaking out when what they have to say may fall on unwelcoming ears in their institutions.

Student complaints tend to fall into three categories.[25] There are complaints about failure to deliver promises (breach of an institution's contract with its students) for example, by not providing a published course; complaints about 'the quality of their experience', which may include incompetent teaching or lack of books in the library; and complaints about 'academic judgements of their work'. 'When the internal procedures within an institution are exhausted, the student should have access to an independent tribunal not involved in the original decision, who can review the way the case has been handled and, in non-academic matters, the decision that has been taken . . . We support the use of reconciliation and possibly formal arbitration' (15.59).

Recommendation 60 is that the arrangements for handling complaints from students should 'reflect the principles of natural justice'; be 'transparent and timely; include procedures for reconciliation and arbitration; include an independent, external element; and . . . are managed by a senior member of staff' (*cf.* 15.57). This last is a provision whose purpose is opaque, and, if case experience is anything to go by, it would not by any means always be protective of the interests of the student. Further, the issue of procedures is legally a mare's nest. Student 'whistleblowing' is a very different affair from staff whistleblowing, for students are extremely vulnerable and they do not have standing to challenge the university in the way its employees may.

So it is, as a rule, those with 'nothing to lose' and those with a conscience who blow the whistle – and sometimes those without a conscience who act out of revenge for damage done to their own careers. In either case, a whistleblower is dangerous because he cannot easily be 'bought off'.

10

Resolving Disputes

Dispute resolution becomes necessary when a problem is allowed to get a foothold. The most common way for that to occur is when a challenge is met by defensiveness and the attempt to persist in the challenged course of action. Those whose role is to deal with the dispute are likely also to be managers of the staff whose conduct is being questioned. They commonly react by seeking to defend their staff rather than to ensure a fair resolution of the matter. That rapidly leads to impasse (if the challenger is resolute) and to attempts at reprisal or dismissal (if he is resolute *or* if he is easily intimidated) and then to the courts (if he is indignant). The expectation that public money will be saved by resolving the matter internally may not be high.

'My appellate judges make proper decisions. Your grievance arbitrators inject their own values. His National Labor Relations Board is full of political prejudices.'[1]

Dispute resolution attempts are often perceived differently by those at the receiving end and those who seek to mediate and those who have to put procedures into operation in the first place. It is right that there should be no requirement that the process should be that of a court. There is a place for informality and a great deal to be said for finding the shortest way to a solution compatible with justice.

In any situation needing reconciliation three elements have to be held in balance. There will be *substantive* issues of right and wrong, reasonableness and unreasonableness; there will be *procedural* issues to do with ensuring that neither party has an unfair advantage over the other; there will be *institutional* questions about the structures within which it is alleged that something has gone wrong, and the authority of any rules which it is alleged have been broken. These last are the hardest to speak about in universal terms (for power structures are diverse between institutions, and within a given institution, they can vary enormously in different sorts of administrative arena). But the overarching requirements of fairness transcend an institution's powers to determine its own regulations and procedures, and it is always an absolute requirement that the complainant or accused is given fair treatment.

This pattern of interrelationship engaged the theorists of the school of 'legal process theory' or 'process jurisprudence' in the USA of the 1950s and 1960s.[2] An attempt was made to contrast the characteristics of the 'dispute resolution' model and the 'public law' model, in the following terms. The first has a focus on specific cases involving individuals; the judge is passive; the remedy is specific; each episode thus dealt with is distinct. On the 'public law' view, the parties are *bodies* of interested persons or groups; the judge active; the remedy broader; and the concern is with the implications of the case for others.[3] In this period of US debate, two ways of looking at the functions of courts thus stood in opposition. 'Courts exist to furnish a peaceful mechanism for the resolution of private disputes.' 'Courts' can, on the other hand, be seen as 'agents for the creation of public norms to guide social life.'[4] The *public* character of a trial is essential, both in its being seen to be open so that justice can be done; and, in a common law country, in its making (in the records of the trial) a contribution to the literature of authority on which later decisions may come to rest.

Disputes in universities have tended to take place at the extreme 'private' end of the scale, with complainant or accused often very isolated and suffering profoundly from not having any other with which to compare his case. Those trying to resolve disputes suffer in the same way from lack of awareness of the wider implications. It would clearly be in the public interest for comparisons to be made and 'public norms' to be established.

A fundamental distinction of types of dispute resolution procedure is between those which are devised voluntarily and those which are imposed by the state or some other authority. It can be possible to have both on offer and for the disputants to choose which route to follow. That choice is sometimes open to a complainant in a university who may go to court or try to achieve a resolution through internal procedures. However, there the options are more strictly 'public' and 'private' systems of dispute resolution than 'voluntary' and 'imposed'.[5] The complainant who uses the internal route will find himself subject to regulations and following procedures in whose devising he has not himself had any say. And he may be forced to follow those before he can have recourse to the courts, which can in its turn create for him the problem of being out of time.

Fuller identifies two fundamental options for the ordering of society: organization by common aims and organization by reciprocity.[6] The second involves trading, or doing a deal between parties which both have sanctions at their disposal. A junior employee complains of managerial misconduct, and finds himself under discipline. The managers or administrators may use their superior power in the hierarchy to 'run' the 'trial' and effectively make it impossible for their own conduct to be examined on all fours with that of the junior. That has the effect of placing him at a disadvantage. He cannot insist on fair 'play in action' on his own authority, because he is not an equal partner in deciding things. Reciprocity looks hollow in those circumstances.

Within both the divisions of 'private' and 'public' dispute resolution so far sketched, there are several possible further models or approaches.

1. There may be a formal procedure laid down in advance, of either discipline or grievance, which is followed to the point where there is adjudication by an officer appointed within the rules of the procedure to make the final decision. That is the pattern of the Model Statute imposed on the old universities under the Education Reform Act 1988.
2. There may be a purely voluntary process of mutual agreement where unions and management settle a dispute round a table on a more or less equal footing. That can happen in universities, but it is unusual for it to work in resolving a dispute concerning an individual. Its normal place is in 'wages and working conditions' negotiations.
3. There may be agreement by the disputants to appoint an independent third party to settle the dispute. That again requires the disputants to begin on a more or less equal footing, because otherwise the stronger party will be unlikely to agree to let a third party resolve things, and the weaker party may have no say in who is to do the resolving.

Conciliation involves a conciliator, who explores the degree to which either side is likely to give way. Adjudication looks at vested rights, and therefore to the evidence for the existence of those rights. This means going to precedent and 'the application of rules which are supposed to exist' already.[7] Adjudication has the character of 'a father attempting to assume the role of judge in a dispute between his children over possession of a toy'.[8] 'Administration' is the use of a discretionary power which allows the administering body to decide the matter. This involves the application of rules which are not strictly vested rights. They can be regulations made by the administering body itself. There can be inquiry of the type conducted by Sir Richard Scott into the 'Arms for Iran' affair, where the purpose is to uncover cover-up and reveal misbehaviour by those in positions of power.

The 'voluntary' methods have the virtue of allowing (in principle) the operation of goodwill, the cultivation of good working relationships and the possibility of a future climate of mutual understanding and cooperation. Discipline and grievance procedures, even where they are successful, have the danger that they leave the disputants with a memory of conflict; there has to be a 'loser', and it is hard for those who have been involved to come out of it with a sense that face has been saved on both sides.

Again, the key distinguishing features include whether or not the parties stand on an equal footing and can therefore be deemed to be reaching a resolution to their mutual satisfaction; only where that is so can the process be truly voluntary.

Sir Gerald Brennan said in his opening address to the Australian Law Forum in July 1996:

> The AAT was intended not only to give better administrative justice in individual cases but also to secure an improvement in primary administrative decision-making . . . External review is only effective if it infuses the corporate culture and transforms it . . . bureaucratic intransigence would not be moved unless errors were clearly demonstrated and a method of reaching the correct or preferable decision was clearly expounded.

The desirability of universities approaching dispute resolution in this spirit and with these objectives is obvious enough. Getting primary decision-making right is of immense importance. Failure to do so is the starting point of dispute after dispute. So, in the interests of accountability we need to look deeper than the adequacy of the fail-safe mechanisms in procedure and of the procedures themselves, to the mindset of university administrators. A change in the climate of expectation is needed.

The requirements about procedures

Procedures are important, however. New universities do not need to keep to the Model Statute devised by the University Commissioners and binding on the old universities under the Education Reform Act 1988. The new universities created by the Further and Higher Education Act 1992 were left free to make up their own rules for discipline and grievance procedures. Some did so at once; some left it until a case arose; some have changed their rules during the conduct of a case; some have folders containing the previous rules of constituent hitherto separate colleges, still imperfectly reconciled with one another. Some are in the barest outline, some are more detailed.

The Model Statute itself has room for improvement. One of its weaknesses is the personal powers it gives to the vice-chancellor as judge at the final stage of a grievance process. There could easily arise a situation where no internal remedy was available where a vice-chancellor made procedural errors – perhaps quite innocently – or became prejudiced by anger and resentment against a lecturer and was therefore guilty of bias. It might be that there was no remedy. In one case – in a new university, so not one legally bound by the Statute – a lecturer sought to bring a grievance case against a vice-chancellor because he believed his impending dismissal had been unfairly handled. But it was the vice-chancellor who had been responsible for the alleged unfair handling. The vice-chancellor wrote to him[9] to say that he would not entertain a grievance case against himself, and that since he was the final arbiter in all grievance cases that decision was unassailable.

Another unsatisfactory feature of the provisions of the Model Statute is the difficulty of calling to account where the procedures it lays down are not properly followed. That again is not uncommon, because such procedures are rarely used, universities' solicitors are not likely to have relevant experience, and administrators charged with carrying out the procedures commonly make mistakes out of sheer unfamiliarity with what they ought to do under the rules.

It may, therefore, be a reasonable requirement that a university have someone to monitor complaints who is on 'no one's side', and that it be seen to keep its procedures under review so that outdated and confused practice does not simply get repeated.

Are there diminished requirements of fairness in handling disputes internally?

There are no absolute rules of natural justice beyond the *nemo iudex* and the *audi alteram partem* principles. There can be circumstances where these requirements are high and others where *even* these can be partly waived. Lord Denning felt concern in the *Profumo* case that he had had to act as 'detective, inquisitor, advocate and judge'. In the Denning and Scott Inquiries alike, one person was sitting alone and therefore without the benefit of anyone to consult, or simply to talk things over with, and was also having to discharge more than one function. That was also true when Sir Michael Davies acted on behalf of the Queen as Visitor at the University College of Wales at Swansea.[10] Sir Michael Davies heard both sides, but there was no opportunity for either side to comment on what the other had said. Lord Howe of Aberavon criticized the procedures adopted at the Scott Inquiry, especially the failure to hear from the defence. Sir Richard Scott's reasoning was that an inquisitorial inquiry is not an adversarial proceeding. These are all on the face of it breaches of the *nemo iudex* rule.

In *Pergamon Press Ltd* [1971] 1 Ch. 388, the duty of fairness was held to extend to an inquiry as well as to a trial. 'Although the inspectors' function . . . is investigatory not judicial, they must, in view of the consequences which may follow from their report, act fairly. In *Pergamon* (at 389) it was held that part of the duty of the inspectors 'to act fairly' consisted in giving 'anyone whom they proposed to criticise or condemn in their report a fair opportunity to answer what was alleged against him'.[11] As Lord Denning put it: 'I take it to be axiomatic that the inspectors must not use the evidence of a witness so as to make it the basis of an adverse finding unless they give the party affected sufficient information to enable him to deal with it.'[12]

In the *litis contestatio* of a trial, there is a test of strength, and it is therefore important that the weaker party (the accused or anyone criticized in a way likely publicly to damage reputation) should have his side heard and should have a chance to meet allegations against him and should know that his judge is unbiased. There was no understanding in *Pergamon* that detailed procedures could be laid down which ought to be binding in every inquiry. Indeed, provided they were acting fairly, the inspectors were to be 'masters of their own procedure'.[13] The presumption in an inquiry is that the person or persons appointed to inquire are wholly independent and experienced and will ensure that they attend fairly to the claims of both sides of the case.

Similarly, in an internal hearing there may, in practice, be a low threshold of expectation in this matter of required procedures, but without that protection. *Maxwell v. Department of Trade and Industry* [1974] 1 Q.B. 523 refers to the *Pergamon* decision – so as to assert the general principle that a board or committee must act in good faith and fairly and listen to both sides but is not bound to proceed as if it were conducting a trial. In *Maxwell*, Lord Denning said (at 536) that in an inquiry those making the report should 'put to a witness the points of substance which occur to them – so as to give him the chance to explain or correct any relevant statement which is prejudicial to him'. There was no requirement to put tentative conclusions to the witness for him to rebut.[14]

The Times, 1 May 1997, reported on the case of a manager sacked for gross misconduct by a privatized utility which had not told him what was alleged against him or by whom. Sir Richard Scott ordered the company to disclose the third party's name to the sacked manager; he would then be able to sue for wrongful dismissal or for libel. What had happened was on the face of it a clear breach of a rule of natural justice universally regarded as fundamental.

Even within an organization as large as a university it can be very difficult to find someone uncontaminated by interest, prejudice or prior knowledge. There are thus practical difficulties in settling a dispute within an institution, in finding persons who can come with fresh and unprejudiced minds to the task of achieving a fair settlement:

> An official charged with allocating television channels wants to know of one applicant 'what kind of fellow he really is' and accepts an invitation to a leisurely chat over the luncheon table. The fact of this meeting is disclosed by a crusading legislator. The official is accused of an abuse of judicial office. Charges and countercharges fill the air and before the debate is over it appears that nearly everyone concerned with the agency's functioning has in some measure violated the proprieties that attach to a discharge of judicial functions.[15]

In general, there must always be a balance between strict procedural requirements and circumstances which may call for them to be moderated. Lord Reid spoke in *Ridge v. Baldwin* [1964] A.C. 40 (at 65) of 'what a reasonable man would regard as fair procedure in particular circumstances'. We are a very long way from consensus about what should be required in a university's discipline, grievance, appeal and dispute resolution processes.

We must place among the most important of those circumstances the scale of the consequences for individuals under scrutiny or being tried (for it is as important to be fair to the seniors as to the juniors). Where consequences of a mistake will be more serious there ought, arguably, to be a higher requirement of procedural rigour.[16] But the tendency is the other way, towards diminishing those requirements in internal procedures.

Internal methods of dispute resolution

The autonomy of universities over their own affairs is well-established, and it is not restricted to their academic affairs. It extends to their treatment of staff and students to a degree which may interfere with individuals' rights under the law.

Grievance procedures and harassment codes

The grievance procedures of universities, whether under the Model Statute and statutorily binding, as in the old universities, or freely-conceived and under no regulation, as in the 'new' are frequently flawed, in ways which have already been touched on.

The harassment code is a relatively new device, largely regulated by developing conventions and public expectations about the treatment of disadvantaged groups, such as the disabled, racial minorities and women, and by the legislation designed to protect their interests. It includes a protection against bullying in the workplace (which may affect any employee, not only those in the aforesaid categories). It normally allows the person alleging harassment to define conduct unacceptable to him, with the proviso that it must also be behaviour which would seem to a reasonable person to constitute harassment.

The problem with such protections is that it may be difficult to protect complainants from retribution or retaliation or reprisal. It is a brave complainant who speaks up. To 'win', in the sense of getting the problem put right often provides only a temporary solution or respite. In one case, the head of department retaliated by seeking to renew a short-term contract with the complainant on terms much less favourable than those on which others on the same contract were to be treated.

Visitors

It has consistently been ruled in UK and Commonwealth cases that if there is a visitor and if the matter can be construed as purely domestic, the courts cannot intervene.

In *Balfour v. Balfour* [1919] 2 K.B. 571 (at 578), and in numerous other cases since involving universities, it has been argued that there exist domestic matters which are not justiciable by the courts.[17] The Council and Academic Board 'are making judgements very much within their statutory powers . . . of "entire management of, and superintendence over" the University'.[18] This is a separate question from whether judgements are unassailable, but it might be used as an argument that even if they were assailable because contaminated by bias or because not expert, they might still be unassailable because 'domestic'.

So, are academic judgements justiciable at all if they are taken by or on behalf of a university? In examining academic judgements a court may seek to establish whether the events and circumstances surrounding the forming of those judgements include elements into which it is entirely proper for the court to look, because they do not fall into a specialist or 'professional' province. But it is also possible to raise the question whether that makes the decision no longer strictly 'internal' to the university. That view was expressed in *Page v. Visitor of Hull University*: 'Nor do I accept that all the questions referred to a visitor involve such arcane learning that only those intimately aware of university affairs can begin to understand it, the judges of the land not being able to appreciate the issues.'[19]

The special claims of universities to remain free from interference with their academic judgements depend upon a fusion or overlapping of these two grounds, about which there has been some muddled thinking.

In *Rigg v. University of Waikato* we read: 'the challenge is to actions taken within the powers which the University undoubtedly had under the Act and the contract. The challenge is made by reference to standards which are internal to the University system rather than to standards which are required by law. The substantive issues appear to us to be essentially "non-justiciable 'in-house' issues".'[20] This is linked with the principle that the setting of such standards is one of the things a university has to do in order to fulfil the purpose for which it exists. In *Herring v. Templeman* [1973] 2 All E.R. 581, a student teacher challenged his removal from a teacher training college – not a university – on grounds of academic failure. He argued that the governing body's decision was *ultra vires* and therefore null and void. Hoffman J. argued (at 591) that, far from being *ultra vires* the institution was discharging its primary duty in making such a judgement.

> [T]he dismissal of a student teacher for failing, in the opinion of those charged with the task of forming an opinion, to match up to the standard required of a teacher is the inevitable duty of an educational establishment which holds examinations and passes out students whom it considers fit to be teachers. The training of a student teacher and the assessment of his competence is the main and indeed the only object of a teacher-training college.

But in *Rigg* it is the *system* which is deemed to be the arena within which the decision is properly and unassailably exercised, and not the institution.

It is argued first that universities are special in needing to have a great deal of freedom to run their own affairs because of what they do in defending the truth and engaging in scholarly inquiry independently of inappropriate influences. This depends on a doctrine of the separation of powers. If defenders of the truth can be put under instructions not to defend it they may be prevented from doing so.

But universities also educate students. So there is a second argument for autonomy which is founded on the existence of a 'private' or 'domestic' relationship of teacher and taught in educational institutions. It has been said of schools, too, that in this latter respect the 'content of educational societies involves a special factor which is not present in other contexts – namely the relation of tutor and pupil'.[21] Is that relationship essentially 'domestic'? Are the roles of 'educator, adviser and friend' incompatible with interference by the courts,[22] so that professional judgements formed in the discharge of those roles cannot be reviewed by the courts? There is the further difficulty that this argument is applicable in principle to all educational institutions, while those about academic judgement belong more strictly to higher education. And it is not usually argued that schools have, or should have, autonomy in the same way as it is argued for universities.

Yet, it is in connection with, and in discharge of, this role that universities give degrees, and professional qualifications. Those take their work into an arena where the private relationship, the domestic arena, issues into the public domain.[23]

The personal and private character of the relation of student or member of staff to university is not in any case unassailably the university's exclusive business. It may be relevant that the consequences to the student or member of staff of the decision being challenged are very great. 'A final year medical student should be entitled on personal grounds to know that an end to his potential career has been decided upon by the University for reasons that are entirely justified and by methods that are demonstrably fair and appropriate.'[24]

The exclusivity of jurisdiction of the visitor is one area in which the autonomy of universities is well-established. It has consistently been ruled that if there is a visitor and if the matter can be construed as purely domestic, the courts cannot intervene. Yet, it has not always been true that a complainant wanted to be free to appeal to a visitor, because that may be not a freedom but a constraint. In *Oakes v. Sidney Sussex College, Cambridge* [1988] 1 All E.R. 1005, a student was anxious to show that he was not subject to the jurisdiction of the visitor, because he wanted his case to be considered by the courts.

The principle justifying the argument that visitorial jurisdiction is exclusive appears to be that an eleemosynary or charitable body has, or is deemed to have, a founder, who determines its aims and establishes domestic rules by which these are to be achieved, *and these are entirely its own.* In *Thomas v. Bradford University* [1987] 1 A.C. 795, Sir Richard Kindersley said 'with regard . . . to any breach of trust committed by the corporation . . . or any contracts by the corporation, *not being matters relating to the mere management and arrangement and details of their domus* then indeed this Court will interfere'.[25] In *Patel v. University of Bradford Senate*[26] it was argued that, 'the Visitor has sole and exclusive jurisdiction, and . . . the courts have no jurisdiction over the matters within the visitor's jurisdiction'.[27] It is suggested in *Thomas v. Bradford University* that the domestic concerns 'those matters which are governed by the internal laws of the foundation'.[28] As Diplock, L.J. put it in *Thorne v. University of London*, 'actions of this kind relating to domestic disputes between members of London University (as is the case with other universities) are matters which are to be dealt with by the visitor and the court has no jurisdiction to deal with them'.[29]

Hoffman J. said in *Hines* that, 'irrespective whether the courts would be as well or better qualified to deal with the particular case, a dispute has the necessary domesticity if it involves members of the corporation and the interpretation or application of its internal rules, customs and procedures'.[30] Examples could be multiplied, but in case after case the rule is that if the matter is internal it is none of the courts' business.

That does not mean that it is allowable for a university to make laws about anything at all and claim not to be accountable for them except to the visitor.[31] There has to be true 'domesticity', and that has not yet proved a helpful or tidy distinction in modern cases. Jurisdiction has had to be defined case by case, precisely because 'domesticity' may not be found to be the same thing in every instance. The intervention of a court would be possible only if an appropriate legal duty of a public nature in the University, and a correlative legal right in the applicant, be shown to exist. Even if there is no express statement of such a right, it may be deemed to 'flow from the nature or character of the University'.[32]

So, in practice, 'the Visitor is not free from all control by the courts' even where his jurisdiction is exclusive. Specifically, he can be compelled to exercise his jurisdiction by mandamus, or restrained by prohibition if he exceeds it. Normally, however, certiorari will not lie,[33] because the courts will not adjudicate in matters which lie within his jurisdiction.

However, there are exceptions to the reservations about certiorari. Lord Griffith argued in *Page* that 'in the light of the modern development of administrative law, the High Court would have power, upon an application for judicial review, to quash a decision of the visitor which amounted to an abuse of his powers'.[34] In *Thomas v. University of Bradford* [1987] 1 All E.R. 834; [1987] A.C. 795 it was accepted that judicial review by way of certiorari does lie at least to restrain an abusive process. There is jurisdiction to correct errors of law, since 'illegality' is one of the accepted heads of judicial review.[35] And exclusivity was in fact tested by judicial review in *Re Wislang's Application* [1984] N.I. 63. But in *Norrie*, Cooke J., held that even if it could be argued that the courts had a power of review of a visitor's decision, that should be exercised reluctantly. He stated that deference requires that even where it can, a court should 'be slow to interfere'.[36]

There seem to be three main arguments against exclusivity. The first is the 'Alsatia' argument: 'There must be no Alsatia in England where the King's writ does not run.'[37] 'If the individual's rights are affected he should be entitled to the same protection by the courts as he would be in respect of the decision of a wide range of other tribunals and bodies to whom decisions involving a question of law are assigned', it was argued in *Page*.[38] In the early cases, the question about exclusive jurisdiction was framed so as to ask whether a plaintiff might have a right of resort to an assize of *novel disseisin*. It was argued that that might well be so if a plaintiff 'has no other remedy', for example, where the master of a hospital was ousted by its visitor 'without just cause'.[39]

The second argument against exclusivity depends on the first. This is the 'subordination' argument; it allows that the visitor has a jurisdiction, but not *alongside* that of the courts; his falls under the *higher* jurisdiction of the courts, and is for that reason not exclusive. 'I do not regard the jurisdiction of the Visitor as exclusive but rather as subordinate to that of the Courts',[40] said Woodhouse P., in *Norrie*. The University of Otago Ordinance 1869, s. 1, which survives as a Schedule to the 1961 Act, states that the University shall 'answer and be answered unto in all the Courts of New Zealand'. In *Norrie v. Senate of the University of Auckland* the court of appeal stressed that the courts have the inherent jurisdiction to control all inferior tribunals.[41] Cook J. took the view that 'the mere existence of the Visitor's jurisdiction does not seem an adequate reason for treating as ousted the ordinary and prima facie all-embracing authority of the Courts of general jurisdiction over justiciable disputes'.[42] Visitors' decisions have been reported. It can then be asked whether visitorial decisions can establish precedent and if so what is the weight of that precedent. There is, therefore, a question about their standing in the 'hierarchy of precedent',[43] and unless it is to be suggested that they can outweigh decisions of the courts they must presumably have a subordinate place.

The third argument against exclusivity is the public policy argument. 'For important reasons of public policy private agreements made between parties which attempt to set up a substitute system of justice or oust the jurisdiction of the Courts will not be countenanced.'[44]

In England, visitorial jurisdiction is abolished by the Education Reform Act 1988, s. 206(1) in disputes about the appointment, employment or termination of contract of academic staff. The thinking here was, presumably, that the law provides a remedy that it would be inequitable to deny to employees of universities when other employees have it. Under the same Act, the Model Statute is to cover redundancies, dismissal for good cause, appeal and grievance procedure in the old universities, even if they had visitors. So some, but not all, of the areas in which the old universities used to be able to make their own laws are placed under statutory control, and some, but not all, of the areas of visitorial jurisdiction are interfered with. Visitors of Oxford and Cambridge colleges are not affected by this legislation.

So it cannot now, if ever it could, be maintained that all visitors have, by virtue of being visitors, the same powers and functions. The law appears not entirely clear-headed here too in its continuing assumption that there is some such generic thing as a visitor. The mere intention to appoint a visitor continues to confer visitorial powers *entière* unless there is express restriction, and that still implies that there is a standard 'set' of such powers. But at the University of Kent the duties of the Visitor are prescribed, so the 'set' can be varied.

So we need to consider in outline what these may be. There is traditionally an interpretative function of the visitor, which derives from the founder's legislative authority. In the interpretation of statute it is always regarded as important to seek to determine the intention of the legislator. There appears no reason why that principle should not also hold in the interpretation of domestic law. However, where no founder other than the Queen acting by Royal Charter can be identified it can hardly be said that it is the founder's personal intentions which are being expressed when the university subsequently makes rules for its own internal use. The Model Statute has not been subject as yet to interpretation and test in a body of visitorial or public case law. There is one ruling in a case at York.

Davidson J. in *Ex parte McFadyen* (1945) S.R. (N.S.W.) 200 (at 202) distinguishes four branches of the *subject matter* of the jurisdiction of a visitor: questions concerning the validity of elections to membership; mutual rights and obligations of the corporators; amotion from or deprivation of fellowship, etc; maintenance of *order, but* confined to offences against the foundation *instrument.* The problems of accountability with which we are primarily concerned are not those to do with admission to membership or fellowship, or removal from it, but those which have to do with behaviour of senior officers in the discharge of the 'mutual rights and obligations' and the 'maintenance of order'.

In *Norrie v. Senate of the University of Auckland* [1984] 1 N.Z.L.R. 129 (at 131) there is reference to the concept of a 'manner' of visitation. The New Zealand University Act 1874, s. 29 places a restriction on the visitor in asserting that he 'shall have authority to do all things which appertain to Visitors in such manner as shall be from time to time directed by the Governor, with the approval of the Senate of the said University'. There are various areas in which the *manner* of the visitation is specified.

It is common ground in the authorities that a visitor may not act *ultra vires.* He might, arguably, be doing so if he made a decision for which there was no basis. However, it is open to question whether he is accountable *within* the sphere of his exclusive jurisdiction. A Church of England bishop may act 'as he thinks fit' in making a disciplinary decision.[45] This appears to apply to university visitors too. The University of Otago in 1869 established the Superintendent as Visitor with 'authority to do all things which appertain to Visitors as often as to him shall seem meet'.[46] It was pointed out in *Murdoch University v. Bloom,* that 'the Governor of the State of Western Australia, "shall have authority to do all things which appertain to Visitors as often as to him shall seem meet"'.[47] In *Page v. Visitor of Hull University* we have: 'a judge who makes what an appellate court later regards as a mistake of law is not "abusing his powers" but exercising them to the best of his ability'.[48] There is an area of real concern about accountability here, for a visitor can always argue that he did what he thought best, and that was what he was required to do. That would make it hard to show that his discretion had not been properly exercised and he had acted *ultra vires.*

The *procedural* restrictions on visitors seem to be as unclear as those relating to reasonableness. A visitor 'need not proceed according to the rules of common law so long as he pays regard to the positive forms prescribed by the statutes regulating the foundation'.[49] On the other hand, he does not appear to be completely free to disregard the rules of natural justice or the wider modern requirement of fairness.[50] In *Norrie*, Cooke J. held that 'when any question of law or natural justice is concerned the Courts retain, I think, their full jurisdiction notwithstanding that the dispute arises in University affairs'.[51]

The visitor cannot be asked to intervene until all avenues below him have been exhausted.[52] But his supervisory, and under them appellate and review functions seem well-established. The Education Reform Act 1988 does not interfere with the visitor's authority to hear appeals or to hear and redress grievances. Universities on whom the Model Statute under the Education Reform Act 1988 is binding are free to appoint their visitor as the person to hear appeals under the Statute, but that remains additional to and separate from his visitorial function.[53]

There is also arguably an 'arbitrator' function. It was ruled in *Norrie* that the visitor has: 'practical responsibilities as a kind of continuing arbitrator to deal with and resolve problems affecting the university even when the answer might involve contractual or other issues of law . . . he may do so . . . on the basis of an *original jurisdiction* or in an *appellate* capacity or on a *supervisory basis in the administrative law* sense'.[54]

Provision of visitors is inconsistent across higher education. Not all universities have them. In Oxford and Cambridge, the colleges have them, but not the universities. A review not only of the availability of the visitor but also of the powers and jurisdiction of the office would need legislation, particularly in view of the long history of precedent establishing the exclusivity of visitorial jurisdiction.

The rationale for visitorial jurisdiction is that a visitor is a domesticated animal. He deals with private laws. It might well be that a general-purpose troubleshooter for higher education would not be strictly a visitor because he could not fulfil all the classic criteria of the office. If visitorial help were to turn into a facility available across higher education, there might be a case for providing a general visitor who could act for any university. The Queen *de facto* discharges that function for many universities already. But she acts for each university and not collectively for all those of which she is visitor. If a visitor could act in any university on request, would all the precedent on exclusivity fall?

So it can usefully be asked whether there is a visitorial role to be inhabited in a university if there is no visitor; and does that role, or elements of it, take a form which can be 'transferred' to another kind of officer with a supervisory role in a university, or shared with other universities? If the 'domesticity' of the visitor is central to his function, that makes it hard to see, prima facie, how he could become an officer shared with other institutions. Lord Hardwicke, C.J. said in Dr Walker's case (1736) Cas.t.Hard. 212 that in eleemosynary bodies 'they are bound to obey' the visitor, 'as the members of a family are bound to obey the master.'[55]

Advantages and drawbacks of having a visitor

The visitor's jurisdiction depends not on whether he is the best *means* of resolving a dispute but whether he is deemed to have the best *right* to do so. However, it has frequently been argued in support of the courts not calling a university directly to account that the visitor has many advantages, and that he may, in fact, be the best means. It has been pressed a good deal in the literature that the visitor is quick, cheap and final. A *locus classicus* on this is Lord Hardwicke in *Attorney-General v. Talbot* (1747) 3 Atk. 662 (at 674): 'it is a more convenient method of determination of controversies . . . it is at home . . . and . . . it is a much less expense than suits at law, or in equity'. In *Patel v. University of Bradford Senate* [1978] 3 All E.R. 841 (at 852) Megarry, V.-C. said that the visitorial system can determine a matter 'informally, privately, cheaply and speedily; and give a decision which, apart from any impropriety or excess of jurisdiction, is final and will not be disturbed by the courts'. 'It provides a practical and expeditious means of resolving disputes', agreed Lord Griffiths in *Thomas v. University of Bradford* [1987] 1 A.C. 795 (at 825). It is hard to say whether the argument from speed and convenience remains strong, since cases in which university visitors have been resorted to remain few. Where the visitor is the Queen and the Lord Chancellor's office acts for her, things do not necessarily move quickly, and indeed the rationale for the function of a visitor may be undermined by the delegation of the task.[56]

An overriding consideration in the decisions not to interfere with the visitor's decision has been that 'finality would be lost'.[57] So one advantage of the visitor is that his decision is decisive. That is an advantage, however, only if there can be confidence in its being taken fairly and without the university denying access to the visitor or refusing to disclose relevant evidence (for a visitor has no powers to order disclosure).

Students or members of the academic staff of universities who have sought remedies through the courts in the past have frequently run up against the problem of the exclusive jurisdiction of visitors.[58] A body without a visitor may thus afford its members, and especially those of its members who are also its employees, a better remedy than one which has a visitor. An employee in a university without a visitor has rights of access to the courts which may be taken away by the existence of a visitor from those employed elsewhere. It has been argued that it is prima facie unfair that university teachers should be denied an access to the courts which other teachers have, just because they happen to be employed in an institution which has a visitor.[59] 'It would be an anomalous situation if a person, simply because he was a member of a university, was denied access to the courts although other employees of the university were not denied that right.'[60]

The ground rules of employment law could restrain a university as employer only if it could be shown that the requirements of employment law override the right of a university to do as it pleases with its employees in matters domestic. A frustrating case is *Re Wislang's Application* [1984]

N.I. 63. This was concerned with the termination of an employee's appointment at the end of a period of probation and had it been possible to test the issues we are discussing it would have set a useful precedent. A lecturer in anatomy was appointed subject to an annual assessment of his teaching, research and scholarly ability. This was done by his head of department and his senior colleagues. There was a negative assessment and he was not confirmed in his post. The matter went up a ladder of appeals to the visitor and then to judicial review. In the end, the case turned on questions of exclusivity of visitorial jurisdiction. The lecturer faced the problem that his dismissal could be deemed an entirely domestic affair. Students, too, can be caught in this trap. In *Thorne v. University of London* [1966] 2 Q.B. 237, it was held that a claim concerning the marking of examination papers was for the visitor to decide upon because it was a domestic question.

External dispute resolution

Ombudsman?

In Canada, most universities have their own ombudsman, to whom a complainant has automatic, direct and speedy access. In the UK, it seems more likely that the provision of an ombudsman would be of a single officer to serve the needs of dispute resolution in all universities. Such an ombudsman would have the advantage of being seen by all parties to be independent. An ombudsman can have a statutory authority, but, correspondingly, his remit will be limited by statutory provision, so much will depend on what that statutory provision is. If employment cases are excluded, a high proportion of disputes will be beyond his reach, and there will be the additional problem of the need to settle the question of 'the type of case this is',[61] before a 'route' can be chosen (industrial tribunal, county court, high court or ombudsman).

It may become a problem if there is one central ombudsman that a flood of cases will make it necessary to operate some system of 'triage' or filtering so that cases cannot in practice be dealt with quickly.

An ombudsman needs a system of control, for example, by making him subject to Parliamentary scrutiny. It is also important that thought is given to the mode of appointment of any ombudsman, whether he is to be 'local' to a university or general, to ensure a real and clearly-perceived independence and impartiality.

The maintenance of a public file of cases taken to a university ombudsman would present a number of difficulties. Individuals concerned would have to be assured of the protection of confidentiality over personal details. Nevertheless, means might be found of making such a file a way of enabling future cases to be resolved on a consistent basis and of creating the spectre of a 'blacklist', onto which universities will not wish to get too often. The existence of an ombudsman might thus be an incentive to watch one's back.

It can affect the outcome of a dispute which route is taken by the complainant in the first instance. In the UK, under the Parliamentary Commissioner for Administration Act 1967, s. 5(2)(b) to go to court, or even to have access to a remedy by that route, is to rule out resort to the ombudsman. So there may be inconsistency in the availability of remedies, which cannot be fair to the complainant.

The exchange of cases between court and ombudsman is a commonsense possibility which appears at present to be beset with mechanical difficulties. Lord Woolf proposed in *Access to Justice* (1997) that:

> The relationship between the ombudsman and the courts should be broadened, enabling issues to be referred by the ombudsman to the courts and the courts to the ombudsman with the consent of those involved.
>
> The ombudsman should be able to refer points of law (including questions of statutory interpretation) to the courts.
>
> Compensation recommended by the ombudsman should be enforceable through the courts.

An ombudsman appears to be subject to judicial review (*R. v. PCA, ex parte Dyer* (1994) 1 W.L.R. 621), but it would make better sense for a dissatisfied complainant simply to have the right to go to a court if the ombudsman cannot help him.

A panel of independent arbitrators

The ombudsman's method of proceeding differs from that of the courts in being inquisitorial rather than adversarial. There are advantages in that, in allowing for a degree of informality and flexibility and commonsense in addressing the problem.

Appeal to (one of) a panel of independent arbitrators or an independent review body which might operate in that manner, is under discussion at the time of writing.[62] In one or two cases a senior figure has been willing to accept an invitation to step in informally, with the consent of the parties, talk to those concerned, point out mistakes and get a rapid solution to a problem which may have been rumbling on for years.

The Nolan Committee's proposal was for the setting up of an independent system of review of disputes. Its *Second Report* excludes 'personal grievances, those connected with terms of employment of individuals, decisions of promotion boards'. It is unclear whether the exclusion of personal grievances is intended also to exclude instances where the formal invocation of grievance procedures has gone wrong, procedurally or in some other way. (It is far from uncommon for an individual who seeks to invoke a grievance procedure to find himself under discipline.) Terms of employment should clearly be excluded in so far as they are the terms on which an individual was appointed. He signed a contract which, presumably, he read first. But in-service changes in conditions of service have been imposed throughout the sector and there are issues which need examining about the distance an employer can travel away from the original contract without itself being in breach of contract. These can be, and increasingly are, being tested in court, but it would be better and cheaper to do it through a system of dispute resolution. The exclusion of decisions of promotions boards are excluded because on the face of it these are matters of academic judgement. But, as emerges elsewhere in this study, things may be much more complex than that.

So there is a danger that the Nolan Committee's limitations of remit may not give adequate scope to any new system of independent dispute resolution, unless these categories are carefully reviewed.

Conclusion

The problem remains that the universities are autonomous, and no system could work without their individual cooperation case by case. Even where there is a visitor he does not have powers to order discovery. A visitor cannot compel the university to act on his decision. Without legislative change, that would remain the case if the investigators were independent arbitrators or an ombudsman. A system of dispute resolution in universities which does not meet all reasonable needs would be an expensive waste. It would be undesirable for a 'miscreant' university to be able to claim that any new system of dispute resolution had no more legitimate interest (because the matter remains private) and therefore no more authority to call to account in a given situation than visitors or courts have at present in universities where there is a visitor.

The hurdle which has to be jumped is the redefinition of the boundary which surrounds the privacy of a university's affairs. That means looking again at its proper sphere of autonomy so that without losing the freedoms without which it cannot continue to serve its purposes as a university, it loses the licence to behave as it chooses in the treatment of its academic staff and its students.

Part 3

Standards: Accounting for Academic Decisions

Introduction

One of the functions of a university is the awarding of degrees. A degree ought to be worthless if it is not an indicator that its possessor has knowledge or skills. It cannot show that unless there is public confidence in the degree-awarding institution. So behind the question of the standard of a degree lie all sorts of questions about the standards of the teaching and research of the staff who teach the students who work for it, and the ways in which academic judgements are arrived at and tested, whether they concern students or staff.

When the scholar making the judgement has power to determine outcomes for the person upon whom judgement is being made, there is an inequality in the encounter which throws into question whether the review is in truth peer review at all, precisely because it involves an inequality. In the case of a degree committee or board of examiners making a decision about a student's grade, expert judgement is deemed to be being applied to a student's work, where the student is, by definition, not equal in expertise with the examiner. In the case of a PhD that line is blurred. This is original work, and the student ought to be more expert in this area than his examiners or he cannot have fulfilled the requirements for the degree. However, in certain respects his examiners remain his superiors because they can judge things like the quality of his writing and the cogency of his case, from their longer experience as scholars.

The presumption is still that the student is not, prima facie, likely to be a better judge of his work than his teachers. In *Norrie v. Senate of the University of Auckland* [1984] 1 N.Z.L.R. 129 a final-year medical student who had failed at the end of his course sought to challenge the university's decision to refuse to allow him to enrol the following year so as to retake his final examinations. The court went along with the assumption that the academic judge or judges know better than either the student or the courts. The

High Court does not act as a court of appeal from educational examiners said Diplock L.J. in *Thorne v. University of London.*[1]

However, a further factor increasingly enters into the judgement of students. Universities can set desirable outcomes in terms of numbers and proportions attaining a certain degree, inflate grades and require, by what may be an essentially managerial fiat, interference with academic judgement. The courts might properly intervene here to question whether such essentially administrative 'policy-making' was interfering with a proper liberty to make academic judgements on a truly expert basis. Similarly, in the academic judgements made upon staff seeking promotion, or academics applying for appointments, factors other than academic judgement may enter in.

Accountability can be hard to achieve where such additional considerations are not spelled out; or, indeed, may not even be consciously in the minds of the judges at all. There is the compounding problem of the secrecy which protects the confidentiality of references and examiners' comments and makes it hard for a complainant or appellant to discover the reasons for his failure.

11

The Value of a 'Degree'

A letter from fifteenth-century Oxford, where certain Bachelors of Arts were trying to call themselves Masters, speaks of the subversive efforts of those who would confound the distinctions of degrees in the University.[1] It is of the first importance for a university to keep a watchful eye on the standing of its degrees, both within and outside the institution. Academic standards were at issue in a letter from Oxford to the King at the end of the fifteenth century, denying that it is possible to get a doctor's degree in Cambridge for a smaller fee.[2] Degree-giving powers under the Cambridge Statutes of 1559 depend on consent by the Master and Fellows of the College, and that too is a mode of making accountable.[3]

A student at a university gets, as his reward for study, a degree or diploma. The definitive 'qualification' for a university to award remains the degree, the mediaeval *gradus*. The *Dearing Report* envisages the honours classification system gradually being replaced by a 'lifetime file' of progress of each student (R 20). On this model, student portfolios (R 20), would include: 'a transcript recording student achievement which should follow a common format devised by institutions collectively through their representative bodies; a means by which students can monitor, build and reflect upon their personal development'. This is a business concept which would not fit well either with the fumbled experiments in essay writing at the beginning of a student's career, or with the processes of infinite subtlety and complexity with which the mind of a mature scholar works upon a piece of research.

It has always been a correlative of the autonomy of universities in the UK that each gave its own 'degree' and that degree-awarding powers were a mark that the body in question really was a university. The situation is rather different in continental Europe, and these assumptions, hitherto fundamental in the UK, can now be questioned there too.

Incorporation was a possibility for Master Peter Courteney, Dean of Exeter, who in fifteenth-century Oxford was admitted to the same degree as he had at Padua.[4] But, in general, Oxford and Cambridge have long recognized only one another's degrees and those of Trinity College, Dublin for such purposes of incorporation. The incomparably more liberal idea of transferable credits was already being floated in the 1970s. Transferability depends either on each university agreeing to recognize the credits awarded by others, or upon a national system of accreditation with a common point of reference. However, that would deny the universities their autonomy in the award of degrees.

In the UK university world of the 1990s the question whether universities can automatically recognize one another's results as equivalent in this way is being raised acutely by the suspicion that some universities are achieving higher standards than others. For a main difficulty in the arena of quality assurance has become the public perception that the degrees of some universities mark higher standards of achievement on the part of their students.

Recommendation 25 of the 1997 *Dearing Report* suggested to the newly established Quality Assurance Agency in the UK that its early work should include: 'work *with* institutions to establish small, expert teams to provide benchmark information on standards, in particular threshold standards, operating within the framework of qualifications . . . work *with* universities and other degree-awarding institutions to create, within three years, a UK-wide pool of academic staff recognised by the Quality Assurance Agency, from which institutions *must* select external examiners'.

This had the disadvantage that it left it far from clear whether the monitoring of standards would in fact be academic or managerial. It also hovered between acknowledging academic autonomy and denying it. The 'with' recognizes the autonomy; the 'must' denies it.

To all this, two types of solution are, at present, proposed. The first is to seek to set standards against which all universities can be measured, with the intention that they shall all seek to achieve them. The National Union of Students in its submission to Dearing said that 'it is vital for the development of higher education and for student confidence in the system that a degree from University X is considered to be of an equal standard to that from University Y'.[5] The second is to accept that not all universities can meet the same standards and to construct a system in which that is acknowledged. But that route presents immense difficulties, not least in how to deal with institutions in which the best departments are capable of preparing students for a better level of degree than the worst, and how to get those low down the list to accept their position, for a low-rated institution giving low-rated degrees will not be attractive to able students who can 'shop elsewhere'.

An institute of higher education may give the degrees of another institution which is a university, and then franchise those degrees on its own account, as the Southampton Institute of Higher Education did with the 'Athens campus' which was so notoriously in the news in 1996–7. There have been worrying instances of such franchising being alleged to provide very inadequate provision of teaching or facilities, and of standards being extremely low. There have been cases where it has apparently not been made clear to students enrolling for such courses that the parent institution was not itself a university but was granting the degrees of another university. The standing of any such 'sub-contracted' degree is that of the degree-awarding body at the top of the ladder.[6]

It seems non-contentious that a degree certificate will be of a value which depends on the standing of the authority which issues it. So what entitles an institution to degree-awarding powers? A crude preliminary approach is to ask whether it is big enough to be stable. In 1921, when Reading University College sought to become a university, its first petition for a charter did not succeed, and the College received a letter from the Clerk to the Privy Council to explain why. There was a problem about numbers – too few students – and about finance, because the College's annual income was held to be too small.[7] In the 1992 Act numbers were still taken to be a defining characteristic, on the basis of which an institution could be deemed to have a claim to be a university.

However, numbers and financial backing are recognized not to be all that is needed to make a university. Since the 1992 Act there remain a number of colleges and institutes trying to gain university status, which may be large and financially secure enough on those measurements alone, but where that has not been deemed to be enough in itself.

Adoption of the title of 'university' is not enough on its own. A college which is an integral part of a university can, in law, quite uncontroversially and legitimately be a 'university college' (as is the case with the four university colleges of the University of Wales, at Cardiff, Swansea, Bangor, Aberystwyth). The Further and Higher Education Act 1992, s. 77, further makes provision for the use of the word 'university' in the title of an institution in circumstances where 'power is conferred by any enactment or instrument to change the name of any educational institution or any body corporate carrying on such an institution',[8] or where 'the educational institution is within the higher education sector', then 'if the power is exercisable with the consent of the Privy Council, it may (whether or not the institution would apart from this section be a university) be exercised with the consent of the Privy Council so as to include the word "university" in the name of the institution and, if it is carried on by a body corporate, in the name of the body'.

The vexed relationship between the title and the identity of an institution is partly spelled out in the Further and Higher Education Act 1992, s. 77: 'Any educational institution [but not here *body corporate*? see note to s. 1 of Further and Higher Education Act 1992] whose name includes the word "university" by virtue of the exercise of any power as extended by subsection (1) above is to be *treated as a university* for all purposes.'

The CVCP Working Party on University College Title, under the Chairmanship of J.F.D. Lauwerys, reported in the spring of 1997. It underlines that an institution may call itself a university only if it has a charter from the Crown; is so entitled by Statute under the 1992 Act; has the title conferred by a private Act of Parliament; if the title has been allowed for use as a 'trading name' or 'business name', through approval by the Board of Trade and the Privy Council, in which last case it is not necessarily a university in law. The use of the title 'university' is thus restricted by law; 'university college' is not, or at least not in an unequivocal manner, and a confusing variety of usages has arisen. It does not appear to be clear whether a university can itself confer the title 'University College' on another, subordinate, institution, or whether there is any legal control over such devices of wording as 'in the university sector' or 'a college of the University of . . .'

Institutions have been adopting the title 'University College' in order to tell the world that they have a status they desire but to which they may not be formally entitled, perhaps to hint that they will soon have degree-awarding powers, or simply as a marketing ploy. Others have been prevented by a parent institution which is itself a university from adopting the title of 'university college' without its sanction. There is bad feeling and frustration, and a danger that the word 'university' will itself be cheapened, with damaging effects upon the reputation of British higher education nationally.

The *Lauwerys Report* suggests a set of criteria. Institutions which are part of a university, as the Colleges of the University of London, might uncontroversially be allowed to use the title 'University College'. Others might petition the Privy Council for permission to use the title in their own right, on the grounds that they have met some, if not all, of the principal criteria for the use of the title 'university'. These would include those having a minimum of 55 per cent higher education work, with at least 300 students in that area and studying in at least five of the HEFCE's 11 Academic Subject Categories. The criteria thus include standards, size and range. A third category might meet these criteria but seek the title 'University College' not in their own right but as dependent institutions of (normally) one university geographically in the same region. There is a concern to avoid duplication of relationships, by requiring that any additional relationship with a different university should involve subject areas where no relationship exists with the principal university.

The *Report* recommends that there should be monitoring, to ensure that such conditions are not met only at the time when the title is granted, but continue to be met. It also recommends the avoidance of forms of words including the term 'university' which are vague and potentially misleading, and looks to primary legislation to control such use in due course.

The power to grant degrees is a privilege not a right, but it is a privilege without which an institution cannot be defined as a university. So this business of the right to the 'university' title is important, and also inseparable from the question of the authenticity of degrees.

That is the formal, if still imperfectly defined, position, but of course anyone can issue a piece of paper and call it a 'degree certificate'. The marketing of such certificates has been a commonplace of the twentieth century. So we ought to ask some deeper questions about what it is that gives a degree 'authoritativeness', 'currency', 'value'.

Modern university charters in the UK contain a clause authorizing the award of degrees.[9] The core understanding here is, again, that a degree is somehow made valid, that is, made a into 'real' degree, by having a recognized authority behind it. Thus, it could be argued that a university in some sense does not confer its own degree, but a degree 'warranted' by the authority which backs its 'setting up' as a university. That is certainly the European situation.

A formal 'degree certificate' will then be of a value which depends on the standing of the authority which issues it. Yet, that standing need not, in principle, be that of a university at all, and historically it has often been a quite different sort of authority. Ironically, it can be argued that the power to award degrees is itself a franchise, in the sense of a power subsisting in someone's hands by a grant from the 'holder of the prerogative'[10] (which in the UK has typically been the Crown). In England, since the Middle Ages, the power to grant degrees has traditionally derived from the Crown, that is, from royal prerogative. Tudor and Stuart monarchs could send a mandate requiring a university to admit someone to a degree whether or not he had fulfilled the requirements, though the universities resisted, and it was by no means clear to them that the power to award degrees did not remain with the Masters, as it had done in the past.[11] In 1689, the King attempted to force the University of Cambridge to admit one Alban Francis to the degree of Master of Arts. The initial objection turned on the taking of an oath, for the candidate was a Roman Catholic, but the more important issue was whether the King had powers to insist at all:

> Mr. Atterbury came down with a Summons from the Ecclesiastical Commissioners to this effect; That whereas complaint was made against the Vice-Chancellour and Senate of Cambridge, for having refused to comply with his Majesties Royal letters on behalf of Mr. Francis, they were therefore commanded to appear, the Vice-Cancellour in Person, the Senate by themselves, and their Deputies before the Lords Commissioners . . . to answer . . .[12]

Royal intrusion in the awarding of degrees might have some justification if the power to award degrees could be considered a grant of royal prerogative, which by this date in England it might.[13] Royal visitations took place, but concerned themselves with property; they were, in effect, audits. But royal, or any outside intrusion into the academic debate or the teaching which went on in the university, was another matter.

And even in England anomalies persist. The Archbishop of Canterbury has been able in principle to grant degrees directly since the Peter Pence Act 1533.[14] The Holy See was able to empower Heythrop College to grant degrees (from 1965).

The royal prerogative is not merely a counterpart to the State's powers over degree-giving as they exist in continental Europe. The notion that the prerogative is 'royal' has, in an English context, certain implications which were strong in seventeenth-century minds, and which continue to linger in association with the status of a degree. The sovereign is the source of 'honour'; according to Lord Coke C.J., 'the fountain of all honour and dignity'.[15] 'All offices under the Crown carry in the eye of the law an honour along with them; because they imply a superiority of parts and abilities, being supposed to be always filled with those that are most able to execute them. And, on the other hand, all honours in their original had duties or offices annexed to them.' So there is an idea of a coupling of being held in respect and displaying competence.[16]

If we move the discussion into the European arena the scene at once looks different and it immediately becomes a central issue that there should be some broad basis of *public* recognition of the degrees. 'Universities which award degrees *recognised by the member states*' are included in the category of bodies which meet the criterion of 'carrying out a public function on behalf of the state'.[17] In much of Europe, State control of universities was a natural development of their foundation by princes under regional control. With this went 'the establishment of a central and formal bureaucracy, the drawing up of formal rules and regulations for its recruitment, its working and for determining promotion and advancement within its ranks. This was set down in the form of administrative law.' There could, in some places, be uniform central control of 'such matters as budget, course structure and curriculum content, as well as de jure control over professorial appointments, which, in essence persists to the present day'.[18]

This creates a precarious balance with academic autonomy, in which the State can, but chooses not to, intervene in such matters as are properly the province of academic expertise.[19]

Whether on the British 'royal prerogative' or European 'State', or on any other understanding, it is in their institutional or formal, their bodily or incarnate role, not in their capacity as 'parts of the community of scholarship', that universities grant degrees. The informal 'community of scholarship' gives recognition, but in informal ways. An individual can present a degree certificate, or he can say 'my paper at that conference was spoken well of and there have been excellent reviews of my last two books'.

Yet, in a sense, even where an authority is deemed to stand behind, a university clearly does award its 'own' degrees, where the monarch or the State does not set the standards which justify the respect, or make the claim to competence demonstrably justified. In the UK, the university examines students it has itself chosen, according to its own rules, setting its own standards. Neither the Crown nor any other authority has, or can have, any part in that. It falls with the proper area of a university's academic autonomy, and this is indeed arguably an area where the university bows to, and stands under, the community of scholarship and where the 'credibility' of the degrees is finally tested. That has not been such an unassailable position in continental Europe.

Complementary to the notion that there must be an authority standing behind to guarantee the degree is an idea of reception or recognition of the degree by the public, and a public which need not consist solely of the citizens of the state in which the university happens to be.

That is not new. In the Middle Ages, degrees of some universities were recognized 'outside' it, by others, so that those possessing them could be considered to have a *ius ubique docendi*, a right to teach everywhere.[20] The licence to teach (*licentia docendi*) nevertheless remained in principle a *local* licence to teach, and no university could have powers to create such a right in any manner which *required* others to accept it. The modern idea of 'licensing' the individual roving researcher would test that ancient set of assumptions, as does the notion of a central accreditation agency for higher education.[21]

In practice, the *ius* became something which the Pope or perhaps the Emperor could confer, so once again 'authorizing' (top-down) can interfere with 'accepting' by public acclaim. That papal or imperial authorizing, like the exercise of the royal prerogative in England, had its drawbacks, for although a university whose degrees were thus recognized acquired a powerful patronage, it was also, in practice, submitting itself to an authority which might choose to interfere in its affairs, at least in the matter of the awarding of degrees.

A degree both affords a guarantee that the person holding it has knowledge or skills and betokens the holding of a rank within a body, a *gradus*, of bachelor or master or doctor. But it is taken to be an indicator of academic attainment with outward reference to the country or the world, and here we have to consider the question of the comparability of degrees given by different institutions. 'The Department wants to see the UK's reputation for excellence in higher education maintained and, if possible, enhanced. In its view, it is no longer sufficient to rely on the award of qualifications without defined standards of attainment', said the Department for Education and Employment in its evidence to the Dearing Committee (para. 8). It asks the Committee to consider:

> whether there is any prospect of achieving common standards in a system where there are some 100 universities and colleges *awarding their own qualifications* and where the subjects studied and the objectives set are so diverse as to make comparisons very difficult. Nevertheless, the Department believes that the Committee should explore the scope for a common framework for qualifications with a requirement that standards are defined.

In the modern world there continue to be two complementary elements making up the credibility of a degree. One is the *giving* of the degree by a recognized institution. The other is its *acceptance* as a 'degree' not only within the body awarding it, but in the country as a whole and internationally, on the basis of the reputation (rather than the mere formal recognition), of that institution as a university. Thus the 'ivy league' universities of the US and Oxford and Cambridge in the UK stand out internationally. The element of a *recognition* of the qualifications of one university by another, and by the community at large, thus always forms a correlative to the *granting* of the degree and the licensing to *exercise* the intellectual skill which the educational process has inculcated.

Calling to account in this arena is, in principle, a matter of recognition and acceptance of degrees. Recognition is a formal act. Acceptance is not. Employers and professions or institutions to which graduates seek to gain admittance may freely choose whether to accept particular degrees. There is an untidy test bed here. The problem is that it will unavoidably operate to some extent on a basis of word-of-mouth, *ad hoc* experience of a few individuals possessing the qualification in question, and general impression. That may be unfair to thosc who have worked for their degrees in the faith that what they were earning would have acceptance as well as recognition.

Quality and quantity

'By their fruits ye shall know them.' There is now a strong public assumption that universities are meant to produce something. More precisely, there is an expectation that they will produce something measurable, in a fixed period of time. Part of the problem with this is that 'outcomes' of the work of universities are extremely long-term and diffusive. Numbers of graduates can certainly be counted, as can numbers of books and articles published. But the graduates will go on for a lifetime growing in skills which were designed to make them independent learners. The books will go on being read; they may be reprinted, translated into other languages. Their full effect, as they are quoted and used in other books, may not be clear for 20 years or longer.

'This work is not of a mechanical character and does not lend itself, either in its methods or in its results, to any mechanically standardised scheme of measurements or to a system of accounting per cent per time unit',[22] asserted Veblen early in the century. Is there any justification for seeking to measure attainment of basic skills while acknowledging that the 'higher' effects of education are partly unmeasurable?[23]

Fruits can be weighed and measured as well as judged sweet or sour. However, evaluation of quality and measurement of quantity are essentially different. A paper on *The Quality of the UK Science Base* produced by the Office of Science and Technology in the Department of Trade and Industry, March 1997, points out that bibliometric analysis of the number of citations of papers published gives a different picture from the Research Assessment Exercise.[24]

In the methodologies of measurement or assessment in the making of peer review judgements academe is but at the beginning of its researches. While it finds out how to tackle the task, however, judgements are being made, on which huge sums of money and titles and rewards of all sorts are being handed out. Broad principles exist within the framework of the law on which such judgements may be questioned and the decision-makers called to account. There is an urgent task of looking at these alongside the decision-making processes which are operating in higher education.

12

Peer Review and Appraisal

Privilege and secrecy in professional criticism

The making of academic judgements commonly involves the framing of views about the quality of the work of *fellow* academics. That happens in appraisal, in promotions processes, in decisions about whether to grant tenure or to renew contracts or award funding, in making appointments, and in writing reviews of books. All these forms of academic 'peer review' imply an equality and a mutual respect between scholars. In a book review that is arguably the true situation. The author of the book can write a riposte, if he feels it to be unfairly assessed by a reviewer, or review the reviewer's own next book in like style if he wants a mischievous revenge. But the appearance of equality may be illusory where one sits in judgement on another in circumstances where appointment or promotion or the award of a grant is at stake, and where the person judged does not know what his 'peer' has said about him and has no opportunity to comment on it.

That is important because peer review is manifestly not an exact science. The HEFCE recognized in 1997 that there was a case for using a bibliometric measure as a rough check that the outcomes of peer review were not distorted by unperceived factors. For the reasons why the courts will not interfere is not because one academic judgement may not be more correct than another, but because it has to be conceded that the courts cannot tell which is which. Even referees in the same field and doing their best to be fair will often be in radical disagreement. Yet, the 'peer review' type of judgement must rest on the assumption that reasonable people possessing the relevant expertise could be expected to rank an individual's work at a certain level.

So our first problem is whether the 'structural' inequality arising between 'peers' where one scholar judges another behind the scenes is something for which there ought in fairness to the one 'judged' be some measure of accountability. A pejorative comment may be true. But it may be false. Or it may be believed by the critic to be true but held by the subject of the critic to be false.

For 'professional criticism' made within a formal structure where academic judgement is needed, the critic is thus not easily brought to book. Is it possible for the subject of the critical or pejorative comment to allege defamation? In general, the answer will be no; unless there is provable malice – and here the threshold is high – such an expression of scholarly opinion remains 'fair criticism'. If the judgement is made in the context of a reference or upon an academic committee, it enjoys the protection of qualified privilege. In *Adam v. Ward*, Lord Atkinson said: 'a privileged occasion is, in reference to qualified privilege, an occasion where the person who makes a communication has an interest, or a duty, legal, social, or moral, to make it to the person to whom it is made, and the person to whom it is made has a corresponding interest or duty to receive it. This reciprocity is essential.'[1]

Where a referee makes a 'peer review' judgement on another scholar in the course of an appointment or promotions process that will be the situation. 'If it is pleaded that a *lie* [my italics] was published on a privileged occasion it is for the judge to determine whether the occasion is in fact privileged, and whether the privilege has been exceeded. There is 'a prima facie presumption of malice arising from a false and defamatory statement prejudicial to the character of the plaintiff'. But the plaintiff would have to prove the malice. And if the communication is privileged 'the presumption is in favour of the absence of malice in the defendant, and in order to rebut this presumption, the plaintiff must show actual malice, and he may no doubt show this by reference to the terms of the libel as being utterly beyond and disproportionate to the facts'.[2] Calling the professional critic to account for harsh words is, therefore, not likely to be easy.

It is now becoming established as good practice that 'the membership of any groups standing in judgement should be published'.[3] That is the beginning of accountability.

'Peer review' in appraisal and promotion

A 1994 Committee of Vice-Chancellors and Principals (CVCP) Report asked the question: 'How can [scholarship] be . . . constrained where it is damaging?'[4] Setting aside the extreme case of research *designed* to destroy life, or likely to let loose plagues on the world accidentally, the notion that any constraint should be placed on scholarship must be inimical to the freedom which is of its *esse*. But it is suggested in this text that appraisal may be used to this end: 'The empirical investigation of the scholarship hypothesis needs to be a priority for all concerned in the quality debate. The immediate aim should be to sort out the various categories both conceptually and empirically and to incorporate the results into both individual and collective appraisals of teaching.'[5] There is acknowledgement here that appraisal is potentially a tool of control. If that can happen, it is necessary to look for mechanisms of accountability here too.

Appraisal began as an imposition on British universities in the late 1980s, which they were forced to accept by the threat of no annual salary rises else. Appraisal was not adopted willingly, partly because it was strongly felt to be of its nature out of keeping with the scholar's task. The fear was expressed that it would become a tool of peer review which could be used to determine career prospects. 'A commitment to improving quality requires a candid, self-critical and open-minded stance on the part of the service deliverers and this is far less likely to be achieved if those deliverers know that the information they are providing may be used to judge them individually in respect of merit pay, promotion, deployment and so on.'[6]

When it was introduced, appraisal was not to be 'assessment'. It was to be an opportunity for colleagues to sit down together and discuss their work in a friendly and cooperative atmosphere. Everyone, senior and junior, was to be appraised alike, and even reciprocally. One of the key features was the notion of an agreement between appraiser and appraisee that the appraisee would seek to achieve certain things by the time of the next appraisal. There has been a shift towards the setting of objectives by appraiser for appraisee, with which the appraisee may in principle remain free to agree or disagree. That can be a nominal freedom only. If the goals are not met there can now be consequences for the very continuance of employment.

The 'performance contract' approach sets performance objectives; measures whether they have been achieved; reports on their achievement; gives a reward by way of promotion or continuance of the contract, or withholds it similarly. There is perhaps an assumption in the very use of the term 'objectives' that their attainment is capable of being objectively judged.

Setting specific performance objectives depends upon the assumption that there is a determinate character to the quality of what is being measured, and therefore that it is in some sense a quantity.[7] 'The proximate if not ultimate goal of education is the cultivation of excellences and . . . excellences are to be understood as desirable dispositions which are, in turn, informally defined as including abilities, habits, skills and traits of character or personality.'[8]

Moreover, the 'mission statement' of late twentieth-century management systems is constructed on the assumption that there is not only a proper goal of academic activity, but also that that goal moves ever further off as more and further 'development' is required. 'Fitness for purpose' is an older idea in law, and it prefers to take the purpose to have to do with the full realization of a potential, so that there can be an ultimate enjoyment of a good fully grasped at last. It is not that scholarship does not assume that there is something more to learn, but that is quite different from the setting of goals of achievement in the form of 'personal development'.

Talk of aims, results, objectives ends and outcomes,[9] has to do with teleology, and that takes us to an earlier scene. Aristotle is helpful here and so is the mediaeval notion of *habitus*. But the 'management objective' style of the typical mission statement is geared to a commercial 'output', in which measurable products can be pointed to in order to satisfy the public interest. This is a cruder notion than that of Aristotle.

Appraisal up and down

Appraisal began as an exercise in peer review. However, it quickly became the pattern for the employee to be appraised by someone senior to himself in his institution's hierarchy. The record of what was 'agreed' between appraiser and appraisee was soon routinely being made available to others. There is a good deal of variety of practice between institutions over who sees the appraisal materials. The key point would seem to be whether anyone other than those present at the interview sees it; and it seems now to be almost universally the case that someone senior to the appraisee in addition to the appraiser, normally the head of department or dean of faculty, does so. The original, full downward appraisal documents may be kept confidential, but some sort of digest may be made available to promotions committees, with or without the consent of the appraisee. In the document on appraisal produced by the CVCP and the Association of University Teachers (AUT) in 1987 it is expected that the records will be kept by appraisers, appraisees *and heads of department.*

One university argues that because there is need for comparisons of appraisal records, confidentiality must routinely be breached, on a 'need to know' basis. 'Senior officers of the institution' may need to 'satisfy themselves that appraisals have been carried out satisfactorily; that common standards of judgement are being applied . . . This may mean that they wish to see an individual appraisal record for reasons particular to that member of staff.' The tendency to wider dissemination seems clear, and there is a worrying amount of room for abuse.

There was also variation in the length of time appraisal records were being kept in the 1990s. They could be kept for a long period, with the attendant danger of their getting into yet more hands as new officers entitled to see them are appointed to replace the old.

It seems not to be the case that appraisal documents of seniors are ever made available to juniors. That those of juniors are increasingly available to seniors was a disturbingly inegalitarian breach of the key principle of peer review, which is its essential equality. Concomitantly, reciprocal appraisal of seniors by juniors was far from universal in the same period, and a survey conducted in 1996[10] suggests that, at least at that date, although senior persons were appraised, it was usually by someone senior still. The assumption was often being made in forms asking for comments on seniors in the early 1990s that any changes needed were structural not personal, that it is the system which is at fault not the senior appraisee.

Appraisal was intended from the first to be related to 'staff development'. But that implies a division between 'developer' and 'developed'. Leicester had not thought about upward appraisal, but commented in 1996: 'we operate a staff development scheme and a discussion with a more experienced colleague would be more beneficial'. It is striking that this does not routinely include such a process for seniors, and indeed 'development' courses for seniors are strikingly few in most universities' staff development arrangements. Provision for training of those who hold senior positions either when promoted or during their tenure of the office seems thin on the ground at the time of writing.

It can now be expected in many universities that candidates for promotion will be asked to allow their appraisal records to be seen by promotions committees, or that such committees will be given them automatically.

Stirling promises[11] that: 'There will be a formal link between the Careers Development and Appraisal scheme and advancement procedures from the second academic session in which an appraisee participates in the scheme . . . Evidence for Career Advancement will be produced, derived from recent appraisal records [and] submitted through the Head of Department.' So at Stirling there is a standard practice which is not a standard practice at Lancaster. Lancaster underlines this sentence from the national guidelines: 'This should be done by the appraisee and appraiser producing an agreed summary of recent appraisal records', and adds 'it is believed to be a decision best left to the appraiser and appraisee as to whether, and in what form, material from the review exercise should be presented in support of promotion cases.' At Lampeter the rules provide that 'the [appraisal] scheme shall be separate from all procedures directly affecting the status and standing of staff such as probation, incremental progression, merit payments and promotion'. At University College London the position is this: 'The opportunity may also be taken, by agreement between the reviewer and the individual member of staff, to discuss promotion or regrading. This discussion may inform the formulation of a promotion or regrading proposal but it is emphasised that there is no direct link between reviews carried out under the scheme [and] promotion, the award of discretionary payments, or any other formal procedures.' 'It is *only* from regular appraisal that senior members of staff can form a judgement on the ripeness of a member of staff for promotion', says Bath. But having said that, Bath adds, rather contradictorily: 'It should be understood that the appraisal exercise is *not* a promotion exercise.' So there would seem to be a need for a systematic review of what has been happening here.

Appraisal statements were in some places being included routinely in promotions processes in the late 1990s. At Sussex it was acknowledged (1996) that 'the career development and appraisal system' is related to the promotions process 'in several ways'. An indication of possible trouble is one attempt to forestall it, framed a little unclearly as to its purpose, by Warwick: 'Professors Responsible are encouraged by the Committee to adopt reasonably formal procedures, involving consultation with senior colleagues, before deciding on whom to propose for promotion. This process has been made particularly important by the introduction of appraisal.'

In the 'career development' model, which routinely links promotions and appraisal, there is a danger to the ancient assumptions of scholarship, that the scholar is his own person, answerable for his own work to the world of scholarship, speaking for himself and for no master.

13

Forming Academic Judgements

The 'skilled authority'

'It is essential to the proper performance by a university of its functions that it maintain and insist upon high standards of scholarship.'[1] That is a statement which places the setting of academic standards squarely within the purpose of a university. In *Thorne v. University of London* [1966] 2 Q.B. 237 an unsuccessful candidate for the LLB of the University sued it for damages for negligently misjudging his examination papers. He sought an order of mandamus requiring the University to award him a grade which he considered the papers merited. There was held to be no question here but that the University was entitled to set a standard and judge by it. That was its own proper business.[2] In *King v. University of Saskatchewan* there was a striking presentation of the inherent absurdity of allowing the courts to settle a dispute about an academic judgement. 'It is difficult to conceive of a situation which would have the representatives of a law school faculty confronting the representatives of a student in the trial of an issue as to whether a degree should be granted.'[3]

The AUT argues in its submission to the Dearing Committee's Inquiry of 1997 that 'public accountability rightly demands that university staff can be interrogated about their professional judgements'.[4] The context is the debate about quality assurance; but this is a contention which ought to be taken seriously throughout the arena of the making of academic judgements. If the courts cannot properly intervene, as they certainly should not where the 'judgement' is truly a 'professional' one, academe must put its own house in order.

Academic judgements may be made in various contexts in university decisionmaking.

1. Some involve the granting of degrees: the ranking of examination candidates; the awarding of doctorates, including higher doctorates.
2. Some involve the making of appointments: the selection of a candidate for an academic post or Fellowship.

3. Some concern selection for advancement within an existing 'job' (although, as we shall see, that may now constitute 'giving a new post' to the person promoted).
4. Others concern the sifting of applications for research funding or for competitive grants, and of those some may fall within the decision-making remit of a single university and some will not. The Research Councils of the 1990s and the British Academy's Humanities Research Board consider applications from all universities. But scientific PhD grants may be made in such a way that a specified number of them may be entrusted to a head of laboratory or a head of department to award to candidates of his choice.

These decisions based on academic judgements are not all of the same kind.

1. Some are competitive; some are not. In principle, examination candidates are being judged against a standard not against one another. In a given year perhaps all students might get first class degrees.
2. In some cases candidates are being judged against one another as well as against a standard of excellence, as in applications for a job.
3. Some are decisions upon the committee's or adjudicator's peers; others – as in the case of the marking of examination papers – are the judgements of experienced practitioners upon the work of those who are still apprentices to scholarship.
4. Some involve the exercise of judgement in a specialized area; others the making of comparative judgements across several specialist areas.

There are complex issues of evaluation here which are not in themselves legal; but there are also questions which the law can address.

In the UK there tends to be a different attitude to expertise from the one commonly encountered in the US. There is a US culture of respect for expert opinion. A television advertisement in the US may simply claim, 'Research by leading experts in some of our top universities says . . .'. A UK television advertisement will be more likely to use irony or mockery to make its point because disrespect wins more sympathy than respect in that culture. The crux is whether expertise is being deemed to carry authority in itself. The mild teasing of an ironic advertisement tests any assumption that it does. But if that is the cultural reality it is not the legal reality.

In *R. v. Board of Education* [1910] 2 K.B. 165 (at 170) reference was made to the Education Act 1902, s. 7(3) with the comment:

> if any question arises under this section between the local education authority and the managers of a school not provided by that authority, that question shall be determined by the Board of Education . . . They are the skilled authority appointed by the Act, and there is no appeal from their decision . . . They were not bound to take any evidence at all . . . the Board are the sole judges of fact and of law.

Two elements are being recognized here – the concept of 'authority' and the concept of 'skill'. The authority to make the decision derives in part from the skill or expertise of the decision-makers and in part from their having been entrusted by statute with the task of making the decision. But the reason why they were entrusted with it was that they were deemed to be competent, 'skilled', so that that would appear to be the load-bearing point.

The advent of a class of professional managers is beginning to throw up new questions here. Such managers are, by training, experts in nothing but management, although some of them may by chance have additional professional skills. It has been pointed out that in the NHS this separation of expertise specific to the profession in question from a non-specific 'managerial' expertise may even be dangerous, because it interferes with expert decision-making without being itself subject to the controls which normally operate on that decision-making.[5]

And there can be circumstances in which an admixture of academic and other considerations is unavoidable. For example, in a period of cutbacks, various principles might be considered for selecting staff who are to go: last in, first out; those teaching fewest students; oldest to go first; youngest to go first; those whose subject area is deemed academically least prestigious; those who have not yet published books long in preparation and therefore have nothing to show for their research as yet; those who earn least for the university by way of research grants. Giving priority among these considerations involves making judgements, only some of which are purely academic. There was a controversy in 1997 over admissions to Pembroke College, Cambridge. Should children of former students, especially those who had made large contributions to the College's fund-raising efforts, be given preferential treatment? Was there a duty to 'old members'? Could a place be 'bought'? These are non-academic considerations which might be allowed to influence what purported to be an academic judgement as to the suitability of a candidate for admission. Would it make any difference if such preference operated only where candidates were in other respects absolutely equal?[6] Even then there would be an admixture of non-academic with academic considerations. So the question whether what purports to be an academic judgement can have its authority diminished by the perhaps unavoidable presence of such factors is a pragmatically awkward one.

Is a 'managerial' task essentially 'unsuited to determination or to judicial review?',[7] asks Lon Fuller, from a US vantage-point. If that can be argued, it raises the question whether this is on the same ground as that which takes professional or expert judgements to be unreviewable by the court. A managerial decision is arguably not in the same sense an expert decision, and if it, too, cannot be judicially reviewed there are manifest dangers of accountability for the exercise of what is at base an exercise of authority as 'power'.

Within certain employment structures in modern UK universities it may be increasingly possible to interfere with that freedom to judge by requiring professionals to submit to managerial wishes. In principle that could be justified. 'One good reason for managerial intervention would be if managers knew more about quality than most of the professional service deliverers.'[8] But there is the strong (and older) counter-argument that: 'Scientific inquiry cannot be pursued under direction of a layman in the person of a superior officer.'[9] Managers are now seeking access to that control.[10] The managerial superior is not necessarily a layman. He may be, or once have been, a member of the profession in question. But in some disciplines it is possible to get very quickly out of date, and for any such ex-professional the change of priorities may encourage the putting of other considerations in front of academic ones.

'A collective expert evaluation of quality':[11] a less than expert decision

Let us come back to academic expertise itself. If professional academic judgement is to be deemed unassailable because it is 'academic' then the academic competency of the judges must be something it is possible to be very sure about. Academic judgements are *expert* judgements, and it can therefore be argued that they cannot be made by those who do not have the relevant expertise. If it can be shown that those who make them pretend to an expertise in doing so which they do not in fact possess, it would seem that they could not be defended as expert judgements.

In the *Institute of Dental Surgery* case which arose out of the Research Assessment Exercise of 1992, the people who made the decisions about the ratings of departments, that is the members of the panels, were beyond dispute suitably qualified. They were genuinely experts, and an effort was made to ensure that any gaps in their collective expertise were filled as necessary. In the circular letter issued to all interested institutions on 6 March 1992 (telling them the rules in advance) there was a promise that there would be specialist expertise in the assessment. 'Each unit of assessment will be assessed by a panel with appropriate specialist membership', with 'specialist advisers to cover specific areas as required'.[12] The selection of members of the 1996 panels was again recognized to be important if they were to be credible as expert assessors.

There were, nevertheless, weaknesses in the process. The 1996 method used was to begin by appointing Chairs. These were selected by the chief executives of the funding bodies.[13] About half had served as Chairs in the previous exercise and in the other cases the outgoing Chair made recommendations. Again, about half of these recommendations were panel members from 1992. So, a quarter of the Chairs had no previous experience of the RAE, and those who had were beginning to form quangos.[14]

The Chairs themselves made recommendations for membership of the panels, 'from the nominations received in response to consultations with some 1,000 outside bodies – subject associations, learned societies, and others interested in the conduct of research from a primarily subject-focused viewpoint'. There were terms of reference determining the choice – personal eminence; the need to cover the subject field; the need to show 'sectoral/geographical balance' (this last presumably designed to exclude a preponderance of Oxford and Cambridge members).

But it is not clear from the RAE Manager's *Report* whether these 'recommendations' were adopted without further ado, or whether there was any revision of the lists and, if so, by whom. If the Chairs indeed had discretion to select the panels, that must somewhat undermine the value of the efforts to get as wide a constituency as possible to provide nominations.[15] There is a potential problem of at least a perception of the operation of patronage.

There can be comparable uncertainties about appointments to appointment committees or promotions committees. It is not known on what criteria the members of the Cambridge promotions committee were selected in the years up to 1998. No list of their qualifications was published to the University. There was no opportunity for members of the University's governing body, the Regent House to 'own' this committee, for example, in the way it owns the 'Septemviri', or ultimate court of appeal in disciplinary matters, whose names have to be published before their appointment.

In appointing Electors to Established Chairs in Cambridge names are put forward by various bodies (Faculties, the General Board). The Nominations Committee (often knowing nothing of these persons) checks for internal–external and 'gender' balance. The Council glances at the result and nods it through. So there is no way of ensuring that patronage does not create a body of Electors with preferences which affect candidates' chances.

Gender balance may be important but it is not necessarily true that women members of a panel or committee will be – or should be – especially vigilant for the welfare of women candidates for promotion or appointment. Senior women are still in the late twentieth century atypical beings and do not represent a 'constitutency'. It is not logical to insist on gender balance and not on racial balance or a balance of the disabled and those who are not disabled. It is also important that considerations of 'balance' of a sort which rest on a notion of 'representing a constituency' are kept separate from the question of relevant expertise.

If a promotions committee or an examination board coopted unqualified people and accepted their judgement that board's decision would not be a demonstrably professional judgement; though the board could argue that it had exercised its professional judgement in deciding to coopt (for example) local businessmen. A case in point already mentioned in the University of Cambridge in the mid-1990s was the inclusion among the Electors to a medical Chair of an NHS manager.

In the University of York a case went to the Queen as Visitor in 1997 in which the complainant alleged that a promotions committee including no one in his field had decided his case was not good enough for external referees to be consulted, which was the preliminary requirement before promotion could be awarded. At another university a vice-chancellor gave a lecturer conflicting reasons for denying him consideration for promotion.

A promotions or tenure committee or examining board which is so small that it cannot possess sufficient expertise to pronounce on the academic quality of all candidates in all subject areas might easily find itself in a position where it would be hard for it to show that its judgements were unassailable *because* they were professional academic judgements, since they would manifestly not be academic judgements.[16]

In *R v. University of London Visitor*[17] a PhD student had challenged the University's refusal to award her the degree on the grounds that it had appointed examiners who were not competent. The Visitor said that he had no duty to interfere in matters involving expert – here scientific or technical – judgement. The student applied to the High Court for judicial review, on the grounds that the *choosing* of examiners is not in itself an exercise of purely academic judgement. The university argued successfully that it had followed its procedures correctly in appointing the examiners.[18] But the underlying issue remains real enough, since that judgement did not address the question whether such decisions about the choosing of examiners itself requires the application of an appropriate professional expertise and whether if examiners are appointed, even by the proper procedures, who are not possessed of the relevant expertise, they make judgements the courts cannot assail.

There is, then, a crucial tension between the need for bodies of experts, professionals with knowledge on which others cannot 'know better', to be free from inappropriate interference in matters which are properly their own concern; and the need to prevent decisions being taken improperly under that protection, on grounds which are not strictly academic or professional. Those with legitimate interests may be adversely affected by decisions which claim to be made on one basis and are actually made on another.

The judgement of an autonomous institution; the expert judgement of the community of scholarship

That usefully takes us to the distinction between the concept of a professional arena of judgement with which it is not proper for the courts to interfere because they are expert judgements, and an *institutional* arena within which it is not proper for the courts to interfere because the university has autonomy.

In the Canadian case *Blasser v. Royal Institute for the Advancement of Learning* (1985) 24 D.L.R. (4th) 507, it was held that:

> in any university . . . there are certain internal matters and disputes that are best decided within the academic community rather than by the courts. This is so, not only because the courts are not as well equipped as the universities to decide matters such as academic qualifications, grades, conferring of degrees and so on, but also because

these matters ought to be able to be decided more conveniently, more quickly and at least as accurately by those who are specialists in educational questions of that kind. In addition, of course, there is every good reason not to risk compromising the essential independence of universities by undue interference in their academic affairs.

The first two arguments turn on the presumption that internal matters are purely academic. The last two arguments are weakened by a failure to distinguish between 'institutional' academic decisions, that is academic decisions taken within a university, and 'community of scholarship' decisions, that is, academic decisions taken within a wider scholarly arena. No Venn diagram would make a university coterminous with the academic or scholarly profession. Universities themselves acknowledge a difference when they appoint external examiners or use external referees by way of 'peer review' of candidates for promotion. Therefore, there could be a professional judgement arrived at outside the university which might challenge that which had been arrived at within it.

A university appears to be free in law to set its own standards, because they fall within the 'academic' sphere. However, in recent UK practice there has been very active Government monitoring of standards both of teaching and of research in the Research Assessment Exercise and the departmental Teaching Assessments, both of which have established a grading which runs across the board between universities. Universities have not been free to refuse to take part in these exercises, if only because, unless they did so, they would be denied funding. The legitimacy of doing this while universities remain in law solely responsible for their own standards does not come into question unless there is direct interference with the conduct of academic affairs on the basis of such monitoring, but there is clearly scope for that to happen in the future. There was a suggestion in the 1997 HEFCE Consultation on the RAE that there should be moderation of marking standards in future, in the interests of accountability.

Standards and objectivity

Gut reaction: a spurious objectivity?

It was reported in the press in May 1997 that the judges in the 1997 NCR book award did not read all the books considered themselves; they depended upon a team of readers to make them summaries. Blake Morrison, himself a judge in another book prize competition, was quoted as saying, 'A reader's synopsis is just like a blurb . . . It gives you no idea what is inside. You've got that, and then you rely on reviews and gossip. Maybe the NCR hasn't got it right.' 'Reviews and gossip' are the basis of many decisions made by academics upon one another, for there must be a sense in which a referee asked about the quality of a colleague's work for promotions purposes is being asked to 'gossip', or will have had his own judgement worked upon by the gossip of others. Referees are usually anonymous. They may be in professional competition with an author. There may be personal dislike of a fellow scholar. Even where there are no base motivations, there are infinite possibilities of misconception and the making of judgements without adequate expertise.[19]

Experts consulted in one review made comments like these: 'What little information I have leads me to suggest';[20] 'I have the sense that';[21] 'I believe'.[22] Value judgements thus based on the most tentative of evidence, little more than a gut feeling, may yet have huge and unreviewable consequences for those whose careers are affected. For it is difficult to rationalize subjective decisions ('assessments of that nature are made day in, day out in every walk of life').[23]

Even where more substantial reasons are given for an academic judgement, questions may be begged about the validity of those reasons. A review of performance in one area of research included these comments:

> A number of weaknesses . . . are evident in the research record. Some studies could be strengthened by more technical analysis. Professional standards of technical rigour have also, at times, been ignored in favour of a political or ideological proposal. Significant multidisciplinary efforts are relatively rare. Attention to the economic history of development has been neglected. Although a number of institutions excel in their practice of consultancy, the practice contributes relatively little to research.[24]

That assumes that technical analysis is good, an ideological stance bad; a multidisciplinary approach good; neglect of the background of economic history bad; use of what has been learned from practice good. All this may be true, but these assumptions are not examined, or perhaps even consciously recognized to be mere assumptions.

In some areas, there have been moves to devalue whole approaches within a discipline. In the area of scholarly inquiry known as 'development research' already cited:[25] '"Grand issues" of the development process still command attention in the UK, and this raises the question of whether development studies are too "soft" and whether only the "hard" analytical core of neoclassical economics now matters . . .'.[26] One criticism of this kind of relegation of a whole area of a subject, like that of an entire subject as a 'soft option', is that it breaks the rule of mutual respect in the community of scholarship.[27]

Measurement

Academic judgements are *value* judgements. Value judgements must at least be founded on evidence which is itself factual. If it can be shown that those facts were inaccurate or inaccurately assessed, appeal might lie against the judgement based on them. In the RAE, the research was to be measured against what was in intention 'an absolute standard'.[28] In Cambridge, P 14651, sent to candidates proposed by their faculties for promotion in 1996, speaks of 'the required academic standard'. The Notice of 4 December published in the *Cambridge University Reporter* says: 'The Board believe that the standard used to determine promotion is a matter of the collective judgement of the committees involved in the process in relation to objective criteria, and that it is not possible to define a universally applicable standard.' The last contention goes against the promise of measurement against a standard. These two statements would appear to be in conflict. But in any case, they are incoherent; they seek to set 'judgement' against 'standard' as though the forming of judgement were an alternative to the establishing of a standard.

Measurement, tabulation, is quantitative. There is a basis of commensurability, on which one can create a rank order. At the same time academic judgement is always in some part qualitative.[29] 'The control of quality lies at the heart of the notion of professionalism . . . autonomy to set entry and practice standards is a distinguishing feature of those occupational groups . . . which are most widely accepted as "professional".'

Competition

It does not cost a university anything (except perhaps in reputation) to give more first class degrees. But in the case of judgements affecting academic staff the problem generated by scarcity of resources may be (for example) that not everyone who deserves it can be promoted. What is a university's duty when resources are limited? This situation is touched on in *Ex parte Forster re University of Sydney* [1963] N.S.W.R. 723 (at 728) in relation to students and the supply of places on courses.

This brings us to the question of value judgements which are also comparative judgements between the successful and the unsuccessful, where both meet a required standard; and also in cases where incommensurables are being compared, as in an attempt to decide whether an astrophysicist is better than a linguist where only one of them can be promoted.[30] In *Thomson v. London University*, 33 L.J. Ch. 625 the question was whether one examination candidate could be ranked above another. In an examination candidates must normally be given a mark. Some marks must be higher than others. So candidates once marked can be listed in a ranked order for their performance in the same examination. But that assumes a common basis of comparison.

Objectivity and collectivity

A committee's judgement is collective. This makes the difference that whereas an individual may be quite free within the law to make capricious decisions, for example, about where he will leave his possessions in his will, a public authority or its committees must 'act reasonably and in good faith and upon lawful and relevant grounds of public interest'. Its discretion is 'never unfettered'.[31]

> It seems to us disingenuous to talk . . . about the impossibility of 'disaggregating the collective view', when that view was an aggregate view in the first place. Schiemann J's reference in *R. v. Poole BC, ex p Beebee* [1991] 2 P.L.R. 27 at 31 to 'the theoretical difficulties of establishing the reasoning process of a corporate body which acts by resolution' does not bear directly on what in our judgement is more correctly viewed as a collegiate than a corporate decision. To suggest that the panel's conclusion cannot be explained without 'undermining the whole purpose of a peer review assessment' seems to us, with respect, to devalue the assessment process.[32]

In the *Institute of Dental Surgery* case the problem of the type of expert judgement which is made by a committee was thus glanced at, though only in passing.

There are, as was indeed pointed out by Schiemann J. in *R. v. Poole Borough Council ex parte Beebee* (1991) 2 P.L.R. 27 (at 31), 'theoretical difficulties of establishing the reasoning of a corporate body which acts by resolution'. But the *Dental Surgery* case would seem to offer a ground for distinguishing between a collegiate or collective decision-making, for which reasons could certainly in principle be given, and the corporate decision.

In the *Institute of Dental Surgery* case it was commented:

> To suggest that the panel's conclusion cannot be explained without 'undermining the whole purpose of a peer review assessment' seems to us, with respect, to devalue the assessment process. It would take a great deal more than this to persuade us that experienced and distinguished academics, *whether individually or collectively*, cannot assign reasons for their own judgement . . . Each panel member will have had reasons for his or her own initial rating, and in discussion each will have been in a position to advance those reasons and to modify them *in the light of the reasoning of others.*[33]

The questions raised here go to the heart of the problem of the method by which what individuals think becomes what a group holds. The ideal is unanimity. The next best thing is consensus, defined as reaching an agreement in which some may join by changing their minds, others by ceasing to press a contrary view. Failing that, a vote may be taken, after which the 'losers' give way. The worst option must be horse-trading, in which some members of the committee sell out on their honest view in return for a favour.

Giving reasons which explain how the opinions of many become a single opinion will be easiest at the top of this range of possibilities, hardest at the bottom.[34]

It is reasonable to ask whether all the members of a committee based their decisions on the same criteria, and weighed them against one another on the same principles, so as to eliminate all factors other than a difference of opinion among the decision-makers. It might be possible to show that there was inconsistency in the *application* of criteria among the members of the committee. This might be shown to be so even if a given committee had set consistent criteria.

Bias, prejudice and malice

Even if there are strong and solidly academic grounds for thinking well of someone, he can be denied recognition by promotion, or fail to get a job for which he has applied, because other considerations are allowed to outweigh his merits or his merits are diminished by talking them down.[35] Outcomes can be 'fixed'. On a promotions committee, one member of the committee may have a personal prejudice in favour of a given candidate and thus wish to exercise patronage; or another, a specialist in a candidate's own field, might belong to an opposing 'party' within the discipline and therefore be disposed to think ill of the type of work done by the candidate. All the dangers inherent in the getting of references apply alike to the decisionmaking of committees.

On a grant review panel the subject under discussion is the project not the person. Nevertheless, the *persons* proposing to carry out the projects are themselves being evaluated for their suitability to do what they are asking to be given money to do. A Swedish study suggests, on the evidence of outcomes, that 'peer reviewers' engaged in the disbursement of such grants for research are frequently influenced in their judgement by factors other than the quality of the work they are considering. Because in Sweden the Freedom of the Press Act gives individuals access to all documents held by state and municipal authorities the researchers were able to get access to documents dealing with the evaluation of applicants. They warn that 'an in-depth analysis of other peer-review systems can be achieved only if the policy of secrecy can be abandoned'.[36]

The authors of the Swedish study concluded that men and women with equal scientific productivity did not receive the same 'competence' rating by the Swedish Medical Research Council reviewers.

> For a female scientist to be awarded the same competence score as a male colleague, she needed to exceed his scientific productivity by 64 impact points . . . This represents approximately three extra papers in *Nature* or *Science* . . . or 20 extra papers in . . . an excellent specialist journal . . . [So] a female applicant had to be 2.5 times more productive than the average male applicant to receive the same competence score as he . . . Our study strongly suggests that peer reviewers cannot judge scientific merit independent of gender.

A similar distortion was created by awareness on the committee that a given applicant had some link with one of their members. 'An applicant lacking personal ties with the reviewers needed to have 67 more impact points . . . to be perceived as equally competent.' Swedish Medical Research Council protocols do not allow a reviewer to participate in the scoring of any applicant with whom there is an 'affiliation'. But the 'neutral' committee members compensated by raising their scores when judging applicants affiliated with one of their peers.

In small ponds a project may become self-propagating. An example is the Ij story. The theory that suppressor factors existed became fashionable in immunology in the 1970s. The Ij cell was identified as a candidate, but it remained a postulate, and no such cell was ever found to clone. When in 1978–9 it became possible to clone molecules it became increasingly clear that the hypothesis was wrong. But by then money had followed money and it was embarrassing and professionally difficult for the scientists involved in this work to draw back and admit error.

The authors of the Swedish study comment how 'being of the female gender and lacking personal connections was a double handicap of such severity that it could hardly be compensated for by scientific productivity alone'. These 'effects of prejudice and comradeship' are indicators of a submerged iceberg of a problem over objectivity in peer review.[37]

Unreasoning prejudice may well not be conscious.[38] But it may be perceptible to others, who may be able to use it to their own ends. When grant applications are forwarded to research councils and other grant-awarding bodies, the astute choice of referees by administrative officers can often determine whether a grant is obtained or not. Some individuals known to be 'old softies', may be chosen because they can be relied upon to favour a given application. Others – especially the relatively young – may be known to be concerned to show off their own expertise, to a degree which may interfere with the assessment of a grant proposal. A similar tendency to machismo and showing off may manifest itself more widely in the work of the committee reviewing the grant applications, so that the discussion turns on the need for its members to be seen to 'know their stuff'. These tendencies can also be consciously 'used' to determine outcomes.[39]

If the chances of 'insiders' or 'known' candidates are affected by positive or negative prejudice in reviewers, there is also the problem of the disadvantage suffered by the 'outsider'. It was Medical Research Council policy in the mid-1990s to help beginners, defined as first-time applicants within five years of obtaining tenured posts. That is similar to the Leverhulme Trust and British Academy practice of giving grants and fellowships to holders of such posts. It has the drawback that able and productive scholars who have been unable to get a permanent post in a period where there are simply not enough university posts on offer, may become ineligible for funding from early middle age.

Being an 'outsider' may be a much subtler business, involving various forms of exclusion or marginalization. At present, a complaint that that has happened may be hard to sustain, precisely because it does not involve anything the complainant can prove, or even put a finger on. It may simply be a matter of leaving someone off committees, ensuring that the small additional items of 'service to the University' which look good on a curriculum vitae are not available; or, conversely, someone is damned because he or she has given so much such service that – it is alleged – research output has suffered. Peer review is so inexact a science that the same individual and the same body of work can be rated high or low with equal plausibility and an outcome can always be justified with a sequence of reasoning which it is hard to fault.

14

Ensuring Sound Procedures

In the UK at the time of writing the public sector benchmark for good practice in peer review is the Research Assessment Exercise. This is run by the Higher Education Funding Councils, a group of statutory bodies, divided into the geographical parts of the British Isles. It seeks to establish on a comparative basis the research quality of the departments of all British universities, so as to provide a baseline from which public funding of university research may be calculated. The assessment is done by peer review, that is by coopting leading academics in each field onto a panel, to judge the work of their fellows in the field. This obviously gives an advantage to universities who supply members for these panels, not in that they will favour their home universities – there are protections against that – but in that such persons will get the hang of the exercise and what is required from inside. Cambridge held a debriefing after the 1996 Exercise in which it brought together its members on the panels to see what it might learn to its own advantage for the future.

The use of academics to do the work of statutory bodies also crosses the line between the academic and the public policy worlds.

The RAE deals with departments not individuals and there are clearly differences in the appropriate methodology for peer review when it concerns the work of a whole department and not that of a single scholar. However, several of the panels admit to having rated individual scholars in an attempt to get a sense of the work of a department. So no firm line was drawn. In what follows the Research Assessment Exercise Manager's *Report* is taken as a basis for analysis of the problems, for its value as a stocktaking exercise at a crucial stage of development of the methodology of assessment in the UK.

Procedural requirements of those making decisions based on academic judgement

The first line of defence against 'fixing' is having clear published principles designed to ensure that the procedure is sound.

'That is not correct' and 'that is not fair' are complaints which challenge academic judgements on legally distinct grounds. In one case the court or other adjudicating authority is being asked to look at the merits of the decision, in the other at whether the decision is within the law. The first says the judgement is incorrect substantively, out of keeping with the facts on which it claims to be based, or unreasonable in all the circumstances. The second contends that it was arrived at in a way which was procedurally flawed or which is against the law in some other way. The distinction is a little like that in logic between a true and a valid conclusion of a syllogism.

In *Re Polten and the University of Toronto* [1976] 59 D.L.R. (3d) 197, a student unsuccessfully contended that his work had been inaccurately assessed in the sense that the 'expert opinion' had been in error, or that the standards set had been too high. The courts are rightly reluctant to address that kind of complaint. They recognize that they cannot have relevant expertise. The right of *appeal* under the rules of natural justice may not exist against an academic judgement. In *Hague v. University of British Columbia* (1969) D.L.R. (3d) 120, it was held that the University's Senate 'through regulations, can determine the number of course appeals and can limit the right to appeal a particular course mark'.

They are much more willing to look at *procedural* flaws. In *Thomas v. University of Bradford* [1987] 1 A.C. 795 the case turned solely on whether correct procedures had been followed.

In the procedural arena, the concept of fairness has largely replaced talk of natural justice in the courts in recent decades. This has the advantage that it permits of application outside a judicial or quasi-judicial arena and therefore applies to administrative decisions.[1] In *Re Racal Communications Ltd* [1981] A.C. 374 (at 384, 390–1); [1980] 2 All E.R. 634 (at 639, 644–5) Lord Diplock said that the decision in *Anismic*[2] that a breach of natural justice is a jurisdictional error applied to decisions of administrative tribunals or other bodies made under statutory powers. In such cases there was a presumption that the statute conferring the power did not intend the administrative body to be the final arbiter of questions of law.

Things can sometimes be set in an explicitly quasi-judicial rather than administrative frame for consideration when academic judgements are being made, and that might still be helpful in its implications for the standards of fairness required. In *Vidyodaya University of Ceylon* it was held that:

> 'if someone has the power to determine what the rights of an individual are to be, then a duty to act judicially arises simply from the nature of the power'.[3] In *Glynn v. Keele University* it was held that the powers of the vice-chancellor to suspend a student were so fundamental

> to the position of a student in the university that they could not be regarded merely as a matter of internal discipline; accordingly the vice-chancellor was acting in a quasi-judicial capacity when he exercised them.[4]

But even if the matter was not obviously disciplinary it might be important that something significant for the individual, such as his future career, was at stake. In *Re Harelkin and University of Regina* [1979] 96 D.L.R. (3d) 14, a student was told, on grounds of which he was not advised so as to be able to answer the accusations made against him, that he must give up his course. It was held in this case that the natural justice rights to personal audience and being given the opportunity to contradict prejudicial statements must be honoured even where the question is not one of discipline but of academic performance.

But *nemo iudex* (bias)[5] questions also arise in connection with *procedures* for academic decisionmaking. In *Orr v. University of Tasmania* [1956] Tas. S.R. 155 (at 160) we find: 'I am quite unable to understand how it could be thought that a professor could teach, examine, recommend for prizes and honours, or present as a fit and proper person to receive a degree, a student who has in her academic life been his mistress.' That is a blatant case of bias in favour. But there can also be bias against. In *Ex parte McFadyen* [1945] 45 N.S.W.R. 200, a student alleged that he had been failed in an examination because an examiner had a grudge against him, over a matter not connected with his academic performance.

The problems may be structural in this procedural arena rather than personal. It was argued in *Rigg v. University of Waikato* [1984] 1 N.Z.L.R. 149 (at 151) that:

> the objective and independent bystander might consider that those members of the Council and the Academic Board who were also members of the School of Science might be unable to give genuine consideration to the issues which remained for their decision . . . the presence of the Vice-Chancellor and . . . a member of the School of Science . . . during the Council's deliberations . . . certainly gave the appearance of bias.

This sort of situation, where senior officers of a university act as accuser and judge, or act as judges when they have a clear personal vested interest, is extremely common.

Yet, a university may be allowed to permit bias because of the sheer problem of finding enough officers to act. In *King v. University of Saskatchewan* (1969) 6 D.L.R. (3d) 120 (at 131) special allowance was made over bias, as was the case in *Re Paine and the University of Toronto* (1982) 131 D.L.R. (3d) 325 (at 331), where members of a tenure committee were allowed to act even though they had previously formed 'general opinions' as to the candidate's suitability for tenure:

> The tenure committee does not sit as a tribunal, acting only on the evidence placed before it. The members act on their own knowledge of the candidate, as well as the assessments and references that are provided to them . . . as a matter of course they must all, in the course of their association with the candidate, have formed general opinions as to his suitability for tenure, and it makes little difference whether that opinion was expressed before or at the meetings of the committee.[6]

'Knowing the candidate' is here, paradoxically, not deemed a source of bias which may disadvantage the candidate, but a necessary qualification for judging him. But on a committee where some candidates are personally known to membership of the committee and some are not, that argument could not apply, for what does not apply in the case of all candidates cannot be a necessary qualification for forming a judgement which decides among them.

In *Re Schabas and Caput of University of Toronto* Pennell J. held that 'subject to evidence of actual bias, I am of opinion that the Court should be reluctant to say that a presumption of bias can arise in so far that it relates to the personnel of a quasi-judicial body where the composition of the tribunal is specifically authorized by the legislature'.[7] But here the membership would have to be of the *ex officio* sort to fit the brief. That is to say, such a committee would have to be made up of (say) the vice-chancellor, the deans, the heads of department. It would not apply if it were made up of assorted persons appointed to 'represent' (say) fields of study or 'constituencies' of some other sort.

The evidence

Comparing like with like

The first task in forming an academic judgement is to assemble the evidence on which it is to be based.[8] Standardization is a first step to achieving commensurability. But that has to be done in recognition of unavoidable differences. For example, it would be unfair to require all candidates for promotion to show evidence of international recognition if some did not work in areas where that was a possibility. Alongside the problem of 'locating' an area of study runs that of the competence of the judges. 'Researchers should have their work assessed by others capable of understanding it – something necessary to inspire the confidence of those being assessed.'[9]

Interdisciplinary work presents special problems of commensurability. The HEFCE conducted its Research Assessment Exercises, on which future funding was to be based, on the assumption that areas of study could be classified. It was decided that it was impossible 'to make separate provision within the panels for all forms of cross-disciplinary work or for comparatively small emerging disciplines'. But not all work was in fact capable of being located within the available boundaries. HEFCE commented that, 'The panels were . . . strongly discouraged from "marking down" work purely on the basis that it did not sit squarely within their discipline.'[10] That implies that there may have been some tendency to do so. They had to be told to be careful to 'give credit for the extent to which research activity spanning or drawing upon several disciplines achieved more than the sum of its parts'.[11]

There is a difference between multidisciplinary and interdisciplinary research. Assessing work which is merely multidisciplinary may be tackled by ensuring that representative expertise is available on, or to, the panels. That will not work for interdisciplinary work which is forging a new discipline. This is likely to be amongst the most truly original work; for that reason, it may be the hardest to 'rate' by existing scales and criteria. Those who engage in it are likely to have had to overcome resistance in their institutions and to be persons of considerable intellectual courage. Those who have made their mark by getting published are a group likely to be pre-selected for excellence.

A single interdisciplinary monitoring group would have the advantage that it could seek to protect against the marking down of interdisciplinary work (p. 10 (49)). It would have the disadvantage that it would become a presumption that all interdisciplinary work has something in common in being 'interdisciplinary'. That is far from clear. All it may have in common is crossing arbitrarily defined subject boundaries devised for syllabus or administrative convenience, and changed within universities over time for reasons which do not necessarily have anything to do with the internal intellectual economy of the subject areas.

The question goes to the heart of 'quality'. For to do something well is to do it in the manner appropriate to the kind of activity it is. (It would be inappropriate to apply techniques of critical appreciation appropriate to English literature to the resolution of a problem in mediaeval logic.) Ought not the rethink now needed, and indeed in hand in a new HEFCE survey at the time of writing, tackle the question of the nature of a discipline at this fundamental level well in advance of the next exercise? Aristotle's *Posterior Analytics* is still a useful starting point.

Special circumstances or contaminating factors?

It might be argued that it is part of the remit of an academic judgement that considerations extraneous to academic quality can, paradoxically, be 'relevant considerations' in assessing it. In *King v. University of Saskatchewan* [1969] 6 D.L.R. (3d) 120, a student sought to appeal against refusal to award a degree. A special appeal committee had recommended that: 'while [the applicant] has not fulfilled the requirements for graduation in Law either according to the old merit point regulations or the new average regulation, nevertheless the Committee recommends that, due to the exceptional circumstances surrounding the case and for compassionate reasons, this student be awarded the Bachelor of Laws Degree'.[12]

Dyslexia used to cover only a difficulty with spelling. It is now often extended to include difficulty with putting words together grammatically or difficulty in putting thoughts in order. But these difficulties may also simply be a sign of limited ability, which examiners would routinely penalize. So dyslexia would be a special circumstance because it is a handicap. But it might require rather careful definition before it was clear whether in a given case the handicap existed. So much turns on what such exceptional circumstances amount to.

It is also necessary to ask whether including them on grounds of fairness to the candidate they apply to might result in disadvantage to other candidates with whom that candidate is in competition. If the grading of examination candidates was the issue, that problem would not arise. If the decision involved choosing between persons who were in competition with one another for promotion or for an appointment, the compassionate allowance made for one might disadvantage another, and some account would need, in fairness, to be taken of that consideration.

In one Australian case there was an attempt to establish distinct areas, circumstances which might count towards the mitigating of an adverse academic judgement and circumstances which might not:

> The past unsatisfactory performance may be evidentiary, for instance, want of intellectual capacity for the course or of insufficiency of application to the study of the subject . . . the Faculty, in an attempt to establish some principles for its guidance in dealing with the many cases which were expected to arise, had considered that 'demands of employers, pressure of employment, time devoted to non-university activities' were not acceptable as 'good cause'.[13]

When factors of this kind are admitted the question of 'special circumstances' abut onto the area of relevant considerations. In *R v. Aston University Senate, ex parte Roffey*,[14] some students failed referred examinations and were sent down. At a meeting: 'each individual's marks were considered in the light of information available on record cards or known to those present. This was not confined to academic matters, but included the fact that one student was labouring under acute personal and family difficulties, that another had an impediment of speech' and so on.[15] So extraneous, non-academic matters were allowed to enter into consideration. At the same time, matters which would have been relevant were not considered. The students understood that the papers in question did not 'count' towards their degrees: 'The examiners who reached the decision were wholly unaware of the widespread allegations that the students had been misled by members of the staff as to what was at stake when they prepared, or failed to prepare, for the examinations.'[16]

It is well-established that the failure to take into account relevant considerations, the entertaining of irrelevant considerations, and the related failures to be faithful to a proper purpose and to act in good faith allow challenge in the courts.

Academic judgement and money

Financial constraint is not necessarily irrelevant if it is stated in the university's promotions procedures as a limiting factor on the number of promotions, because then the university will have stated it openly. Nevertheless, as soon as it is conceded that financial considerations come into the decision, it could be argued that the judgement of a promotions committee ceases to be a purely academic judgement, and that might in itself be a ground of challenge. If a university's criteria for promotion thus mention only academic considerations, while the university's practice is to make promotions on a basis which always includes non-academic considerations at least of a financial kind, this may prove to be significant in law. In every instance where the candidate is deemed to have met the required standard this must be so, since it will always be true that the committee which made the final choice decided on financial grounds not to promote him,[17] not on the grounds that he was not of a sufficient standard. However, it is also true that the committee will be able to try to claim (unless there are very rigorous requirements about giving reasons) that there were purely academic grounds for preferring other candidates to him, and that in that sense the decision was purely academic, although it was *also* true that even if he had been deemed promotable on academic grounds there would not have been enough money to promote him.

This point about the academic irrelevance of financial constraint may prove to be less clear-cut than it seems in another way, too, because a promotions committee may redefine the 'standard' each year in such a way that the number deemed to meet it precisely matches the number for whom the money is available to pay for promotion. Cambridge did that for many years in the early 1990s, before publishing the admission that it was denying promotion to academic staff who deserved it. Where the stated criteria have to do with having an 'international reputation' of unspecified dimensions, or with an undefined 'satisfactory performance' in teaching or administration, it is clearly going to be difficult to quantify or objectify what is required in such a way that the decision could be challenged on the grounds that a financial consideration operating as an irrelevant factor was the reason why a candidate was not promoted.[18]

On the other hand, the existence of a financial consideration is also relevant to the question whether the promoting committee as a whole could be shown to have made a policy decision in advance of the consideration of the candidates which would be prejudicial to the chances of some of them by prejudging the outcome. A considerable proportion of those considered by such a promotions committee cannot hope to be promoted, however outstanding their record, where there has already been a decision that factors other than the purely academic will be brought into play. This preempts the proper exercise of the discretion of the committee and destroys the academic purity of that discretion. If that can be shown, it would seem that all those rejected candidates who were deemed to have met, or more than met, the standard, would have grounds to complain that the committee had claimed to make academic judgements which were not pure academic judgements.

Judgements contaminated by damning with faint praise or hints of criticism

In *Norrie v. Senate of the University of Auckland* [1984] 1 N.Z.L.R. 129 (at 137) it was contended that the decision was influenced not only by factors which were irrelevant, but also by 'inexact or misleading statements' ('virtually failed twice') and criticisms in response to which the student should have been given an opportunity to speak. So the academic judgement here could be held to be contaminated in a number of ways which may be of wider relevance.

Inexact or misleading statements may bring together errors of judgement and errors of fact in ways so subtle that they will not easily be distinguished. In a US teaching assessment, it was found that 'an instructor who can teach charismatically but non-substantively for a brief period on a topic about which he knows nothing can be rated very favourably' in a student questionnaire.[19] Opportunity to answer criticism becomes highly important in the face of such factors when they work negatively. But it may need to go further if it is not even clear that what has been said is, in fact, a criticism. Damning with faint praise may be decisive in a close competition.

In *Norrie* two other problems were touched on. There were personal assessments which the court deemed not to be 'directly academic considerations'.[20] There could, for example, be a contention that someone was unable to get on with his colleagues. This could affect a decision about promotion or a decision about making a probationary contract permanent. That might well be pertinent to a lecturer's ability to do his job. On the other hand, breakdown of working relations can be created readily enough by a senior who wishes to damage a junior, and who has a perhaps decisive say on a promotions or appointments committee. So the lecturer might not deserve that slight on his professional conduct.

Academic and moral judgements

In *Orr v. University of Tasmania* [1956] Tas. S.R. 155 (at 159) where a Professor was dismissed for seducing one of his students it was accepted that the University had a right to dismiss for neglect of duty, misconduct or inefficiency.[21] The contention that moral issues need to be taken into account when making academic judgements may also arise from a complainant.

'This appellant . . . made many contentions which were not solely related to his attainment of academic qualifications' including 'that there was a breach of ethics which amounted to a value judgement.'[22]

Is the morality of the candidate a proper element to consider in forming an academic judgement? Lord Goddard C.J.'s inquiry 'whether a person is a fit and proper person to be appointed or retained as a teacher at a university'[23] would seem to cover both moral fitness and capability. The second of these falls into the class of academic judgements of fitness for the job, the first not so clearly so.

Academic and moral judgements – competency and conduct – are often confused, and that is of importance in law under the provisions of the Education Reform Act 1988 which allow a lecturer to be dismissed on the one hand under a disciplinary procedure for misconduct and on the other hand (without following a disciplinary procedure) on grounds of capability.

The area of overlap may be grey. A lecturer might do his job adequately but fail to do it in a 'well-rounded' way. 'Personal development' was a vogue notion of managerial theory in the 1990s, but the ethical dimension was not central to it. More usually taken into account were 'skills' (specialist/transferable); attitude (persistence, independence, receptiveness); and knowledge (of a specialist area of cultural heritage). But those criteria which take (professional) expertise as 'ability to do things' are not necessarily concerned with 'what a person is'. Is competence merely being able to do things, 'arguably to the detriment of knowledge, understanding, and all-round development'?[24] Is that a moral failing or a failing of capability? It goes, after all, to 'the whole person'.

Moral judgements may certainly be relevant to the academic assessment of a teacher or researcher. He may be in the *habit* of seducing his students, trading sex for better marks, and that would be an exploitation of a position of trust. An honest scholar does not plagiarize, so it is important to his scholarly credibility that an academic is honest in his use of sources.

But not all sound moral qualities are unequivocally good things in a scholar. Rigour and thoroughness are, arguably, scholarly virtues, but an excess of these good qualities is not necessarily a virtue – as evidenced by the scholar who becomes unable to finish a book for decades because there is always something more to recheck. Further down the line of scholarly virtues which have scholarly vices on their reverse sides are flexibility (or a tendency to keep shifting ground?); originality or boldness in the framing of hypotheses (or rashness, lack of judiciousness?); faithfulness to good practice (or lack of innovativeness?); such qualities may be read either way, as academic vices or academic virtues.

Judgement and speculation

Is it proper for prediction of future performance to be included in an academic judgement? In *Vaneck v. Governors of the University of Alberta* [1975] 5 W.W.R. 429, the decision not to grant tenure was challenged. The Alberta

Faculty Handbook (106.6) makes reference to the requirement that 'a successful candidate for tenure must have exhibited satisfactory performances during his probationary period and should be considered worthy of advancement' and that it is 'the responsibility of a tenure committee to examine all aspects of the appointee's contribution, to assess *his probable continued progress* [my italics] and to make a recommendation based thereon'.[25] So there were two elements in the decision. The candidate had to show he was capable of doing the job adequately and that he would do so, and even improve, in future. A personal Chair is both a recognition of achievement and an act of trust that the person recognized is not going to drop off from that level. It is assumed that the world's view of him will continue to be high. But it is not assumed that he will write another book.

The 'futurity' issue has arisen elsewhere in connection with student performance. In *Norrie v. Senate of the University of Auckland* [1984] 1 N.Z.L.R. 129 (at 137), arguments turned partly on the making of an academic judgement about the likelihood of a student subsequently passing final examinations he had already failed once. This is clearly a judgement about standards, though the issue of 'future reference', which must always arise when a student is not allowed to retake an examination, has not usually been so sharply focused. The underlying rationale appears to be that past performance is an indicator of capacity for future performance. But it is not logically the same thing to predict improvement upon that performance.

Convenience

Is the consideration of convenience a proper additional factor to take into account in forming an academic judgement?

> There are certain internal matters and disputes that are best decided within the academic community rather than by the courts. This is so, not only because the courts are not as well equipped as the universities to decide matters such as academic qualifications, grades, conferring of degrees and so on, but also because these matters ought to be able to be decided more conveniently, more quickly and at least as accurately by those who are specialists in educational questions of that kind.[26]

It would seem a dangerous concession that a decision could not be challenged because it had been taken in a certain way for the sake of speed, when the accompanying contention that that had not affected its accuracy could not be challenged.

'The exercise of discretion' and 'following the rules'

What is to be done about these difficult matters when decisions have to be made? For they are not easily or tidily resolved. 'The life of the law has not been logic: it has been experience', said Oliver Wendell Holmes,[27] making the familiar point that logic in legal reasoning is the servant of the end in view. A case can, more often than not, be argued either way. But what he says also carries the implication that a judicial decision may also be a decision made by a decision-maker who is taking a personal as well as his 'official' view.

Salmon has argued in a classic study that 'for good and sufficient reasons, the Courts which administer justice are constrained to walk in predetermined paths . . . They are bound hand and foot in the bonds of an authoritative creed, which they must accept and act on without demur.'[28] The question is whether that excludes an exercise of judicial discretion in which a judge might say, 'this is how it seems to me',[29] and feel it proper to give his personal view of the way circumstances are to be weighed. For it is clear that that is possible, since judges do disagree in the hearing of appeals and in other contexts.

The thing does not have to be seen in black and white terms.[30] Yet, there must remain to the 'judge' some element of choice. A judge has to take one construction or another of a statute or a precedent and state a preference. In this sense at least he has to form an opinion.[31]

A judge is a practised decision-maker who understands very well what he has to take into consideration in arriving at his decision. This may not be true of the administrative decision-maker in universities and colleges when there is a battle on a committee, or a point to be scored, and the issues become blurred under such irrelevances.

Someone makes rules within a university. Sometimes it is not clear who has in fact made them or upon what authority.[32] Sometimes their existence is not 'discovered' until someone raises a difficulty. Sometimes what has in fact happened is that a decision is made by an individual exercising a discretion which he may (or may not) have had entrusted to him by the university, and when it is challenged he seeks to say that he was only following the rules. So the relationship between making rules and exercising discretion is at the heart of internal decision-making of the muddled sort on which universities often operate.

The letter written by the head of department in *Vaneck v. Governors of the University of Alberta* [1975] 5 W.W.R. 429, to support the case for refusing tenure was described as 'in part . . . the opinions of the writer'.[33] In *Re University of Melbourne, ex parte Simone* [1981] V.R. 378 (at 395 and 396) the case was also acknowledged to involve the forming of an opinion. 'Opinion' need not imply the balance, judiciousness, the possession of relevant expertise and the possession of relevant information which the claim that a judgement is an academic judgement would presumably require if it was to be well-founded, and it is a vexed question how it would relate to the exercise of discretion entrusted to a decisionmaker through some formal process.

The law in its present state suggests some guidelines. The exercise of a discretion by a decision-making body is an exercise of choice. It is different from a 'duty', about which there is no choice, merely obligation. It involves both 'power' and 'responsibility'. The 'responsibility' is to exercise the 'power'. But it is a responsibility with concomitant restrictions, which require the power to be exercised within limits. So discretion has to be exercised in determining where those limits lie, as well as in keeping within them once defined.

There are well-trodden paths here. It is not possible to make a rule which will improperly impede the exercise of a discretion. A body may be held to decline jurisdiction if it decides under the dictation of another body.[34] The interplay is between the interests of individuals affected by the decision-making and the authority to make the decision. A tribunal entrusted with a discretion must not, by the adoption of a general rule of policy, disable itself from exercising its discretion in individual cases.[35] A body may decline jurisdiction if it decides by reference to a predetermined rule of policy without giving any genuine consideration to the merits of the case before it.[36] Moreover, a competent authority may not fetter the exercise of its discretion by the adoption of a fixed rule of policy. A competent authority may fail to exercise a discretion because it has failed to appreciate the amplitude of its discretion. A competent authority may, for example, misconceive the scope of its own powers by disclaiming competence to take other relevant factors into account.[37] Discretion cannot be allowed to take a decision-making body beyond its powers, even if those who are affected give their consent.[38]

Nor can it be interfered with by responsibilities or obligations arising from some other source. Discretion must 'not be fettered or hampered by contracts or other bargains or by self-imposed rules of thumb'.[39] It must certainly not be a matter *simply* of personal opinion. Discretion must, above all, be objective, uncontaminated by 'private affections'.[40] Lord Halsbury gave a classic definition on this point in *Sharpe and Wakefield*: '"Discretion" means when it is said that something is to be done within the discretion of the authorities that that something is to be done according to the rules of reason and justice, not according to private opinion . . . it is to be, not arbitrary, vague and fanciful, but legal and regular.'[41]

Yet, 'discretion' frequently tends to be read as 'unfettered discretion' alike by officials who claim it, and by committees pointing to the exercise of their discretion in the interpretation of rules. The law frowns on that. Discretion 'must be exercised within the limit, to which an honest man competent to the discharge of his office ought to confine himself'.[42]

The main principles are that:

1. a decision-maker has 'a broad discretion as to the factors which are to be taken into account before a decision is made';
2. that discretion is restricted only if 'the governing statute clearly requires that a particular factor must be considered or must not be considered'.

There is not, however, an unfettered discretion to determine what is or is not a relevant consideration. In *Tesco Stores Ltd v. Secretary of State for the*

Environment [1995] 1 W.L.R. 759, Lord Keith held that 'it is *for the courts*, if the matter is brought before them to decide what is a relevant consideration. If the decision-maker wrongly takes the view that some consideration is not relevant and therefore has no regard to it, his decision cannot stand and he must be required to think again.' 'Once the decision-maker has *properly* determined the range of relevant considerations, the weight to be given to each consideration is a matter within its discretion and a decision will only be struck down as unreasonable where it is so unreasonable that no reasonable decision-maker could have made it.'[43]

So, getting the range of relevant considerations right is important.

'Advice', 'decision-making' and relevant expertise

In the UK Research Assessment Exercise of 1997, sharp distinction was maintained between 'advice' and 'decision-making'. Each panel 'could set up subpanels if it wished' but 'these were to be advisory with the main panel retaining the responsibility for deciding ratings in all cases'.[44] 'Where subpanels were established these were required to work in a way which did not allow members who were not on the main panel access to anything done by the main panel after receiving their advice.'[45] 'Most panels were advised by specialist advisers whom they asked to provide advice on the quality of work in particular areas within their field which they did not feel able to cover adequately.'[46] But: 'it was left entirely to the panel in each case to decide what advice was required and whom to approach'.[47] What does not appear to be clear here was how the panels could know what advice was required and whom to approach if they lacked the expertise in the subject area which would have allowed them to identify it.

These distinctions within the arena of academic judgement had a counterpart in the distinction which had to be made between academic and managerial judgement. '[T]he role of panel secretaries as advisers and as guardians of procedural integrity'[48] was again kept separate from that of the decisionmakers themselves. The ground rules were clearer here because the panel secretaries would not (except by coincidence) be able to lay claim to relevant expertise and the fundamental distinction between the roles of a 'civil servant' and a 'minister' would apply.

Explaining what you are doing and why

There was a strong emphasis in the UK's 1996 Research Assessment Exercise on 'transparency of approach and process'. This began with the publication of draft procedures in advance.[49] It seems likely in the light of the 1996 RAE Manager's *Report* that publishing in advance the way the considerations are to be weighed against one another may also now be a requirement.[50]

Establishing the facts

When a decision-maker has to take on board a good deal of evidence a problem arises about reading it all. The RAE panels faced the question of 'what approach to take to the assessment of works not read by any panel members, in order to reach a sound and robust overall view of the quality of output in a submission'.[51] 'Very broadly, panels in the humanities and social sciences tended to read more widely than those in science, engineering and medicine; and the latter group were often more confident in their ability to assess the quality of listed outputs by reference to their medium of publication.'[52] But that throws back the decision-making on to editors of refereed journals and the referees they use. It brings us into an arena of vicarious decision-making which may be dubious in law.

'In all cases where panels read selectively, they avoided crude sampling but tended instead to target researchers and topics with which no one on the panel was already familiar, and works in unfamiliar media and imprints where assessment by reference to medium of publication was problematic.'[53] The idea here was evidently to make good any gaps in knowledge on the part of the panel. But targeting unfamiliar topics may mean moving into areas where the judgement cannot be expert.

Getting hold of items to read proved to be a practical problem, especially because it was particularly work in obscure journals which was most likely to need scrutiny.[54]

These admissions in the RAE Manager's *Report* do not, on the face of it, tell a wholly satisfactory story of the establishing of the facts by decision-makers making academic judgements in areas where the establishment of the facts is inseparable from the making of a value judgement.

Resolving disagreement among referees

There is a further problem, to do with the resolving of *conflicts* of evidence. In the allocation of Research Council money, the longer the period for which funding is needed and the larger the sum involved, or the more international the area from which they are drawn, the more referees it is felt to be appropriate to consult. That, too, has a drawback, for to make the number of voices greater is to make it more likely that some of them will be dissentient. It is a fact of common experience that academic referees do not agree with one another with any degree of consistency.

On a grant review panel there will normally be a primary and a secondary reviewer who has responsibility for taking a detailed and considered view of a specific application. The whole panel has available to it all the papers for all the applications. If there is disagreement between the first and second reviewer each will give reasons for his view and time will be set aside so that the matter can be more fully discussed. If there is serious discrepancy the primary reviewer will probably get his way.

Consistency

In the 1996 RAE 'The need for compliance with guidance and criteria, and for the clear recording of panel decisions, was reinforced through the use of "checklists" drawn up by the secretaries to monitor and record that each submission was considered in the same way as the others in the same unit of assessment and against the full criteria set.'[55]

Discrepancies from emerging patterns were noted and looked at:

> The panels looked for evidence that individual staff listed as research active may have achieved significantly more (or less) than their sub-area viewed as a group, and for cases where the reasons for apparently low productivity needed to be considered, and such cases were taken into account in building up an overall quality profile against the rating scale.[56]

The intention here was to ensure not only that there was consistency in the *way* judgements were arrived at but also (perhaps paradoxically) that all relevant circumstances were taken into consideration.

Forming a judgement: the machinery

The RAE does not come out well in some aspects of its use of procedural machinery. 'The most significant variance in [the panels'] approach to the assessment process was in *how far they read the cited works* . . . and in the extent to which they formed an initial view, individually or collectively, on the quality of the works cited by individual staff or sub-groups.'[57] To call for evidence and not examine it is a fault.

It can also be a fault to create and disappoint legitimate expectation. Legitimate expectation began as a notion deriving from procedural promises.[58] Those to whom promises are made by decision-making bodies can reasonably expect them to be kept (although 'official statements of policy . . . may cancel legitimate expectation, just as they may create it').[59] But a person whose interests are affected may wish to claim that a legitimate expectation has been created which goes beyond procedure to the substance of the decision,[60] and that might be relevant in a promotions or tenure or examination case.

He might also argue that in disappointing that legitimate expectation the decisionmaking body has gone beyond its powers. For a decisionmaking body to make a decision without good reason, just because it can, takes its actions *ultra vires.*[61] Lord Scarman argued in *R v. Inland Revenue Commissioners, ex parte Preston* that 'unfairness in the purported exercise of a power can be such that it is an abuse or excess of power'.[62]

Legitimate[63] expectation has to be set beside rights. The first may exist where the second do not. This may be so where a promise has been made by a decision-making body (as in a 'mission statement') but not honoured, and where an existing practice is discontinued without informing those it affects, as, for example, in a decision rigidly to exclude certain categories of evidence which were previously admitted at the discretion of the decision-maker. Where either of these had happened it might be shown that the decisionmakers 'had been guilty of conduct equivalent to a breach of contract or breach of representation'.[64] *Casson v. University of Aston in Birmingham* [1983] 1 All E.R. 88, reports a case in which two applicants to the university complained that they had been admitted to a course which proved in the end not to be available.

There may also be a case for saying that someone who has wished to make representations to a decision-making committee determining whether or not he is to be promoted or given a long-term contract has a legitimate expectation of consultation.[65]

Attorney-General for New South Wales v. Quin (1990) 170 C.L.R. 1, has become a load-bearing case in the development of the doctrine of legitimate expectation. A Stipendiary Magistrate argued that he had a legitimate expectation that he would be appointed as a magistrate along with his colleagues when a new court system was introduced in New South Wales.

Quin's case in the High Court was that he had a legitimate expectation that he would be treated in the way his former colleagues had been treated; he should not have to compete with fresh applicants. If the adverse report had not been taken into account he would have been appointed along with his former colleagues and on the same terms as they were. He lost this case. It was held that his only legitimate expectation was that the contents of the adverse report would be disclosed to him. But that itself was a substantial point.

A number of themes came into play in this case, but among the most significant was the recognition that when some decisionmaking task is entrusted to a public authority, and the promise in practice it makes is the source of a legitimate expectation, 'the repository is bound to have regard to the promise or practice in exercising the power'.[66]

Procedural fairness is a complex area; but the ground rules are well-established. The main problem with the internal procedures of universities for making promotions or appointments, is lack of awareness of those ground rules. There is an educational task, to be coupled with a change of culture which will make it unacceptable not to create procedures which are adequate to ensure fairness.

15

Reasonableness

The relationship between 'being reasonable' and 'having reasons' is not tidy. Everyone who has been an examiner or served on any committee making academic judgements is familiar with the gut feeling, the level below the conscious, at which the elements in the basis on which the decision is being reached 'gel' together. And something does not necessarily have to be justified by conscious or stated reasoning in order to appear reasonable to the ordinary person. In *Post Office Counters Ltd v. Heavey* [1989] I.R.L.R. 513, the EAT held that the Industrial Tribunal had 'confused the burden on the employer under s. 57(2) [of the Employment Protection (Consolidation) Act] of "showing" the reason for dismissal, with the requirement in s. 57(3) that the employer act reasonably in treating that reason as sufficient for dismissing the employee'.[1]

However, if something appears unreasonable or if its reasonableness is challenged, it becomes necessary to explain the reasoning behind it. And presumably a 'reasonable' decision must by definition be capable of being explained by reasoning if it is challenged. Moreover, there are circumstances, and surely decisions which claim to be based on academic judgement must be among them, where there must be conscious reasoning in advance of the decision, and where, therefore, in principle, reasons certainly ought to be *able* to be given, even if they do not *have* to be given.

In *R. v. Higher Education Funding Council, ex parte Institute of Dental Surgery* [1994] judicial review was sought in an attempt to challenge the decision to give the Institute of Dental Surgery a lower grade in the RAE than it believed itself to deserve, a decision which struck at more than the self-esteem of the Institute because it resulted in a cut in its funding. It was held that: 'academic judgements were not in a class of case where the nature and impact of the decision itself required that reasons be given as a routine aspect of procedural fairness but were in a class where some factor would be required to show that in the circumstances of the particular decision, fairness required reasons to be given'.[2] The circumstances of this decision meet the requirements of openness of procedure and of demonstrable relevant expertise in the decision-maker, so that it could *only* have been challenged on its 'merits'. That left things on a knife edge.

The broad tendency of recent cases in this area moves towards the requirement to give reasons, though there is still no general duty to do so. In *R. v. Royal Borough of Kensington and Chelsea, ex p Grillo* (1996) 28 H.L.R. 94, Neill L.J. held against the reasoning of Sir Louis Blom-Cooper, sitting as a deputy judge, that there was a general duty to give reasons 'wherever the statutorily impregnated administrative process is infused with the concept of fair treatment to those potentially affected by administrative action'. Neill L.J. took this to go too far. But in *R. v. Mayor, Commonalty and Citizens of the City of London and another, ex parte Matson* (1996) 8 Admin. L.R. 49, the issue of reasons was decided the other way, again by Neill L.J. A candidate for the post of alderman was refused admission on the ground that he was not a suitable person to discharge the duties of office. The Court of Appeal found that it was unlawful in this case to refuse to give reasons. This is important because there were no fundamental rights involved and no obvious aberrance in the decision. The Court in this case was influenced by the fact that it could be argued that a *reasoned* decision was appropriate in this situation, where there was an electoral context, the decision was public, Mr Matson's reputation was likely to be damaged, and the decision caused uncertainty (at 63–4).

Among the reasons why it was held that reasons should have been given in *Matson* was that:

> there was no way of knowing whether the court of aldermen had accepted the explanation which the alderman elect had given in respect of a specific allegation of prior inappropriate conduct on his part . . . the basis of the decision may have been either that the alderman elect lacked the necessary positive qualities, or that the court of aldermen was dissatisfied with his answers to some particular questions . . . in the absence of reasons, neither the alderman elect nor the councillors could know whether he should *stand again* for election . . . the alderman elect's rejection was bound to cast a shadow on his reputation . . . the giving of short reasons by the court of aldermen would not impede the court in the exercise of its powers, but would, on the contrary, enable it to ensure that its decisions in every case are sound, manifestly just, and in the interests of the City.[3]

'There was no way of knowing' is the crucial statement, because of the nature of the things which there was no 'way of knowing'. That could be helpful in an 'academic judgement' case because a candidate for promotion or an applicant for a job would need to know whether his case was hopeless; he has had a slur cast on his reputation; the outcome is public.

It has sometimes been asked whether there could be a shift either way from *Wednesbury* standards, involving a conceptual movement either towards a lower or towards a higher threshold of unreasonableness? In *R. v. Secretary of State for the Home Department, ex parte Brind* [1991] 1 A.C. 697 (at 757, *per*

Lord Ackner), it was held that there are rights with which there can be limited discretion to interfere. 'In a field which concerns a fundamental human right – namely that of free speech – close scrutiny must be given to the reasons provided as justification for interfering with that right.'

Attempts have been made too to lift the level of *Wednesbury* unreasonableness to that of 'manifest absurdity', in cases involving national economic policy. It remains unclear how 'manifest absurdity' would differ from irrationality at the normal *Wednesbury* level.[4]

So it may be that this will not approve a fruitful line of development. But further decisions in this area may tip the balance, if that defence cannot be mounted.

It became clear in the course of the High Court leave hearing in *R. v. University of Cambridge, ex parte Evans*[5] that: 'No method appears to have been laid down for the orderly evaluation and comparison of commentaries on the candidates.' The use of criteria and evaluation forms by the committee was voluntary. No minutes were taken, merely notes, at the hand of the Secretary-General, who was not a member of the committee but only its Secretary. These were never ratified as Minutes by the committee, for the committee never met again. At no stage could each member of the committee or the committee as a whole have given reasons for the decision in any recorded form, either so as to allow candidates to answer any criticisms (and no candidate was interviewed) or so as to allow candidates to appeal (and there was no appeal).

In *Doody* it was argued that: 'Fairness will very often require that a person who may be adversely affected by the decision will have the opportunity to make representations on his own behalf either before the decision is taken with a view to producing a favourable result, or after it is taken, with a view to procuring its modification, or both.'[6] The *Doody* rule could not have been satisfied by the University either prospectively or retrospectively, even if it had allowed candidates to be interviewed or to appeal, because candidates could not have known to what points held against them they were to address themselves.

It matters that the 'outcome' of the making of an academic judgement should have 'accuracy . . . on the substance of the case'.[7] It is a long way from a perception that the wrong choice has been made between two candidates for appointment or promotion, to being able to say that it is unreasonable on a *Wednesbury* basis. But it may be impossible even to begin to argue that it is unreasonable unless the reasons for the choice are given. Candidates not given adequate reasons may 'in effect be deprived of their rights of appeal'.[8] To deprive someone of any grounds for appealing a judgement when such grounds exist may be an abuse of power.[9] That takes us to the area of giving opportunity to make representations. It is a fundamental principle of natural justice that both sides must be heard. If candidates are rejected without being interviewed and without being told of allegations made against their work by referees they may be entitled to argue that that rule has been broken.

In *ex parte Evans* there was no need for the court to require reasons for it to become apparent that there were no reasons to be had. The inadequacy of the procedures as they were revealed at the hearing made that plain, but that did not eliminate the need to look at the question of the requirement to give reasons in this context.

The University of Cambridge[10] not only failed to have any reasons; it refused to accept that it had any duty to do more than assert that it had acted correctly: 'The giving of reasons may be inconvenient, but I can see no reason at all why it should be against the public interest: rather the reverse. That being so, I would ask simply: is refusal to give reasons fair? I would answer without hesitation that it is not' (*Doody v. Secretary of State for the Home Department* [1993] 3 All E.R. 92, [1994] 1 A.C. 531, at 564, [1993] 3 W.L.R. 154, HL). It is well established that it is not acceptable for a decision-maker merely to assert that it did no wrong: 'Authorities assist neither themselves nor the courts if their response is a blanket assertion of having acted in accordance with law or one which begs the question.'[11] So it could not have been sufficient for the University merely to say that it had acted properly although it could not explain how or why.

That attempt was in fact made by members of the General Board speaking in a Discussion of the University's Parliament, the Senate, on April 29 1997. 'The Board and the Committee are entirely satisfied that . . . the necessary procedures have been followed, and the Regent House can be assured that the General Board officers concerned with the exercise have shown the highest standards', reassured Professor M. Pepper.[12] Professor D.H. Mellor said that 'none of the matters that were presented' to the General Board gave him 'any reason whatever to doubt the propriety, good faith, and the constitutional correctness of what had been done'.[13]

An external member of the promotions committee, Professor Hugh Williamson, came over from Oxford to speak in this internal debate, which he had standing to do because he remained a member of the Senate of the University of Cambridge. He admitted the possibility that the objection might be raised that the University's published procedures are inherently flawed, so that, even if followed, they are bound to lead to an inequitable conclusion.[14] But Professor Pepper denied that even if that were so, any authority could have power to intervene. The system of promotion, he claimed, 'is one of the most significant issues which is within the power of the Regent House to decide without the interference of outside bodies or events'.[15] (He made this claim in the knowledge that application had been made for judicial review.)

'A requirement to give reasons [can] no longer be regarded as exceptional.'[16] But there remains no general requirement, so it still has to be established case by case whether reasons can be required.

Sedley J. addressed the thus load-bearing question of what gives a decision 'importance' by listing three reasons why unsuccessful candidates need to know why they have failed:

1. 'First and foremost it will tell them where to concentrate their efforts.'

That is of especial value in the Cambridge situation (and there will be others like it in promotion processes elsewhere) because in Cambridge there is now acknowledged (*Reporter*, 25 June 1997) to be a queue of persons who deserve promotion but for whose promotion the University has not made provision in its budget.

So it is unlikely to be possible for such candidates to be told that they need to add to their achievements in order to succeed, since many of them have already more than amply met the criteria now (after some years' campaigning by the 'reformers') explicitly laid down by the University. They could presumably only be told that some other candidate had been preferred to themselves. But that, arguably, would not be an adequate reason if they were not told why. They could not be told directly what it was about the successful candidate which had made him preferable, or what it was about their own performances which had made it seem to the committee less worthy than his, because that would involve disclosing matters the other candidate might properly consider to be his own private business.

So the requirement to perform better, embedded in this first ground rule for the giving of reasons, contains within it, in circumstances where there is a competition, much matter for further unfolding in the arena of the making of comparative judgements; and in the area of the confidentiality a candidate may expect to protect him from having his performance exposed to his colleagues through the making of comparisons to them in the giving of reasons concerning their own candidatures.

The defence of confidentiality is often used by decision-makers who do not wish to have to explain themselves. There is authority on that: 'Information . . . may be confidential. But that does not mean that the applicants are not to be given a chance of answering it. They must be given the chance, subject to this qualification: I do not think that they need to tell the applicants the source of their information, if that would put their informant in peril, or otherwise be contrary to the public interest' (*R. v. Gaming Board, ex parte Benaim* [1970] 2 All E.R. 528, C.A., at 534). In promotions cases the confidentiality consideration is rather different. It has to do with the problem that if referees write in confidence they write differently from the way they write if they know their comments will be shown to the subject of those comments. But that does not remove the requirement that candidates be given the chance to answer at least the substance of criticisms, even if they may not know their source.

2. 'Occasionally', continues Sedley J. in the judgement in *ex parte Evans*: 'it will become apparent that the decision-makers have misapprehended or overlooked something relevant – a fault which will not necessarily make the decision reviewable but may well be open to correction on a future application.'

This is a provision which lies securely within the established area of procedural requirements, for it is the duty to ensure that everything relevant has been taken into consideration. It surely implies that a right of appeal must follow a duty to give reasons to those whose interests are affected, in case the reasons should reveal a flaw which makes the process unlawful.

Until 1997, the University of Cambridge offered unsuccessful candidates no 'feedback' and there was still in 1998 no appeal against what proved in practice to be 'decisions', not 'recommendations' of the central promotions committee. In *R. v. Secretary of State for the Home Department, ex parte Fayed* [1996] 1 All E.R. 228, it was ruled that the fact that under the British Nationality Act 1981 the Home Secretary was not required to give reasons for refusing an application for British citizenship, did not relieve him of the obligation to be fair. Fairness dictated that, while he need not give reasons for his decision, he ought in some circumstances to inform the applicant beforehand of new matters weighing against the grant of naturalization, so the applicant could address him on those matters. Lord Woolf M.R. said that the applicants had never been told what aspects of their applications had given rise to difficulties or reservations. Without information as to this it would be impossible for them to volunteer information to support their applications. The refusal of their applications was damaging to their reputations and deprived them of the substantial benefits of citizenship. 'The public rejection of Mr Matson is bound to cast a shadow on his reputation' (*R. v. City of London Corp, ex parte Matson* (1995) 8 Admin. L.R. 49, C.A., at 63). The factors of damage to reputation and deprivation of benefit are very strong considerations in the denial of promotion in the University.

3. 'Above all, perhaps, the giving of reasons demonstrates that proper care has been taken over something of critical importance to the standing and career of each candidate.'

This is the nub of the 'importance' argument. It allows the case to be mounted that there were procedural flaws at least at the level of failing to do everything which ought to have been done (if not at the level of negligence), for if the decisionmakers cannot say *why* they arrived at their decision, it follows that they also cannot say *how*.

Again there is authority: 'The giving of reasons may amongst other things concentrate the decision-maker's mind on the right questions; demonstrate to the recipient that this is so; show that the issues have been conscientiously addressed and how the result has been reached; or alternatively alert the recipient to a justiciable flaw in the process' (*R. v. Higher Education Funding Council, ex parte Institute of Dental Surgery* [1994] 1 W.L.R. 242, D.C., at 256; [1994] 1 All E.R. 651). '"What was the true purpose for which the power was exercised" can only be established when it is clear to what the decision-makers' minds were being addressed' (*R. v. Inner London Education Authority, ex parte Westminster City Council* [1986] 1 All E.R. 19 (at 37) quoting de Smith).

There have been two cases since the *Dental Surgery* decision, both discussed in Sedley J.'s judgement, in which there have been attempts to address the difficulty which logically follows if reasons can, on these principles, now be required. These are particularly important in the context of promotions and appointments decisions. The decisionmakers may say, 'it is not that we did not have reasons, but that these reasons are, of their nature, inexpressible'. They may say this on two kinds of grounds.

1. The first is that the decision necessarily includes elements of gut feeling. There is a complex interaction of factors below the conscious level predisposing the scholar to approval or disapproval, and he may not be able to bring them all to the surface, even if he tries.

That is perhaps no more than saying that academic judgements are *value* judgements. But even value judgements – perhaps especially value judgements – must be presumed to seek to be objective. They must at least be founded on evidence which is itself factual. In the RAE of 1992, the research was to be measured against what was in intention 'an absolute standard'.[17] But the realities of the forming of academic judgements appear not always to meet this requirement.

This brings us again to the question of value judgements which are also comparative judgements between the successful and the unsuccessful, where both meet a required standard; and also in cases where incommensurables are being compared, as in an attempt to decide whether an astrophysicist is better than a linguist where only one of them can be promoted.[18]

A judgement about the quality of an individual's performance is made either against a notional standard, or against the performance of other candidates, by ranking them. If it is made against the performance of others there ought to be an identifiable basis of comparison. In *Thomson v. London University*, 33 L.J. Ch. 625 the question was whether one examination candidate could be ranked above another. In an examination, candidates must normally be given a mark. Some marks must be higher than others; so candidates once marked can be listed in a ranked order for their performance in the same examination. But that is not the same exercise as ranking them against one another by direct comparison of candidates and without the assistance of numerical marks.

2. The second reason decision-makers may give for declaring their reasons inexpressible is that the decision was made not individually but collectively.

A committee's judgement is collective. This makes the difference that whereas an individual may be quite free within the law to make capricious decisions, for example, about where he will leave his possessions in his will, a public authority or its committees must 'act reasonably and in good faith and upon lawful and relevant grounds of public interest'. Its discretion is 'never unfettered'.[19]

In the *Institute of Dental Surgery* case the problem of the type of collective expert judgement which is made by a committee was thus central.

> It seems to us disingenuous to talk . . . about the impossibility of 'disaggregating the collective view', when that view was an aggregate view in the first place. Schiemann J's reference in *R. v. Poole BC, ex p Beebee* [1991] 2 PLR 27 at 31 to 'the theoretical difficulties of establishing the reasoning process of a corporate body which acts by resolution' does not bear directly on what in our judgement is more correctly viewed as a collegiate than a corporate decision.[20]

There are, indeed, 'theoretical difficulties of establishing the reasoning of a corporate body which acts by resolution'. But the *Dental Surgery* case would seem to offer a ground for distinguishing between a collegiate or collective decision-making, for which reasons could certainly in principle be given, and the corporate decision, for which that might be less easily done.

In the *Institute of Dental Surgery* case it was commented:

> To suggest that the panel's conclusion cannot be explained without 'undermining the whole purpose of a peer review assessment' seems to us, with respect, to devalue the assessment process. It would take a great deal more than this to persuade us that experienced and distinguished academics, *whether individually or collectively,* cannot assign reasons for their own judgement . . . Each panel member will have had reasons for his or her own initial rating, and in discussion each will have been in a position to advance those reasons and to modify them *in the light of the reasoning of others.*[21]

In *R. v. City of London, ex parte Matson* (1995) 8 Admin. L.R. 49, Swinton Thomas L.J. brought (1) and (2) together. He distinguished between the articulation of 'a factual basis for a decision' and 'assessment' of that factual basis which, must, involve a value judgement. He said: 'I do not believe that any judgement involves the articulation of *inexpressible* value judgements. Assessments of that nature are made day in, day out in every walk of life.' He placed that view of the practicalities in the context of the forming of a decision by a group or committee or panel: 'I do not believe that it would be unduly difficult or arduous for the aldermen to give a collective reason for their decision.'

The collective character of a decision made by a committee lies not in unanimity of opinion, for a decision may be unanimous even if those sharing it have different reasons for sharing it; but in a balancing of factors in which some will seem more important than others to certain members of the committee: 'True it is that individual members may have considered differing factors.' That is likely to apply to any collective decision. All this takes further forward the line of thinking adumbrated in the *Institute of Dental Surgery* case that it cannot be accepted that 'experienced and distinguished academics, whether individually or collectively, cannot assign reasons for their own judgement'.

The business of the requirement to give reasons needs to move forward on clear principles. It is a very important requirement, not only to those whose interests are affected, but also because of its potential for curbing the excesses and confusions which frequently attend administrative decision-making. In the *Dental Surgery* case it was pointed out that 'in the absence of a prior principle irreconcilable or inconsistent decisions will emerge'. 'From the tenor of the decisions principles will come'. Principles can begin to emerge even from apparently conflicting decisions.

Arguably, the next step is a free-standing obligation in the form of a duty to give reasons and the concomitant requirement that the business of the requirement to give reasons be 'infused with the concept of fair treatment to those potentially affected'.[22]

Can a decision be challenged because it seems *merely* an expression of opinion?

In *Weinberger v. Inglis* (1919) A.C. 606, an attempt was made to allege that a decision was arbitrary and capricious and based on irrelevant considerations. It was held that because the decision-makers had exercised the discretion in good faith their decision could not be challenged. But in this case there was a clear burden upon the applicant, explicitly set out in the procedures, to show that there were special circumstances excepting him from a rule which would otherwise normatively apply. He was of German extraction and at this time there was a policy of the Committee of the Stock Exchange to exclude from membership those who were enemy-born. They laid down a procedure to be followed in such cases. Applicants who fell into this category were to be placed on a separate list and told that they could send in, for the Committee to consider, a statement of any special circumstances they deemed to obtain in their own cases. Candidates were to be interviewed by the Committee, but no questions asked by candidates at these interviews 'with a view to eliciting grounds of objection other than those disclosed or known to' them were to be answered. The court concluded that each case was handled in accordance with the stated procedures and that 'each case received some reasonable degree of individual attention'. The problem was not procedural but had to do with the merits of the case. The candidate had simply failed to establish sufficient special circumstances.

But things have changed since 1919. 'The attainment of fairness' is increasingly seen as the objective in all administrative decision-making affecting the individual,[23] and that is inseparable from reasonableness. 'In my judgement an unfair action can seldom be a reasonable one.'[24] Lord Donaldson held that fairness requires a tribunal to give sufficient reasons for its decision to enable the parties to know the issues to which it addressed its mind and that it acted lawfully.[25] 'One aspect of unfairness may be . . . the inability to know whether an error of law or of process has occurred'.[26] A candidate might complain that it is impossible to know what was discussed by an examining or promoting or tenure-granting committee in reaching its decision, and whether it was done in a lawful manner. This might bear not on the particularities of an individual case, or in any way on the merits, but on the question of the methods and criteria used for all candidates, and thus be procedural and not substantive. It might not be possible for procedural error to be shown unless reasons had to be given.

Giving reasons in advance: publishing the criteria

On 26 March 1997 the CVCP made a submission to the HEFCE on the Funding Method for Teaching from 1998–9. In a section of the paper (N/97/51(a)) it set out a list of principles or desirable attributes for the system. It wanted it to be simple; cost-effective; transparent; predictable; to command confidence; to be 'bottom-up'. It also stressed the importance of agreeing criteria in advance. 'Criteria for determining allocations should be well known and published.' In the *Dental Surgery* case, it told against the duty to give reasons that the procedure had been open, 'widely canvassed in advance and published in circular form'.[27] It had also been made clear what the criteria were, and that proved important.

Measuring like against like: standardization and variation

There is a fundamental difficulty in comparing unlike with unlike where the outcome has to be a single list which purports to have compared the achievements of all those on it in such a way as to be able to rank them. It may be particularly difficult to arrive at criteria on which incommensurable kinds of performance can be ranked side by side. In the Cambridge list published in the *University Reporter* of 7 August 1996 the notion of the 'nature' of the contribution to knowledge seems extremely vague.

a. Originality of research
b. Nature of the contribution to knowledge
c. Significance of the work for others
d. Quality of publications and scholarly communications
e. Intellectual leadership
f. Reputation within:
    the candidate's own field of research;
    cognate disciplines;
    national peer groups;
    international scholarship
g. an effective contribution to teaching.

But criteria may also have to be *defined*. Some RAE panels saw a need to define terms, and distinguished in their criteria statements between 'work of international visibility (but not necessarily of the highest quality) and work of excellence on an international scale of quality'.[28] It is also important that it should be decided in advance how criteria should be weighed against one another.

The RAE Manager's *Report* explains that 'a balance had to be struck between unduly constraining' the 'judgement' of the RAE panels 'and the need to behave and be seen to behave reasonably and consistently',[29] where consistency meant not doing everything in an identical way, but in a way which took account of innate differences in subject matter. The RAE adopted 'a common basic approach, with the panels all working within the same general framework and a standard written presentation of research for assessment'.[30] But it was recognized that different subjects constituted different areas of expertise and that there might be legitimate differences in the way the standardized submissions were to be interpreted according to subject.[31] There is to be a similar allowance in 2001.

The RAE exercise made a distinction between work in humanities and arts subjects, which could have been published over a six-year period, and work in the sciences covering a four-year period. This recognizes subject differences in published outcome over time.

Discipline-specific issues were consciously addressed: 'the balance between uniformity and differentiation of approach . . . reflects the common basic approach and dataset adopted for the exercise while allowing scope for methods to be tailored to genuine subject differences'.[32]

A few panels specified 'additional information to be provided for their subject alone . . . This approach was adopted in particular by some panels which had reservations about the ending of the overall publication count and were looking for additional indicators especially towards the upper end of the quality scale.'[33]

Interdisciplinary submissions presented a severe test of the 'standardization and variation' balance. It is acknowledged in the RAE Manager's *Report* that 'more could reasonably have been done to encourage panels in cognate disciplines to work together. Joint working of any kind was fairly limited.'[34]

'The need to explain (even in the case of inter-panel referrals) in what terms the advice was required to be couched – for example, whether the panel had an interim rating scale and if so how that operated'[35] – also set up tensions within the arena of standardization and variation. 'Panels responding to referrals sometimes found it awkward to look at material in the light of another panel's criteria.'[36]

Because the RAE competition was against a standard only ('the assessments were to focus on quality'), and did not measure submissions against one another, there was less danger of disadvantaging some by having a standardized submission. That is, no HEI stood to lose out against another because it had been forced to leave out certain evidence in its favour by the rules of the standard submission. The appropriate balance between standardization and variation would seem to vary with the danger of disadvantage to some arising from too high a degree of standardization.

The process of giving reasons

Feedback was thought about in the 1996 RAE. It was a sensitive matter, because the *Institute of Dental Surgery* case had come very close to requiring the HEFCE to give reasons for its decision. A blanket decision was taken not to offer routine feedback but to allow for it in particular cases 'where a panel decided that it wished . . . to offer written developmental feedback, in confidence, to the head of an HEI on a particular submission'. 'This decision reflected the limited, summative purpose of the RAE and the fact that it was based on judgemental peer review.'

But there were queries, and some attempt was made to answer them on the basis of the panel's recorded reasons. 'In practice, where institutions have queried a rating, the funding bodies have provided a brief statement of the reasons for the rating drawn from the minutes of the meetings of the panel concerned.'[37]

There was a third possibility, that chairmen or panel members would leak information. 'Many Chairs have been willing to talk to departments in confidence about their rating.'[38] There is no comment in the *Report* on informal feedback given by panel members, and where such members return to their own departments this must be a strong temptation. Anecdotal evidence was strong that some heads of department were informally supplied with individual ratings for members of their departments by those who had been on the panels.

It was recognized by HEFCE that the position on feedback was unsatisfactory and would 'need to be considered further in planning any similar exercise'.[39] Forward planning for 2001 allows for feedback.

The process of giving reasons

Once leave has been granted to apply for judicial review it is usual for administrative bodies to give reasons for their decision, in an effort to end the litigation. That is in keeping with the view that a public body has a duty to 'put all of its cards on the table'.[40] If reasons are required, to what patterns do they need to conform and what requirements ought they to meet?

Giving information

> The key to ministerial accountability must surely be the obligation to give information . . . if, and to the extent that, the account given by a minister to Parliament, whether in answering parliamentary questions, or in a debate, or to a select committee, withholds information on the matter under review, the account given is not a full account and the obligation to account for what has happened, has, prima facie, not been discharged . . . the withholding of information by an accountable minister should never be by rote, should never be based on reasons of

> convenience or for the avoidance of political embarrassment, and should always require special and clear justification.[41]

Sir Richard Scott, in these reflections on the conduct of the Scott Inquiry, allows that there is a question as to how far the information has to be complete.[42] 'To supply information which is known to be less than complete to an audience that does not know it is less than complete involves, in my opinion, a failure to comply with the requirements of ministerial accountability.'[43]

Sir Richard Scott argues that 'a comprehensive review' is needed, both of the list of subjects on which 'the government's refusal to answer questions is still justifiable' and also 'of the conventions governing the obligations of ministers to provide or to facilitate the provision of information to select committees'.[44]

These comments of Sir Richard Scott relate to the question of giving information in the context of an inquiry into the conduct of Members of Parliament and civil servants. There the 'public interest' defence must be strongly in play in any resistance to having to give information when it is asked for: 'Parliament should not be content to be fobbed-off by some general statement about "the public interest" . . . consideration should be given to the appointment of a senior officer of Parliament tasked to inquire into the adequacy of refusals on public grounds to supply information.'[45]

The situation is quite different in the arena of giving the information on which an academic judgement is based. There it related to an individual (candidate) for an examination, a post or promotion, and only to such candidates in the plural if there is a question to be answered about why one person was preferred to another.

Are minutes adequate reasons?

There is no common law obligation to keep minutes of the meetings of corporations. The charters and statutes of pre-1992 universities do not require the keeping of minutes. The articles of government of higher education corporations in the 'new' sector speak of access to minutes as part of the general right to access to proceedings enjoyed by staff and students.[46] But committees of such bodies could not automatically be required to keep minutes or to give all members open access to them.

In any case, 'minutes' would only be 'reasons' if they were drafted so as to fulfil that function. They may be no more than a summary of conclusions reached with no account of the manner in which they were reached, and then minutes could not be adequate reasons.

Explaining decisions

There is a difference between giving an account of expenditure, or of persons consulted or involved in a research investigation or a peer review, or of other factual matters; and explaining why things were done in a certain way, and why that was the best way.[47] Matters of fact and matters of judgement of these sorts can be hard to separate where there is first a need to make a judgement as to whether the facts are facts, and then a need to make a judgement on the facts. For example, in deciding whether there is a case for promotion, it first has to be established what the facts are in support of the case. These are of two sorts – what books, or other research the candidate has to his credit, what teaching, what administration; and what its *quality* is. The first sort many universities allow candidates to have some say in.[48] The second type of 'fact' is actually a 'judgement' or 'opinion', and that is derived from referees and colleagues and the candidate is not usually allowed to see it or to comment on it.

The nature of evidence provided by referees is a crucial difficulty in peer review processes. On the face of it, it is a sensible means of discovering whether a candidate for a post or for promotion is well regarded by fellow scholars. But the referees are also the candidate's scholarly rivals, especially at senior levels. Referees are rarely all of one mind about a candidate and there can be glaring discrepancies of opinion. If that is doubted, it is only necessary to look at the range of opinion in published reviews of a given book. So referee evidence can be unreliable and contradictory.

It can also be hard to keep in sight the fact that referee evidence is only witness evidence, mere testimony, and testimony of the sort which in the Middle Ages was the equivalent of 'character'-witness. In a modern court, an accused person can call witnesses on his own side and his accusers can call witnesses on theirs, but it is essential to a fair trial that the conflicting points in their testimonies are visible to both sides and that the witnesses can be cross-examined. In that way malice, poor judgement and error on the part of the witnesses can be brought out. Where referees enjoy the protection of confidentiality of their identities and their comments that cannot happen.

A parallel situation arises in making appointments. The candidate submits the facts (a curriculum vitae, list of publications). Referees submit references and the appointing committee makes judgements. Once it is established what 'factual' evidence of both these sorts is in play, the next stage is to move to the forming of a judgement upon it, and it is there that difficulties of fairness and accountability proliferate.

Adequate reasons

How full do reasons have to be? A mere list of outcomes as in the list of persons to be promoted, or examination candidates to be 'passed' is not enough. The courts need not be satisfied with information which is so exiguous as to be meaningless.[49] There is a logical problem that if no reasons are given, for example, for not appointing someone to a post or not promoting him, then he cannot allege that negative things were said which he was not given an opportunity to answer (as the rules of natural justice would require if that were so).

The Australian Administrative Appeals Tribunal Act 1975, s. 43(2B) require a tribunal in giving its reasons to set out the finding on material questions of fact and the evidence or other material on which those findings were based. First-level decision-makers face similar requirements under section 13 of the Administrative Decisions (Judicial Review) Act 1977. What has to be stated is the findings of fact, the evidentiary basis and the reasoning process.

That is a good working definition of an adequate set of reasons. Reasons will be deemed inadequate if the appeal court is not able to ascertain the reasoning on which the decision was based; or if justice is not seen to have been done. That suggests that a manifestly absurd decision may be assailable under the Australian legislation on that ground alone. But perhaps more importantly, the presumption is that there is a public interest in the process of reasoning which has decided the case being exposed to the light of day.

R. v. Lancashire County Council, ex parte Huddleston [1986] 2 All E.R. 941 (at 947) Sir John Donaldson M.R. said that when the decisions of local authorities are challenged 'they should set out fully what they did and why, *so far as is necessary, fully and fairly to meet the challenge*'. So the nature of any challenge might determine what would, in that case, constitute adequate reasons.

That means it is not enough to deny that anything was done wrongly.

> No one should suppose that, where leave has been given by the Divisional Court to apply for judicial review on the ground that an authority has taken into account irrelevant considerations or has failed to take into account relevant considerations or has made an 'irrational' decision, it can be regarded as sufficient to say, 'We took into account all relevant considerations and took no account of any irrelevant considerations.' Where leave has been given on any such ground the authority would normally have to explain what it did and did not take into account.[50]

In a challenge to an 'academic judgement' decision this would be an important precedent, because it would require frank admission of the way the kinds of complexity we have been looking at had been handled.

A number of difficulties remain. The first is the question how far reasons can be altered or amended after the event. In *R. v. Westminster City Council, ex parte Ermakov* [1996] 2 All E.R. 302 a council had given reasons for finding someone intentionally homeless which were quite different from the reasons given in an affidavit later. The court held that that was quite different from elucidating the original reasons, and that the contradictory nature of the two accounts was a ground for striking out the decision. This would presumably imply that rationalization after the event of a decision for which there were no consciously formulated reasons at the time would be deemed inadequate. It would be necessary to show that the decisionmakers had had those reasons in their minds at the time of the making of the decision.

Reasons for not giving reasons

In the face of acts of administrative decision-making by managers to which academics may wish to object, it is proving increasingly necessary to ask whether a decision-making body or officer can be required to give reasons for a decision. The JUSTICE-All Souls Review of Administrative Law in the United Kingdom recommended that there should be a general statutory duty on administrators to give reasons for findings of fact on demand.[51] But where fact shades into opinion that may not be sufficient to ensure fairness, and there is much dragging of heels about the giving of reasons in this further area.

It was argued in *Doody* that: 'the giving of reasons may be inconvenient, but I can see no ground at all why it should be against the public interest: rather the reverse. That being so, I would ask simply: is refusal to give reasons fair? I would answer without hesitation that it is not.'[52] What was being pressed for here was not the giving of reasons so that the court could look at the merits of a decision but the giving of reasons so that it might be possible to see whether there had been a procedural error or an error of law which would be properly the courts' concern. In *Doody* it was held to be 'important that there should be an effective means of detecting the kind of error which would entitle the court to intervene'.[53]

There may be circumstances in which reasons could legitimately be refused – special provisions in a statute which make it unnecessary to give reasons. In *R. v. Secretary of State for the Home Department, ex parte Mohammed and Ali Fayed* (1996) *The Times,* 13 March, even in face of an apparently aberrant decision, the reasons were not required by the court. But there reliance was placed upon the British Nationality Act, s. 44(2), which expressly precludes any duty to give reasons. In that situation, the courts may be required to tolerate the admitted unfairness.

It is also a reason sometimes given for not giving reasons that it causes an undue administrative burden. But it is too easy for decision-makers to use that argument in order to protect themselves and to deny those whose interests are affected any means of challenging the decision. In *Matson* this excuse was considered to carry little weight against the importance of not causing unnecessary damage to someone's reputation and not creating a lingering and damaging uncertainty.[54]

The effect of failure to produce reasons, or adequate reasons

If it is found, on the evidence of a failure to produce them when they are asked for, that a decision-maker had no reasons, the decision falls. A court may send the decision back to the decision-maker to be made again, and this time to give reasons for it.[55] But more often there will be reasons already, though reasons which are not adequate.

In *Minister for Immigration and Ethnic Affairs v. Wu Shan Liang* (1996) 70 A.L.J.R. 568, it was held that an administrator's reasons are not to be construed minutely and finely with an eye keenly attuned to the perception of error, and to that extent are to be given a beneficial construction. However, there would presumably be a balance to be struck between this principle and the fineness of the lines to be drawn between, for example, candidates for promotion. So a court may have discretion to make what it will of the reasons or the failure to give reasons when they are required.

The direction in which the law's requirements are moving is clear; and it is increasingly towards requiring accountability by way not only of feedback or the giving of reasons, but also by way of providing avenues of redress if the feedback reveals that a mistake has been made. Accountability is not only about knowing what is wrong; it is also about being willing to put it right. Reasonableness ought to embrace both.

A letter published as a contribution to the *Times Higher Education Supplement* debate on peer review launched in January 1998, from Susan Greenfield, sketches elegantly the crudities of the then existing system.

> Certain scientists with no obviously special qualifications and in accordance with no obvious guidelines, have greatness thrust upon them, whereas others, even long-term recipients of major grants, are never invited to serve [on panels]. Such haphazard selection is ripe for old-boy exploitation . . . [On] the inner sanctum panels . . . the final decisions are made. Yet these discussions are never fully disclosed. Thus seemingly strong referees' reports can be trumped by comments not held to account and delivered anonymously in camera.[56]

That that is a scandal when it is set beside the law's requirements we have been looking at, needs no underlining.

Conclusion

For many at the receiving end of academic judgements, students and academic staff, these issues burn like no others. Upon fair and expert decision-making hang not only the budding careers of new graduates and doctoral students, but also the crowning recognition which is the fulfilment of a lifetime's work in academia, the award of grants to enable scientists to carry on with their work and of honours at the end of it.

Few areas are generating so many challenges, internal and external, from both students and staff. To judge from the often incoherent attempts to give account of what they are doing, encountered at hearings and inquiries from members of decision-making bodies and committees, there is a long way to go in the education of those who make peer-review judgements.

There appears to be very little understanding in universities of the requirements of procedural fairness in these matters and wholly inadequate protection against the admission of irrelevant considerations and other distorting factors.

Perhaps the most important missing element is the requirement to proceed on a basis of respect for others' scholarship. For peer-review is justifiable only if there is a presumption of equality between reviewer and reviewed. That has a place even between examiner and student. It has to do with human dignity as well as with that detachment and reflectiveness which ought to characterize all scholarly endeavour and all the critical activities of academics.

Conclusion

What ought to be a resigning matter in higher education? Sir Richard Scott had cause to reflect as a result of his conduct of the Arms to Iran Inquiry, upon the question what a Minister should do when he is called to account for a proved fault, or for a fault on the part of one of his civil servants. In his evidence to the Scott Inquiry, Sir Robin Butler, speaking as Cabinet Secretary, provided a working definition: 'I am using "accountability" to mean that the minister must always answer questions and give an account to Parliament for the action of his department . . . I am using "accountability" to leave out, as it were, the blame element of it.'[1] He goes on to argue that: 'It is not, I suggest, the willingness of ministers to resign that lies at the heart of accountability, but, rather, the obligation of ministers to give, or facilitate the giving, of information about the activities of their departments and about the actions and omissions of their civil servants.'[2] This is helpful because it places the emphasis not on punishment for wrongdoing but on putting right. A willingness to explain one's actions or decisions would again and again transform situations in universities where there has been muddle or unfairness or victimization, and a dispute has arisen. Sometimes blame is appropriate, but more often than not the situation could have been salvaged, lessons learned and better times ensured by catching things early and not being afraid to be open about what has happened.

Perhaps the key principle is of the rendering of account of a stewardship, as Sir David Maxwell Fyfe argued in 1956.[3] That would fit very well the nature and purpose of a university, as so long conceived; less well with the growing late twentieth-century Western idea that a university is a business.

The Committee of Vice-Chancellors and Principals in the UK showed little resolve in the face of successive government intrusions in the 1980s and 1990s. There has also been a lack of courage in standing up for the things of great importance for which universities exist. What is it a duty to resist? In what circumstances is 'a declaration of educational independence called for'?[4] The lesson of this study may be that those running universities ought to take the view that good governance in universities is protective rather than directive. There is a duty to create and defend an environment within which the work may go on, to keep the intellectual space open, for academics are pusillanimous souls. They need a degree of protection. Intellectual virtues are both 'fragile' and 'tough',[5] suggests Pelikan. They are fragile in that they are carried by extremely imperfect human beings who can be seduced by money and power like anyone else, or – at the other end of the scale – crushed to exhaustion by being forced to carry unreasonable teaching loads.

But intellectual virtues are tough in that, as any scholar will tell you, when those distorting pressures are eased, there is no greater pleasure than getting back into the library or laboratory and getting on with the 'real work'. Out of that return to base will occasionally come an ascent of a new Everest. The struggle is worth it for the rare conquest of an intellectual peak. The cowardly and petty would-be university politician will turn from tormenting those weaker than himself to a saintly dedication as he returns to his research. Unless that is worth the huge cost of it all some of the best minds of their generations live their academic lives in vain.

Notes and References

Introduction

1. Lord Howe of Aberavon (1996). Procedure at the Scott Inquiry. *Public Law* 445.
2. *Ex parte Forster re University of Sydney* [1963] N.S.W.R. 723 at 730.
3. Lewis, R. (1995). Disciplinary dismissals and redundancies in higher and further education. *Education and the law* 7(4): 211–19 at 213 and 219.
4. *R. v. Lancashire County Council, ex parte Huddleston* [1986] All E.R. 941 at 945.
5. *R. v. Lancashire County Council, ex parte Huddleston* [1986] All E.R. 941 at 947.
6. Committee on Standards in Public Life (1996). *Second Report*, para. 102. HMSO.
7. [1986] All E.R. 941 at 945.

Part 1/Introduction

1. Williams, S. (1977). Robbins plus Twenty. *Foundation Oration.* Birkbeck College, London.

Chapter 1 Values and the World of Scholarship

1. Cicero, *Academica,* I.i.
2. Ibid., I.i.
3. Cicero says in the *De natura deorum* (I.iii.6) that he has spent time on philosophy from his youth. His speeches, he points out, often reflect their views (*philosophorum sententiis*).
4. Pelikan, J. (1992). *The idea of a university: a Reexamination.* Yale. Yale University Press. p. 51.
5. Ibid., p. 51.
6. See Preface to my *Old Arts and new Theology* (1983). Oxford: Oxford University Press.
7. See my problems of *Authority in the Reformation Debates* (1992). Cambridge.
8. *De natura deorum* I.iv. 8–9.
9. Ibid., I.iv.8.
10. Augustine, *De Beata Vita.* Green, W.M. (ed.) (1970). CCSL 29: I.5.
11. Barnett, R. (1990). *The Idea of Higher Education.* Society for Research into Higher Education. Buckingham. Open University Press. p. 154.
12. Veblen, T. (1918). *The Higher Learning in America: A memorandum on the Conduct of Universities by Businessmen* (repr. London, 1994). p. 18.

13. Pelikan, op. cit., p. 61.
14. Clark, B.R. (1983). Governing the Higher Education System. *The Structure and Governance of Higher Education*, Shattock, M. (ed.). Society for Research into Higher Education Monographs. Guildford. 19–45, p. 20.
15. Ibid., p. 23.
16. Newman, J.H. (1996). *The Idea of a University*, Turner, F.M. (ed.). Yale. Yale University Press. pp. 5–6.
17. Pelikan, op. cit., p. 58.
18. Veblen, op. cit., pp. 16–17.
19. Ibid., p. 17.
20. Newman to Whately, 14 November 1826, *Letters and Diaries*, Ker, I. and Gornall, T. (eds) (1978). Oxford. Oxford University Press. Vol. I, p. 307.
21. Pelikan, op. cit., p. 59.
22. Newman to Whately, 14 November 1826, op. cit., p. 306.
23. Whately to Newman, 17 November 1826, op. cit., p. 308.
24. Ibid., p. 308.
25. Newman to Whately, 1 November 1828, op. cit., p. 305.
26. See pp. 90ff.
27. 'The main argument for the repayment by the student of part or all of the cost of higher education is *distributional equity*. It is regarded as contradictory to redistributive objectives that the potentially affluent student should receive subsidies from a society the majority of whose members have lower incomes than the beneficiaries of higher education.' Maynard, A. (1985). *Experiment with choice in education*. London. Institute of Economic Affairs. p. 51.
28. Tapper, T. and Salter, B. (1992). *Oxford, Cambridge and the Changing idea of the University*. Buckingham. Open University Press. p. 4.

Chapter 2 Rights and Responsibilities: Academic Freedom and Professional Ethics

1. Betteridge, H.T. (1968–9). Academic Freedom. *Universities Quarterly* 23: 189–202.
2. Price, G. (1983–4). Universities today: between the corporate state and the market. *Universities Quarterly* 38: 43–58.
3. *Utinam quietis temporibus . . . haec inter nos studia exercere possemus*. Cicero, *Academica*, I.i.
4. Newman to Edward Smedley, 10 February 1826, *Letters and Diaries*, Ker, I. and Gornall, T. (eds) (1978). Oxford. Oxford University Press. Vol. I, p. 276.
5. Holmes, O.W. quoted in White, G.E. (1993). *Justice Oliver Wendell Holmes*. Oxford/New York. Oxford University Press. p. 444.
6. Ibid., p. 444.
7. The 1988 Act speaks of 'privileges'.
8. Education Reform Act 1988, s. 202.
9. One bulletin includes the 'right of the teacher to criticize university affairs' as lying 'within the concept of *academic* freedom of expression'. *AUT (UK) Bulletin* (1974) 54: 8, cited in *Rigg v. University of Waikato (Commissaries' Report)* [1984] 1 N.Z.L.R. 149 at 202.
10. *Rigg v. University of Waikato* [1984] 1 N.Z.L.R. 149 at 151.
11. *Rigg v. University of Waikato (Commissaries' Report)* [1984] 1 N.Z.L.R. 149 at 201.
12. See pp. 90ff.
13. *Rigg v. University of Waikato (Commissaries' Report)* [1984] 1 N.Z.L.R. 149 at 195.
14. *Rigg v. University of Waikato* [1984] 1 N.Z.L.R. 149 at 151.

15. Sunstein, C.R. (1993). *Democracy and the problem of free speech.* New York. The Free Press. p. 198. Cf. *Doe v. University of Michigan,* 721 F. Supp. 852 (ED Mich. 1989) *UNM Post, Inc v. Bd of Regents,* 774 F. Supp. 1163 (ED Wis. 1991).
16. Sunstein, op. cit., pp. 197ff.
17. See p. 125.
18. By extension there must be an ethical requirement of protection of the teacher who seeks to defend a student's interests against pressure from senior officers discouraging him from doing so.
19. Sayers, D. *Gaudy Night* (London: Chivers, 1935), p. 256.
20. Ibid., pp. 256–7.
21. Sayers, op. cit., *Gaudy Night* (London, 1935), p. 260.
22. Ibid., p. 261.
23. Ibid., p. 259.
24. Ibid., p. 259.
25. Ibid., p. 258.
26. Newman, J.H. (1996). *The Idea of a University.* Turner, F.M. (ed.). Yale. Yale University Press. Discourse, VI, p. 91.
27. Ibid., Discourse, V, p. 77.
28. Ibid., p. 9.
29. Ibid., p. 8.
30. Ibid., p. 7.
31. Pelikan, J. (1992). *The Idea of a University: a Reexamination.* Yale. Yale University Press. p. 50.
32. Ibid., p. 49.
33. Ibid., p. 50.
34. See pp. 147ff.
35. Now advocates and attornies have always been admitted in the colonial courts by the judges and the judges only. This is deemed to be inalienably a judicial duty. The benchers of the Inns of Court are only 'the agents of the judges in calling to the Bar' *Manning's Sergeant's case* (1840) 139–40, cited in *R. v. Visitors to Lincoln's Inn, ex parte Calder* and *Same v. Same, ex parte Persaud* [1992] W.L.R. 994 at 1004.
36. *Manning's Sergeant's case* (1840) 139–40, cited in *R. v. Visitors to Lincoln's Inn, ex parte Cale* and *Same v. Same, ex parte Persaud* [1992] W.L.R. 994 at 1004.
37. Whincup, M.H. (1993). The exercise of university disciplinary powers. *Education and the Law* 5(1): 19–31, 20.
38. This last point is important, since reasons cannot necessarily be required in a court of law.
39. CAFAS Report. Council for Academic Freedom and Academic Standards. *Raising concerns and handling the consequences* (London, 1996).
40. University of North London Procedures, 8.5.
41. Cases known to the author through work with CAFAS.
42. On the employee's fiduciary duty, see pp. 90ff.
43. *Derbyshire County Council v. Times Newspapers Ltd* [1993] 2 W.L.R. 449, H.L.

Chapter 3 Value for Money

1. I am indebted to Dennis Farrington of the University of Stirling for bringing this clause to my attention.
2. 'It is both intellectually and politically dangerous simply to identify' freedom of inquiry, 'as its latter-day defenders sometimes do, as a corollary derived from

the right of free speech guaranteed by the First Amendment of the Constitution of the United States and by equivalent political constitutions in other states'. Pelikan, J. (1992). *The idea of a University: a Reexamination.* Yale. Yale University Press. p. 48.
3. It appears that Rygge may have voted on Wyclif's side. *Fasciculi Zizaniorum,* Rolls Series, p. 113.
4. Events described in Hudson, A. (1986). Wycliffism in Oxford, 1381–1411, in *Wyclif in his Times.* Kenny, A. (ed.). Oxford. 67–84, p. 67.
5. On this notion, see Pelikan, op. cit., p. 61.
6. *Allocation of the Science Budget.* Office of Science and Technology, 15 January 1997, para. 19.
7. See pp. 133ff, 150, 186.
8. Extract from letter from Edwards, A.W.F. Reader in Mathematical Biology, to the Secretary General of the Faculties in Cambridge, 1989.
9. Pelikan, op. cit., p. 51.
10. Pelikan, op. cit., p. 55, citing Newman, *Idea* II.ix.4.
11. Pelikan, op. cit., p. 51.
12. See pp. 133, 150, 186 on confidentiality.
13. Reported in *The Lancet* (19 April 1997) 349: 1149 and in *Science* (25 April 1997) 276: 525.
14. Reported in *Science* (25 April 1997) 276: 525.
15. The Authors' Licensing and Collecting Society has been an active force in assisting authors to get financial rewards from photocopying of their work.
16. 'Copyright in a work is infringed by a person who without the licence of the copyright owner does, or authorises another to do, any of the acts restricted by the copyright' (Copyright, Designs and Patents Act 1988, II.xvi.2). It is not infringed by the use of the work for purposes of research or education (III.xxix).
17. Copyright, Designs and Patents Act 1988, II.xvi.1e. 'Adaptation' means making a translation, turning a play into something which is not a dramatic work, or vice versa; alteration or arrangement of a computer programme or translation of it; arranging or transcribing a musical work; changing the language or code of a computer program (II.xxi.3).
18. Boydell, C. and Gaunt, R. (1995). Patents and Innovation. *Oxford Innovation News* 15: 8–11.
19. Bainbridge, D. (1994). *Software Copyright Law.* London. Pitman. Bainbridge, D. (1996). *Introduction to Computer Law.* 3rd edn. London.
20. Ducor, P. (1997). Are patents and research compatible? *Nature* 387: 13–14.
21. Gilbert, R.J. and Shapiro, C. (1996). An economic analysis of unilateral refusals to license intellectual property. *Proceedings of the National Academy of Science USA* 93: 12749–12755 at 12749.
22. Ibid., 12750.
23. Ducor, op. cit., at 13.
24. Gilbert and Shapiro, op. cit.
25. Neale, A.D. and Goyder, D.G. (1960). *The Antitrust Laws of the United States of America.* 3rd edn., 1980. Cambridge. Cambridge University Press. p. 15.
26. Ibid., pp. 22–3.
27. Quoted in Neale and Goyder, op. cit., p. 25.
28. Chief Justice Hughes, quoted in Neale and Goyder, op. cit., p. 23.
29. Neale and Goyder, op. cit., p. 29.
30. Gilbert and Shapiro, op. cit., 12750.

31. Ibid., p. 12750.
32. Neale and Goyder, op. cit., p. 288.
33. The attribution of all output to the university where a member of staff is based on 31.3.96 is a matter on which HEFCE says, in a recent letter to Professor Fergus Millar, that it went to some trouble to consult. The alternative envisaged was to attribute the work to the university where the individual was 'located' when the work counted in the assessment was produced. The response to the consultation was apparently strongly in favour of continuing on the current rule, which was in force in the 1992 round. The 'rationale' of this was that the Research Assessment Exercise in 1996 will influence the allocation of resources from 1997 onwards, and ought, therefore, to place those resources at the disposal of the departments where the producers are now to be found.
34. I am indebted to a document produced by the AUT/NATFHE Confederation, *Intellectual Property in the Workplace* (1993) in the form of a report of a conference held in November of that year for reference to two cases, *Stevenson-Jordan v. Macdonald* (1952) and *Noah v. Schuba* (1991).
35. Copyright, Designs and Patents Act 1988, II.xi.2.
36. These examples are taken from *Intellectual Property in the Workplace*, op. cit.
37. Reported in *Science* (25 April 1997) 276: 524.
38. Letter from Gilson, M.K., *Science* 275 (3 January 1997).
39. Letter from de Sa, P. and Sagar, A. *Science* (6 December 1996) 274.
40. But the right is not infringed unless it has been asserted in accordance with section 78. (Copyright, Designs and Patents Act 1988, s.87.1.lxxvii.1).
41. Copyright, Designs and Patents Act 1988, s.88.1.lxxxviii.1.
42. Copyright, Designs and Patents Act 1988, s.79.3a.lxxix.3a.
43. Copyright, Designs and Patents Act 1988, s.80.2a–b.lxxx.2a–b. The exceptions to this specified (s.81.lxxxi) are unlikely to arise on the academic scene.
44. Copyright, Designs and Patents Act 1988, s.82.1a.lxxxii.1a.
45. Copyright, Designs and Patents Act 1988, s.88.4a.lxxxviii.4a.
46. Hillman, H. (1996). What price intellectual honesty? *Confronting the Experts*, Marting, D. (ed.). State University of New York. Albany. pp. 99–130.
47. *Allocation of the Science Budget*, op. cit., para. 22.
48. Copyright, Designs and Patents Act 1988, IV.lxxxiv.1a.
49. Letter from Wooley, C.F. *Science* (6 December 1996) 274.
50. Letter from Levy, G.N. *Science* (6 December 1996) 274.
51. Hillman, H. (1997). Parafraud in biology. *Science and Engineering Ethics* 3: 121–136 at 126.
52. de Sa and Sagar, op. cit.
53. Letter from White, B. *Science* (24 January 1997) 275.
54. Hillman, 'Parafraud in biology', op. cit., p. 126.
55. Reported in *Science* (31 January 1997) 275: 610.
56. Veblen, T. (1918). *The Higher Learning in America: A Memorandum on the Conduct of Universities by Businessmen* repr. London, 1994. p. 5.
57. Ibid., p. 93.
58. Ibid., p. 87.
59. Ibid., p. 88.
60. *Nature* (1 May 1997) p. 387.
61. Higgins, C. quoted in *Nature* (1 May 1997) 387 at 6.
62. Ibid., at 6.
63. Hillman, 'Parafraud in biology', op. cit., at 127.

64. Ibid., at 128.
65. Hillman, What price intellectual honesty? op. cit., at 105.
66. Ibid., at 102.
67. *R. v. Parliamentary Commissioner, ex parte Dyer* [1994] 1 W.L.R. 621 at 623.
68. Fox, J.D. (1997). Leasing the Ivory Tower at a Social Justice University. *Organization and Environment* 10: 259–77 at 259.
69. Soley, L. (1995). *Leasing the ivory tower: the corporate takeover of academia.* Boston South End and Big money on campus. (1997) *Dollars and Sense* 210: 24–7.
70. Fox, op. cit., at 260.
71. Fox, op. cit.
72. *Epistolae Academicae Oxoniensis* (1898) Anstey, H. (ed.). Oxford. Oxford University Press. II.430.
73. Soley, op. cit., pp. 14–15.

Chapter 4 The Public Interest

1. Fisher, H.A.L. (1922). *Royal Commission on Oxford and Cambridge Universities* Appendix 4.
2. See pp. 14–30 on the ethics of scholarship.
3. Jaeger, W. (1939). *Paedeia,* tr. Highet, G. Oxford, remains a classic study.
4. For the sophisticated, philosophy provided in fact what were tantamount to systems and codes for living. At a lowlier 'civic' level came Roman 'civic' religion.
5. Farrington, J.D. (1994). *The Law of Higher Education.* London. Butterworths. 3.6.
6. In Council Directive (EEC) 71/305 'a body governed by public law' is defined as any body 'established for the specific purpose of meeting needs in the general interest, not having an industrial or commercial character'. This does not cover the question of who established them.
7. *Foster v. British Gas plc* [1990] 3 All E.R. 897 at 905.
8. Referred to in *Foster v. British Gas plc* [1990] 3 All E.R. 897 at 905.
9. Shattock, M. (1994). *The UGC and the Management of British Universities.* Society for Research into Higher Education. Buckingham. Open University Press. p. 33.
10. Owen, S.G. (1986). Research funding in *Standards and Criteria in Higher Education,* Moodie, G.C. (ed.). London. p. 140.
11. Veblen, T. (1918). *The Higher Learning in America: A memorandum on the Conduct of Universities by Businessmen* (repr. London, 1994). p. 80.
12. Ibid., p. 81.
13. Ibid., p. 67.
14. Ibid., p. 73.
15. *The Haldane Report* (1918). Ministry of Reconstruction.
16. 'What is rarely mentioned is that Haldane saw this model as a temporary device which would have to be superseded by a different structure, possibly a Department of Intelligence and Research, once government research expanded further.' (Ibid., 35).
17. 'The transition of the research council model from, as Haldane saw it, an administrative compromise with a limited life-expectancy, to an ideological symbol of the necessary autonomy of research to be protected as a sacrosanct principle in a civilized society, was accomplished with remarkable ease in the same way as the University Grants Commission had gained its own mossy respectability. One of the reasons for this and the state's lack of concern was the small amount of public money involved: in 1939, expenditure on the research councils amounted to £1,328,000 (ACSP 1964). In 1947, the research councils

became part of the general responsibility for civil science of the newly formed Advisory Council on Scientific Policy (ACSP). The ACSP advised the Lord President to the Privy Council who was responsible to Parliament for the research councils and their establishments', Tapper, T. and Salter, B. (1992). *Oxford, Cambridge and the Changing idea of the University.* Buckingham. Open University Press. p. 23.

18. Griffith, J. (1989). *Universities and the State: the next steps.* Council for Academic Freedom and Democracy. p. 12.
19. In Kurland, C.G. (1997). Beating Scientists into Plowshares. *Science* 276: 761–2 at 761 the example is cited of the refusal of the pharmaceutical industry to develop a new generation of antibiotics to meet the need which arises as pathogens become resistant to the old ones.
20. Cf. Ibid., at 761.
21. Address by the Chairman of the UGC to the Committee of Vice-Chancellors and Principals (CVCP) 24 October 1980.
22. Rice, C.D. *The Scotsman,* 8 January 1997.
23. *Allocation of the Science Budget.* Office of Science and Technology. 15 January 1997, para. 1. In its submission to Dearing, the confederation of British Industries wanted to see some favouring of research of national strategic importance. See *Special Digest Report* of the CVCP on submissions to Dearing, 1996–7, p. 5.
24. *Allocation of the Science Budget,* op. cit., para. 24.
25. The HEFCE circular of February 1997: *Joint Research Equipment Initiative: HEFCE and DENI Awards.*
26. This HEFCE text was quoted by John Griffith in his article in *The Times Higher Education Supplement,* 7 March 1997.
27. Zemsky, R. and Massy, W.F. Toward an understanding of our current predicaments. *Change* (November/December 1995). pp. 41–9.
28. Trani, E.P. (1997). The changing American college presidency. *Perspectives* 1: 34–39 at 37.
29. The HEFCE circular of February 1997, op. cit.
30. Kurland, op. cit., at 762.
31. Quoted in Shattock, op. cit., p. 30.
32. The HEFCE circular of February 1997, op. cit.
33. Kurland, op. cit., p. 761.
34. Ibid., p. 762.
35. Overseen by the Office of Science and Technology which is part of the Department of Trade and Industry.
36. The HEFCE circular of February 1997, op. cit.
37. The US pattern has a different history from the British one. Boards of control rather than academics established the first American colleges, and that meant that from the beginning non-academics could control academic activities. Trani, op. cit., p. 34.
38. *Review of Institutional Lessons to be Learned 1994–6,* Rowe, P. (ed.) (1997). University of Lancaster.
39. Kurland, op. cit., p. 761.
40. *Allocation of the Science Budget,* op. cit., para. 4.
41. Ibid., para. 16.
42. Ibid., para. 18.
43. See pp. 34ff, p. 60.
44. *Allocation of the Science Budget,* op. cit., para. 28.

Part 2/Introduction

This is a defining characteristic in the 1992 Further and Higher Education Act.

Chapter 5 Structure and Purpose

1. *St David's College, Lampeter v. Ministry of Education,* SI 1948, No. 1655 at 561.
2. Christie, J. (1976). The power to award degrees. *Public Law* 358–96 at 389–90, with a footnote on the sparse literature available on the principles.
3. Whereas, in principle, a monastic scholar was an enclosed scholar and his work left the monastery without him when it was copied for distribution.
4. *Peripateticorum emulator factus sum.* He did not of course understand quite what Aristotle meant by a 'peripatetic'.
5. *Diversas disputando perambulans provincias.* Abaelardus, P. (1967). *Historia Calamitatum,* Monfrin, G. (ed.). Paris. pp. 63–4.
6. *Et nonnumquam superior in disputando viderer.* Ibid., pp. 64–5.
7. In Oxford and Cambridge the move from BA status to MA status still confers lifetime rights of membership in the University. 'Beginners were members of the same organism as the master, because [they were] engaged in learning the same craft.' Marjorie Reeves continues: 'secondly, that there are progressive stages in learning and that theoretically all are open to all; thirdly, that those at the half way stage can teach beginners; fourthly, that because the craft of learning is a mystery the masters must keep a monopoly of it and demonstrate their solidarity in defence of its standards.' Reeves, M. (1969). The European University in Mediaeval Times. *Higher Education: Demand and Response,* Niblett, W.R. (ed.). London.
8. See pp. 139ff.
9. 'Higher education is the the only profession in which the makers of the product hire it back . . . There is a pattern of hereditary succession through cycles of master–disciple relationships. Such a system hardly inspires young men to radical departures or rebel ideas that might distress their seniors.' Dodds, H.W. (1962). *The American president: Educator or caretaker.* New York. p. 126.
10. Jaspers, K. (1959). *The Idea of a University.* Boston. Boston University Press. p. 71.
11. Cornford, F.M. (1908). *Microcosmographia Academica.* Repr. 1922, new edn. Cambridge, 1994.
12. Ibid., p. 3.
13. Ibid., pp. 12–13.
14. Ibid., p. 2.
15. Ibid., pp. 14–15.
16. Ibid., pp. 14–15.
17. Ibid., pp. 14–15.
18. Ibid., p. 17.
19. Ibid., p. 18.
20. Ibid., p. 18.
21. Ibid., p. 18.
22. Ibid., p. 19.
23. Ibid., p. 20.
24. Ibid., p. 21.
25. Ibid., p. 8.
26. Ibid., p. 23.
27. Ibid., p. 10.

28. Ibid., p. 22.
29. Ibid., p. 23.
30. Clark, B.R. (1983). Governing the Higher Education System, in *The Structure and Governance of Higher Education,* Shattock, M. (ed.). Society for Research into Higher Education Monographs. 19–45, p. 20.
31. Ibid., p. 22.
32. Ibid., p. 27.

Chapter 6 Institutional Autonomy: Academics and Managers

1. Veblen, T. (1918). *The Higher Learning in America: A memorandum on the Conduct of Universities by Businessmen* (repr. London, 1994), p. 236.
2. University of Cambridge, Statutes of 1559, Chapter 50,43.
3. *The Cambridge Case, being an Exact narrative of all the proceedings against the Vice-Chancellour and delegates of the University for refusing to admit Alban Francis . . . to the Degree of Master of Arts.* 1969 London. pp. 1–16, p. 1.
4. See *Oxford University Gazette,* Michaelmas term, 1996. See also Tapper, T. and Salter, B. (1992). *Oxford, Cambridge and the Changing idea of the University.* Buckingham. Open University Press.
5. See the discussion of what happened at the University of Lancaster in *The University of Lancaster; Review of Institutional lessons to be learned 1994 to 1996* (1997) Rowe, P. (ed.). Lancaster. University of Lancaster.
6. Reporting in 1998.
7. Statute A of the University's *Statutes and Ordinances* (1997). Cambridge.
8. Education Reform Act 1988, s. 124A.
9. Education Reform Act 1988, s. 124A.
10. Swansea Institute of Higher Education and Southampton Institute of Higher Education were cases in point in 1997.
11. (1996) para. 70.
12. Munro, C. (1987). *Studies in constitutional law.* London. Butterworths. p. 185 (Chapter 9).
13. Noticeable in the funding of science. See pp. 30ff.
14. See articles by Richard Mayou in the *Oxford Magazine* (1997). 145 'After the General Board' and Evans, G.R. '*Fiat iustitia: ruat caelum*'.
15. Caldwell, J.L. Judicial Review of Universities: the Visitor and the Visited. *Canterbury Law Review* 1: 307 at 318.
16. Committee on Standards in Public Life. *Second Report* (1996) para. 104.
17. Statement by the University of Newcastle, submitted to the Committee on Standards in Public Life (the Nolan Committee) and quoted in its *Second Report* (1996) p. 31.
18. Cf. *Guide for Governing Bodies of Universities and Colleges in England and Wales,* (1995) Committee of University Chairmen, and *Guide for College Governors,* (1995). Further Education Funding Council for England.
19. Harlow, C. (1976). Administrative reaction to judicial review. *Public Law* 116–33 at 117.
20. Ibid., at 117.
21. It has been suggested that failure to implement the judgement of a court might count as maladministration, but that has not been directly tested. Harlow, op. cit., at 131.
22. Professor Raj Rao.

23. *Staff communication review at Southampton Institute,* November 1996, conducted by Geoffrey Hall.
24. Ibid.
25. Ibid.
26. Ibid.
27. *The Times Higher Education Supplement,* 21 March 1997.
28. *University of Oxford, Commission of Inquiry (Franks Commission), Evidence* (1965). Oxford. Part 11.
29. Lord Curzon of Kedleston (1910). *Report of the Hebdomadal Council on Principles and methods of University Reform,* pp. vi and ix.
30. *Royal Commission on Oxford and Cambridge Universities* (1922). London. Appendix 1.
31. Tapper and Salter, op. cit., p. 46.
32. Wass Report, Synopsis, *Cambridge University Reporter* (1989). p. 616.
33. *Cambridge University Reporter* (1989). p. 619.
34. Tapper and Salter, op. cit., p. 44.
35. Ibid., p. 44.
36. *Cambridge University Reporter* (1967). p. 345.
37. Veblen, op. cit., p. 94.
38. See pp. 68ff.
39. Veblen, op. cit., p. 94.
40. Wall, A. and Rowden, R. (1994). Managerial accountability, in *Whistleblowing in the Health Service,* ed. Hunt, G. (ed.). London. p. 23.
41. 139, Fourth Week, Hilary Term, 1997, pp. 4–5.
42. Pollitt, C. (1990). Doing business in the Temple? Managers and Quality Assurance in the Public Services. *Public Administration* 68(4): 435–52 at 438.
43. Ibid., at 439.
44. 139, Fourth Week, Hilary Term, 1997, pp. 4–5.
45. The 1988 Act requires that a policy decision is to be taken in advance of the identification of individual lecturers who are to be made redundant.

Chapter 7 Membership, Employment, Office

1. *Great Western Railway v. Bater* [1930] 3 K.B. 266 at 273–4. This has been an important distinction in the cases about the employment status of ministers of religion.
2. *Vidyodaya University of Ceylon and others v. Silva* [1964] 3 All E.R. 865 at 867. And if there is an office there is a right to a hearing if it is proposed to deprive someone of it. Caldwell, J.L. (1982). Judicial Review of Universities: the Visitor and the Visited. *Canterbury Law Review* 1: 307 at 320–1.
3. Dennis Farrington argues that there is no reason why, in principle, membership of a university should not be extended to all staff, not merely the academic staff, though that might throw up some questions about the collegiality of the community of scholarship formed by a *universitas* and the gild as a gild of 'experts' in a skill. Farrington, D.J. (1994). *The Law of Higher Education.* London. 2.77–80.
4. Because they are not involved in the academic work of the University.
5. Some members of the academic staff of Oxford and Cambridge are lifetime members because they are MAs of the University and their membership does not depend upon their employment status. Many have lifetime membership of both universities upon incorporation.

6. It has been suggested that a lingering sense that an educational establishment behaves like a parent has encouraged the courts to take the line that students are not entitled to complain of breach of natural justice in the handling of their complaints. (That argument is weakened by the fact that in England students over 18 are now legally adults.) In *R. v. Aston University Senate, ex p. Roffey* [1969] 2 W.L.R. 1418 it was found that students are entitled to be treated according to the rules of natural justice.
7. *Thomas v. University of Bradford* [1987] 1 A.C. 795 at 799.
8. The powers of a head of department may especially need definition in that respect.
9. Cf. Whincup, M.H. (1993). The exercise of university disciplinary powers. *Education and the Law.* 5i 19–31 at 29.
10. Farrington, op. cit., 2.78 and cf. draft 1994 Statutes of the University of London, cited there.
11. These are listed by Hoffmann, J. in *Hines v. Birkbeck College* [1985] 3 All E.R. Ch.D. 157 at 165.
12. *Re Wislang's Application* [1984] N.I. 63 at 80–1, *per* Kelly L.J.
13. Smith, P.M. (1986). Visitation of the Universities: A Ghost from the past. *New Law Journal* 136: 665.
14. *Murdoch University v. Bloom* [1980] W.A.R. 193 at 198.
15. *Murdoch University v. Bloom* [1980] W.A.R. 193 at 198.
16. Smith, op. cit., at 665–6.
17. *Re Wisling's application* [1984] N.I. 163.
18. *Hines v. Birkbeck College* [1985] 3 All E.R. 156.
19. *Vaneck v. Governors of the University of Alberta* [1975] 5 W.W.R. 429 at 434.
20. In *Vaneck v. Governors of the University of Alberta* [1975] 5 W.W.R. 429 the authority for the university's rules was identified by the court as The Universities Act, RSA 1970 c. 378, and therefore as statutory. But at the same time it deemed them internal and, therefore, outside any possibility of remedy being sought on a basis of breach of contract. 'The committees and their functions were established not as bodies prescribed by statute as a matter of public policy, but rather as a matter of choice in the exercise of a discretion granted by the statute relating to affairs internal to the university.' In *Re Bezeau and Ontario Institute for Studies in Education* [1982] 134 D.L.R. (3d) 99 the committee whose decision was being challenged was a 'promotion and tenure committee', so a single committee may in practice have responsibility for at least these two kinds of decision.
21. *Vaneck v. Governors of the University of Alberta* [1975] 5 W.W.R. 429 at 431.
22. This may not, however, guarantee security. See *Page v. Visitor of Hull University* [1993] 1 All E.R. 97.
23. Though there have been cases lately where even senior appointments have been terminated before the end of a period of probation.
24. *Re Paine and University of Toronto* [1981] 131 D.L.R. 325 at 330.
25. Education Reform Act 1988, s. 204.
26. Education Reform Act 1988, s. 204.
27. Education Reform Act 1988, s. 204(2).
28. This is not, therefore, a case in which the exclusivity of the visitor's jurisdiction was the central issue, but rather one in which it was asked whether there had been an *error of law* on his part within that jurisdiction, in the way he had interpreted the statutes.
29. *AUT v. University of Newcastle* [1987] I.C.R. 317.

Chapter 8 Making the Rules: Internal Legislation

1. Griffith, J. Universities and the State: the next steps. *Council for Academic Freedom and Democracy* (November, 1989).
2. The Model Statute is now incorporated into the statutes of all the old universities, with Privy Council approval required in each case.
3. Instruments of government may be found in Schedule 7A to the 1988 Act, which is now substituted by Schedule 6 to the Further and Higher Education Act 1922. But the actual articles on dismissals are in Annex C (Articles of Government for Higher Education Corporations) to a letter of 3 November 1988 issued by the DES to the institutions to which it applies.
4. Cross, C. and Bailey Cross, S. (1986). *Local Government Law.* 7th edn London. Sweet and Maxwell. p. 107.
5. This dual teleology is Aristotelian; it has to do both with the nature of things and with their ends.
6. Farrington, D.J. (1994). *The Law of Higher Education.* London. Butterworths. 2.75.
7. These reasons are listed by Carr, C.T. (1921). *Delegated legislation.* Cambridge. Cambridge University Press. Chapter 3.
8. On what follows, see, too, Farrington, op. cit., 2.67, p. 58.
9. *Attorney-General v. Great Eastern Railway* (1880) 5 App. Cas. 473 at 478, *per* Lord Selborne.
10. *Amalgamated Society of Railway Servants v. Osborne* [1910] A.C. 87 at 97, *per* Lord Lacnaghten.
11. *Ashbury Railway Carriage Co v. Riche* (1875) L.R. 7 H.L. 653 at 670.
12. *Attorney-General v. Great Eastern Railway* (1880) 5 App. Cas. 473 at 486, *per* Lord Watson.
13. Cf. Laws, Sir John (1995). Law and Democracy. *Public Law* 72.
14. Wade, W.H.R. *Administrative Law.* 7th edn. Oxford. Oxford University Press. p. 859.
15. Wall, A. and Rowden, R. (1994). Managerial accountability, in *Whistleblowing in the Health Service,* Hunt, G. (ed.). London. Arnold. p. 23.
16. The Higher Education Funding Council for England has declared: 'The Council also wishes to look forward and to be able to *shape the distribution* of funds, ensuring that the overall balance of distribution fulfils its objectives and *responds to national priorities.* It therefore wishes to include a *policy* factor in setting the quanta which will allow it to influence the distribution between subjects, based on national needs and international standing . . . In future the Council proposes to look first at whether the institutions themselves *are responding to national needs.* However, it may also wish to reinforce institutional decisions or to anticipate areas of need' (emphasis added).
17. *Patel v. University of Bradford Senate* [1979] 2 All E.R. 582 CA.
18. The Articles of Association for London Guildhall University (55).
19. Ibid., (59).
20. See pp. 90ff. on relationships of obedience.
21. The Articles of Association for London Guildhall University (40(b)).
22. Ibid., (36).
23. Ibid., (36).
24. Ibid., (36).
25. Ibid., (40).
26. Ibid., (40).

27. Kindersley, V.C. in *Thomson v. London University* (1864) 33 L.J. Ch. at 634.
28. Deakin, S. and Morris, G.S. (1995). *Labour Law.* London. p. 213.
29. Wall and Rowden, op. cit., pp. 25–6.
30. See pp. 107–8, 125, 157.
31. In *Re Civil Service Salaries: EC Commission v. EC Council* [1973] C.M.L.R. 639 the Council was required to follow the published guidelines.
32. *Attorney-General of Hongkong v. Ng Yuen Shiu* [1983] 2 A.C. 629, citing *R. v. Liverpool Corporation, ex parte Liverpool Taxi Fleet Operators' Association* [1972] 2 Q.B. 299.
33. *R. v. Home Secretary, ex parte Ruddock* [1988] 1 W.L.R. 1482.
34. *R. v. Civil Service Appeal Board, ex parte Cunningham* [1991] 4 All E.R. 310 at 319.
35. *Lloyd v. McMahon* [1987] A.C. 625 at 702–3; [1987] All E.R. 1118 at 1161.
36. *Oakes v. Sidney Sussex College, Cambridge* [1988] 1 All E.R. 1004 at 1014.
37. Wade, op. cit., p. 875.
38. Ibid., p. 879.
39. Cf. Wade, op. cit., p. 892.
40. De Smith, (1995). *Judicial Review of Administrative Action.* London. Sweet and Maxwell. p. 122.
41. De Smith, op. cit., p. 123.
42. An MPhil student appeal in the University of Cambridge in 1997 raised this difficulty.

Chapter 9 The Rights of the Subordinate and the Insubordinate

1. *Robinson v. Crompton Parkinson Ltd* [1978] I.C.R. 401 at 403.
2. *Fyfe and McGrouther Ltd v. Byrne* [1977] I.R.L.R. 29, *per* Lord McDonald. In *De Buse and others v. McCarthy and Another* [1942] 1 K.B. 156 at 160 'the occasion of the publication was privileged, and . . . ratepayers had a common interest with the council in the publication of the whole of the report of the committee contained in the agenda'. The report in question gave the names of employees who were alleged to have stolen petrol. Two had been convicted of doing so, and they had given the names of others who they said had been 'in it' with them, although those employees had emphatically denied that they had had anything to do with it. The report did not say that the committee had found these allegations proved, but it nevertheless recommended that they should be removed from their existing positions and transferred. Copies of this notice were put up near the Town Hall and sent to all public libraries. The relationship between 'interest' and 'duty' was explored in this case. The Council, it was argued (at 165) had no duty to make the report available to the ratepayers but it might have had an interest. The man in the street might find it unacceptable for such statements to be published in this way just because 'the [local] public' had (arguably) a right to know.
3. Martin, J.P. (1985). *Hospitals in Trouble.* Oxford. Blackwell.
4. Hillman, H. (1966). What price intellectual honesty, in *Confronting the Experts,* Martin, B. (ed.). State University of New York, Albany. pp. 119–20.
5. University of Hull, *Policy on the Reporting of Serious Malpractice and Abuse* (1997) 1.
6. Pilgrim, D. (1994). Explaining abuse and inadequate care, in *Whistleblowing in the Health Service,* Hunt, G. (ed.). London. Arnold. p. 82.
7. See *Cambridge University Reporter* (1997).
8. Cover, M. and Humphreys, G. (1994). Whistleblowing in English Law, in *Whistleblowing: Subversion or Corporate Citizenship,* Vinten, G. (ed.). London. pp. 89–105.

9. McHale, J. (1995). Whistleblowing in American Health Care, in Hunt, G. (ed.) op. cit., p. 125.
10. Howard, J.C. (1988) Current developments in whistleblower protection. *Labor Law Journal* 39(2): 67.
11. Case described in McHale, J. op. cit., p. 123.
12. Ibid., p. 123, citing *Maus v. National Living Centers* (633 S.W. 2d 674 Texa. Civ. App. 1982).
13. Benson, G.C.S. (1994), in Codes of ethics and whistleblowing, Vinten, G. (ed.) op. cit., pp. 54–60.
14. McHale, op. cit., p. 128.
15. Hunt, G. and Shailer, B. (1994). The whistleblowers speak, in Hunt, G. (ed.) op. cit., p. 10.
16. McHale, op. cit., p. 127.
17. Ibid., p. 124, citing *Wartho v. Toms River Community Memorial Hospital*, 199 N.J. Super 8 App. Div. (1985).
18. McHale, op. cit., p. 126, citing *EEOC v. Kallir Phillip Ross Inc.*, 401 F. Supp. 66 71 (D.C. N.Y. 1975) 10 E.P.D. 10 366.
19. Vinten, G. Enough is enough: an employer's view – the Pink affair, in Vinten, G. (ed.) op. cit., pp. 118–32.
20. Ibid., p. 121.
21. Lovell, A. and Robertson, C. (1994). Charles Robertson: in the eye of the storm, in Vinten, G. (ed.) op. cit., pp. 146–73, p. 154.
22. Ibid., p. 158.
23. Ibid., p. 162.
24. Ibid., p. 1667.
25. Of which Dearing identifies two (15.57).

Chapter 10 Resolving Disputes

1. Weddernburn, K.W. (1969). Conflicts of 'Rights' or Conflicts of 'Interests' in Labor Disputes. *Dispute Settlement Procedures in Five Western European Countries.* Institute of Industrial Relations. Los Angeles. 65–90 at 69.
2. Bone, R.G. (1995). Lon Fuller's Theory of Adjudication and the false dichotomy between Dispute Resolution and the Public Law models of Litigation. *Boston University Law Review* 75: 1274–1324 at 1276. Fuller points to the need to distinguish social problems which require executive action for their solution; problems which can best be dealt with by the courts; problems which ought to be addressed by 'planning boards or public corporations'. Fuller, L.L. (1978–9). The forms and limits of adjudication. *Harvard Law Review* 92: 353–409 at 354.
3. Cf. Bone, op. cit., at 1280.
4. Ibid., p. 1275.
5. Giugni, G. (1969). The Public and Private Ordering of Dispute-Settlement procedures. *Dispute Settlement Procedures in Five Western European Countries.* Institute of Industrial Relations. Los Angeles. 24–31 at 24.
6. Fuller, op. cit., at 357.
7. Schmidt, F. (1969). Conciliation, Adjudication and Administration: Three Methods of Decision-Making in Labor Disputes. *Dispute Settlement Procedures in Five Western European Countries.* Institute of Industrial Relations. Los Angeles. pp. 45–65.
8. Fuller, op. cit., at 353.
9. Letter seen by the author.

10. Davies, Sir Michael (1994). *The Davies Report.* Bristol.
11. *Pergamon Press Ltd* [1971] 1 Ch. 388 at 389.
12. *Pergamon Press Ltd* [1971] 1 Ch. 388 at 400.
13. *Pergamon Press Ltd* [1971] 1 Ch. 388 at 389.
14. Ibid.
15. Fuller, op. cit., at 355.
16. *Pergamon Press Ltd* [1971] 1 Ch. 388 at 399.
17. Cooke, J. in *Norrie v. Senate of the University of Auckland* [1984] 1 N.Z.L.R. 129 at 140.
18. *Rigg v. University of Waikato (Commissaries' Report)* [1984] 1 N.Z.L.R. 149 at 193.
19. *Page v. Visitor of Hull University* [1993] 1 All E.R. 97 at 113.
20. *Rigg v. University of Waikato (Commissaries' Report)* [1984] 1 N.Z.L.R. 149 at 194.
21. *Glynne v. Keele University* [1971] 2 All E.R. 89 at 95.
22. Cf. US Supreme Court decision in *Board of Curators of University of Missouri v. Horowitz,* 435 U.S. 78, 55 L. Ed. 3d 90.
23. That has been held to be a consideration in deciding whether an issue which is otherwise clearly a matter of professional judgement is justiciable.
24. Woodhouse, P. in *Norrie v. Senate of the University of Auckland* [1984] 1 N.Z.L.R. 129 at 135.
25. *Thomson v. University of London* (1864) 33 L.J. Ch. 625.
26. [1978] 1 W.L.R. 1488.
27. [1978] 1 W.L.R. 1488.
28. *Thomas v. Bradford University* [1987] 1 A.C. 795 at 821.
29. *Thorne v. University of London* [1966] 2 All E.R. 338; [1966] 2 Q.B. 237, cf. *Patel v. University of Bradford* [1978] 3 All E.R. 841 at 846–7, *per* McGarry, V.-C.
30. *Hines v. Birkbeck College* [1985] 3 All E.R. 156.
31. *Thomson v. University of London* (1864) 33 L.J. Ch. 625.
32. *Ex parte Forster re University of Sydney* [1963] N.S.W.R. 723 at 727.
33. Lord Griffiths in *Thomas v. University of Bradford* [1987] 1 All E.R. 834; [1987] A.C. 795 and *Page v. University of Hull and Visitor* [1993] 1 All E.R. 97 at 100.
34. *Page v. Visitor of Hull University* [1993] 1 All E.R. 97 at 100.
35. *Page v. Visitor of Hull University* [1993] 1 All E.R. 97 at 106.
36. Cooke, J. in *Norrie v. Senate of the University of Auckland* [1984] 1 N.Z.L.R. 129 at 141.
37. *Czarnikow v. Roth Schmidt and Co* [1922] 2 K.B. 478 at 488; [1922] All E.R. Rep 45 at 50, *per* Scrutton L.J.
38. *Page v. Visitor of Hull University* [1993] 1 All E.R. 97 at 114.
39. *Bagg's Case* (1615) 11 Co. Rep. 93b.
40. Woodhouse, P. in *Norrie v. Senate of the University of Auckland* [1984] 1 N.Z.L.R. 129 at 136.
41. See Khan, A.N. (1990). University visitor revisited, I. *Education and the law* 2: 163 at 166.
42. Ibid., see at 166. But even if the High Court may be held to have a supervisory jurisdiction in regard to the visitor, that does not necessarily give it an appellate jurisdiction. Ibid., at 181.
43. *Patel v. University of Bradford* [1978] 3 All E.R. 841 at 846, McGarry V.-C. For an example, see *Ex parte Foster, re University of Sydney* (1963) 63 S.R. (NSW) 723.
44. Woodhouse, P. in *Norrie v. Senate of the University of Auckland* [1984] 1 N.Z.L.R. 129 at 135, citing *Czarnikow v. Roth, Schmidt and Co* [1922] 2 K.B. 478.
45. See my, Episcopal accountability (1998) *Discipline and Justice in the Church of England.* Hereford. Gracewing, Fowler Wright Books.

46. Referred to by Woodhouse, P. in *Norrie v. Senate of the University of Auckland* [1984] 1 N.Z.L.R. 129 at 134.
47. *Murdoch University v. Bloom* [1980] W.A.R. 193 at 199.
48. *Page v. Visitor of Hull University* [1993] 1 All E.R. 97 at 100.
49. Halsbury, *Laws*, 5(2): 419. Cf. *R. v. Bishop of Ely* (1788) 2 Term Rep 290 at 338. Cf. discussion in Sadler, R. (1981). The University Visitor: Visitorial Precedent and Procedure in Australia. Uni of Tas. L.R. 7:2 at 19.
50. Halsbury, *Laws*, 5(2): 419.
51. Cooke, J. in *Norrie v. Senate of the University of Auckland* [1984] 1 N.Z.L.R. 129 at 140.
52. Sadler, op. cit., at 13.
53. Cf. Lewis, R. (1995). Disciplinary dismissals and redundancies in higher and further education. *Education and the law* 7(4): 211–19 at 213.
54. Woodhouse, P. and Cooke, J. in *Norrie v. Senate of the University of Auckland* [1984] 1 N.Z.L.R. 129 at 135–6.
55. The tests of domesticity are reviewed by G.G. Howells (1989). Employment disputes within universities. *Civil Justice Quarterly* 8: 152.
56. *Times Higher Education Supplement* (11 July 1997) carried an article on the question whether the Archbishop of Canterbury could delegate his responsibilities as a university visitor at the University of Kent.
57. *Page v. Visitor of Hull University* [1993] 1 All E.R. 97 at 109.
58. The earliest cases are catalogued and discussed by Smith, P.M. (1981), in University Visitor. *Law Quarterly Review* 97: 610. For recent studies, see Whalley, P.W.F. and Price, D.M. (1994). 'Mischievous anachronism' or a 'swift, cheap and final' form of alternative dispute resolution for universities? *ABCD* 114:7–11 and (1996) Noblesse oblige – a role for the Visitor? *ABCD* 124: 48–53.
59. *Thomas v. Bradford University* [1987] 1 A.C. 795 at 822.
60. *Thomas v. University of Bradford* [1987] 1 A.C. 795 at 801.
61. It is not always obvious whether a dispute between employer and employee is a contractual matter within the employment arena or falls outside it.
62. The Committee of Vice-Chancellors and Principals (CVCP) set up a committee to consider the possibility in 1996, under the chairmanship of the Vice-Chancellor of Oxford Brookes University, Dr Clive Booth. The committee reported in 1998, but confined its recommendations to student disputes.

Part 3/Introduction

1. Diplock, L.J. in *Thorne v. University of London* [1966] 2 Q.B. 242; [1966] 2 All E.R. 339.

Chapter 11 The Value of a 'Degree'

1. Letter 104, *Epistolae Academicae Oxoniensis* (Registrum F): I (1421–57), ed. Anstey, H. 1898. Oxford. p. 127.
2. Ibid., p. 238.
3. *The Privileges of the University of Cambridge* (1824). Dyer, G. (ed.). London. 2 vols., I.172.
4. *Eodem dignitatis nomine, quo Padue donatus es, in nostram Universitatem ascribi posses. Epistolae Academicae Oxoniensis*, ibid., p. 283.
5. See *Special Digest Report* of the CVCP on submissions to Dearing, p. 6.
6. Cf. Dearing Recommendation 23.
7. Childs, W.M. (1933). *Making a University.* London. p. 243.
8. The working concept here separates the institution from the body.
9. Christie, J. (1976). The power to award degrees. *Public Law* 358–96 at 362.

10. Ibid., at 359.
11. Churchill, E.F. (1920). The dispensing power of the Crown in ecclesiastical affairs. *Law Quarterly Review* 38: 297, 307, 310.
12. The Cambridge Case, being an Exact narrative of all the proceedings against the Vice-Chancellour and delegates of the University for refusing to admit Alban Francis . . . to the Degree of Master of Arts (1969) London. pp. 1–16, p. 3.
13. See pp. 144.
14. Owen, T.A. (1972). The power to grant degrees. *Universities Quarterly* 26: 271–82 at 271–2.
15. In *The Prince's Case* (1606) 8 Co. Rep. 1a, 166.
16. Blackstone's *Commentary* (1797), 10th edn., I, p. 272.
17. *Foster v. British Gas plc* [1990] 3 All E.R. 897 at 917.
18. Neave, G. (1983). Regionalization in Higher education Governance and the Regional Dimension: Some Considerations from a European perspective. *The Structure and Governance of Higher Education*, Shattock, M. (ed.). Society for Research into Higher Education Monographs. pp. 133–49, pp. 135–6.
19. Ibid., p. 136.
20. Haskins, G.L. (1941). The University of Oxford and the *Ius ubique docendi. English Historical Review* 56: 281.
21. I am indebted to John Lauwerys for this thought.
22. Veblen, T. (1918). *The Higher Learning in America: A Memorandum on the Conduct of Universities by Businessmen.* Repr. London, 1994. p. 99.
23. Wagner, R.B. (1989). *Accountability in Education: a Philosophical Enquiry*, New York. p. 36. Cf. Pincoffs, E.L. (1973). Educational accountability. *Studies in Philosophy and Education* 8: 136–7.
24. 'The outcomes of the RAE reflect a peer-group assessment panel's estimate of a discipline's own research standing, against a number of subjective criteria.'

    'Bibliometrics looks across the UK as a whole by field and allows citation and publication data to be compared across countries, whereas subject rating deduced from the RAE outcomes are based on an assessment of research by university department' (7).

Chapter 12 Peer Review and Appraisal

1. *Adam v. Ward* [1917] A.C. 309 at 334.
2. *Adam v. Ward* [1917] A.C. 309 at 334–5.
3. 26 March 1997, CVCP submission to HEFCE on the Funding Method for Teaching, 1998–9.
4. Williams, G. and Fry, H. (1994). *Longer Term Prospects for Higher Education.* CVCP Report, Institute of Education, University of London. p. 38.
5. Ibid., p. 38.
6. Pollitt, C. (1990). Doing business in the Temple? Managers and Quality Assurance in the Public Services. *Public Administration* 68(4): 435–52 at 445.
7. Wagner, R.B. (1989). *Accountability in Education: a Philosophical Enquiry.* New York. Routledge. pp. 24–5.
8. Pincoffs, E.L. (1973). Educational accountability. *Studies in Philosophy and Education* 8: 136.
9. Wagner, op. cit., p. 23.
10. See Evans, G.R. and Moloney, K. (1996). *Upward Appraisal.* Council for Academic Freedom and Academic Standards, Report No. 4.
11. Ibid.

Chapter 13 Forming Academic Judgements

1. *Ex parte Forster re University of Sydney* [1963] N.S.W.R. 723 at 728.
2. But the issue of jurisdiction here was not whether the court could thus intervene to change a decision made on a basis of professional judgement, but whether it had any jurisdiction at all where there was a visitor and the matter was domestic.
3. *King v. University of Saskatchewan* [1969] 6 D.L.R. (3d) 120 at 128–9.
4. See *Special Digest Report* of the CVCP on submissions to Dearing, p. 6.
5. Wall, A. and Rowden, R. (1994). Managerial accountability, in *Whistleblowing in the Health Service*, Hunt, G. (ed.). London. p. 32. See Chapter 6[40].
6. Even there, it might be argued that there is a public interest if it is perceived that advantage is being given on the basis of non-academic considerations.
7. Fuller (1978–9). The forms and limits of adjudication. *Harvard Law Review* 92: 353–409 at 355, citing Landis, J.M. *Report on Regulatory Agencies to the President-Elect* 41–5 (December 1960), reprinted in Subcommittee on administrative practice and procedure, Senate Committee on the Judiciary, 81st Cong. 2D Sess, Report on Regulatory Agencies to the President-Elect 41–5 (Comm Print 1960).
8. Pollitt, C. (1990). Doing business in the Temple? Managers and Quality Assurance in the Public Services. *Public Administration* 68(4): 435–52 at 438.
9. Veblen, T. (1918). *The Higher Learning in America: A Memorandum on the Conduct of Universities by Businessmen.* Repr. London, 1994. p. 97.
10. Pollitt, op. cit., at 435.
11. *R. v. Higher Education Funding Council, ex parte Institute of Dental Surgery* [1994] I All E.R. 651 at 660.
12. *R. v. Higher Education Funding Council, ex parte Institute of Dental Surgery* [1994] I All E.R. 651 at 655.
13. *1996 Research Assessment Exercise: Conduct of the Exercise: RAE Manager's Report* (HEFCE May 1997), RAE 96 1/97 (10).
14. The principle that a body can appoint new members is causing problems in the governance of new universities at governing body level.
15. *1996 Research Assessment Exercise*, op. cit. (10).
16. Consulting referees would not meet the difficulty if the committee was not competent to assess the expertise of the referees or to deal with any contractions between them.
17. [1988] Q.B. 322.
18. On these points, see Khan, A.N. (1991). University visitor revisited, II. *Education and the law* 3: 179 at 181.
19. Hillman, H. (1997). Parafraud in biology. *Science and Engineering Ethics* 3: 121–36 at 128.
20. Meier, G.M. (1994). Review of Development Research in the UK: Report to the Development Studies Association. *Journal of International Development* 6: 465–517 at 509.
21. Ibid., at 508.
22. Ibid., at 510.
23. *R. v. Mayor, Commonalty and Citizens of the City of London and another, ex parte Matson* (1996) 8 Admin. L.R. 49 at 71, *per* Swinton Thomas, L.J.
24. Meier, op. cit., at 466.
25. Ibid., 465–517.
26. Ibid., at 466.

27. English Departments fared statistically worse than other comparable large-number mainstream 'conventional' arts subjects in the Research Assessment Exercise of 1996. 11% of English departments were awarded a 5, but 26% of History departments got 5 and 39% of Classics departments.
28. *R. v. Higher Education Funding Council, ex parte Institute of Dental Surgery* [1994] 1 All E.R. 651 at 655.
29. On the idea that quality assurance can include 'identifying those features of a service which are of significance to users and their needs . . . implementing improvements . . . monitoring the situation', see Pollitt, op. cit., at 437.
30. See my *Prospects of promotion: towards a common code of practice.* Council for Academic Freedom and Academic Standards. *Report No. 3,* 1994. Oxford has now made the decision to award titles in recognition of distinction without accompanying pay rises and does not have to make such comparisons.
31. Wade, W.H.R. (1995) *Administrative Law.* 7th edn. Oxford. Oxford University Press. pp. 391–2.
32. *R. v. Higher Education Funding Council, ex parte Institute of Dental Surgery* [1994] I All E.R. 651 at 668.
33. *R. v. Higher Education Funding Council, ex parte Institute of Dental Surgery* [1994] I W.L.R. 242 at 259.
34. The committee as a whole might be held responsible for the aberrant view of one of its members if it had allowed its decision to be influenced by that view.
35. 'Relevancy is always a matter of degree, and . . . however laudatory the reports may have been, the tenor and contents of such a report could [not] go any distance toward showing unreasonableness on the part of the Council. In reaching its decision the Council and its committees had to balance a great number of considerations, of which the contents of these reports, even if favourable, could be only one; and even then, one of little importance.' *Bell v. University of Auckland* [1969] N.Z.L.R. at 1036.
36. Wenneras, C. and Wold, A. (1997). *Nature* (22 May) 387: 341–4.
37. Ibid., 341–4.
38. 'Such an unfair and tendentious assessment of the appellant . . . established "gross and unreasoning prejudice on the respondent's part".' *Horrocks v. Lowe* [1975] A.C. 135.
39. To counter this danger, there is in some fields a growing pressure to keep records of the performance of referees, so that the references themselves can be more efficiently weighed. This record-keeping may not be known to the referees themselves, and it is to be anticipated that there may in due course be problems with the Data Protection Act in this connection.

Chapter 14 Ensuring Sound Procedures

1. *Leech v. Governor of Parkhurst Prison* [1988] A.C. 533 at 573.
2. *Anismic v. Foreign Compensation Commission* [1969] 2 All E.R. 208.
3. 'And secondly, that where the power is a power to dismiss from an office . . . and to dismiss not at discretion but by reason of misconduct, then there is a duty to act judicially.' *Vidyodaya University of Ceylon and others v. Silva* [1964] 3 All E.R. 865 at 875.
4. *Glynn v. Keele University and another* [1971] 2 All E.R. 89.
5. See pp. 163ff.
6. *Re Paine and University of Toronto* [1981] 131 D.L.R. 325 at 331.

7. *Re Schabas and Caput of University of Toronto* [1975] 52 D.L.R. 497 at 505.
8. A document setting out good practice in the forming of academic judgements was published by the Higher Education Funding Council for England in May 1997, in the form of a Research Assessment Exercise Manager's *Report.* This was formulated under a shadow cast over the whole process by the *Institute of Dental Surgery* case arising out of the previous RAE. It was, therefore, framed with a conscious eye on the current state of the law. It has its flaws and its grey areas. But it will be used in what follows primarily for its strengths in setting bench-marks.
9. RAE Consultation Paper, HEFCE, November 1997.
10. *1996 Research Assessment Exercise: Conduct of the Exercise: RAE Manager's Report* (HEFCE May 1997), RAE 96 1/97 (90).
11. Ibid., RAE 96 1/97 (91).
12. *King v. University of Saskatchewan* [1969] 6 D.L.R. (3d) 120 at 126.
13. *Ex parte Forster re University of Sydney* [1963] N.S.W.R. 723 at 728.
14. [1969] 2 Q.B. 538.
15. [1969] 2 Q.B. 538 at 545.
16. [1969] 2 Q.B. 538 at 554.
17. It is conceded that such cases are numerous. 'The quality of proposals for promotion to Readerships or Professorships is consistently high from one year to the next' (*Cambridge University Reporter,* 6 December 1993, p. 239. Cf. *Reporter* of 25 June 1996, where it is conceded that more academic staff deserved promotion than had been getting it.)
18. But it can also be argued that the cost of exercising a discretion is relevant. See Halsbury, *Laws,* para. 76, p. 136.
19. Moodie, G.C. (ed.) (1986). *Standards and Criteria in Higher Education.* London. p. 99.
20. Woodhouse, P. in *Norrie v. Senate of the University of Auckland* [1984] 1 N.Z.L.R. 129 at 138; cf. *R. v. Aston university Senate, ex parte Roffey* [1969] 2 Q.B. 538. In another it was noted that 'irrelevant and damaging personal factors have been allowed to enter into the evaluation'. W.L.R. [1994] at 261.
21. That did not mean, however, that it had no control at all over these matters. It would have undisputed control over the syllabus. But it would not dictate every word of a lecture. But this is problematic if in principle it could declare the lecturer 'inefficient' on the basis of the content of his lectures (let us say that he failed to cover the syllabus by spending too much time on only part of it).
22. *King v. University of Saskatchewan* [1969] 6 D.L.R. (3d) 120 at 128.
23. *R. v. Dunsheath, ex parte Meredith* [1951] 1 K.B. 127 at 132.
24. McKenzie, P., Mitchell, P. and Oliver, P. (eds) (1995). *Competence and accountability in education.* Aldershot. Arena. p. ix.
25. *Vaneck v. Governors of the University of Alberta* [1975] 5 W.W.R. 429 at 431.
26. *Blasser v. Royal Institute for the Advancement of Learning* [1985] 24 D.L.R. (4th) 507. See p. 119 on the 'quick, cheap, final' argument.
27. Holmes, O.W. (1881). *The Common Law.* Boston. p. 1.
28. Salmond, J.W. (1902). *Jurisprudence.* p. 16.
29. Cf. 'Rigid rules in accordance with which justice is administered . . . to the exclusion of the unrestricted judicial discretion of the judges and magistrates to whom this function is entrusted', Salmond, J.W. (1921). *Science of Legal Method.* London. p. lxxv.

30. Holmes, O.W. (1896). The Path of the Law. *Harvard Law Review* 10: 457 at 457 takes an intermediate line.
31. Cass, R.A. (1995). Judging: norms and incentives of restrospective decision-making. *Boston University Law Review* 75: 941–96 at 979. The above citations of Salmond and Holmes are made in this article.
32. See pp. 99ff.
33. *Vaneck v. Governors of the University of Alberta* [1975] 5 W.W.R. 429 at 431.
34. *Ex parte Duncan* (1904) 4 SR (NSW) 217 and *R. v. Stepney Corporation* [1902] 1 K.B. 317.
35. *Schmidt v. Secretary of State for Home Affairs* [1969] 2 Ch. 149 at 158.
36. *R. v. P.L.A., ex parte Kynoch* [1919] 1 K.B. 176, 183.
37. *Hammond v. Hutt Valley and Bays Metropolitan Milk Board* [1958] N.Z.L.R. 720.
38. Wade, W.H.R. (1995). *Administrative Law.* 7th edn. Oxford. Oxford University Press. p. 272: 'no amount of waiver or consent can extend a public authority's powers or validate action which is ultra vires'.
39. Ibid., p. 9.
40. *Rooke's Case* [1598] 5 Co. Rep. 99b.
41. *Sharpe and Wakefield* [1891] A.C. 173.
42. Wade, op. cit., p. 387.
43. Lord Irvine of Lairg (1996). Judges and decision-makers: the theory and practice of Wednesbury Review. *Public Law* 59 at 62.
44. *1996 Research Assessment Exercise: Conduct of the Exercise: RAE Manager's Report* (HEFCE May 1997), RAE 96 1/97 (45).
45. Ibid., (45).
46. Ibid., (51).
47. Ibid., (51).
48. Ibid., (62).
49. 'Detailed guidance on the approach and procedures (including how to complete submission for assessment), and the criteria and working methods to be adopted by each panel, were published well before the closing date for submissions.' Ibid., (6).
50. Ibid.
51. Ibid., (69).
52. Ibid., (69).
53. Ibid., (70).
54. Ibid., (71).
55. Ibid., (62).
56. Ibid., (65).
57. Ibid., (63).
58. The first legally load-bearing use of the expression appears to be by Lord Denning, in *Schmidt v. Secretary of State for Home Affairs* [1969] 2 Ch. 149.
59. Wade, op. cit., p. 525, and see *R. v. Secretary of State for Health, ex parte United States Tobacco International Inc, The Independent,* 4 January 1991.
60. A case in point is *Council of Civil Service Unions v. Minister for the Civil Service* [1985] A.C. 374 at 408.
61. Cf. *Woods v. Secretary of State for Scotland* [1991] S.L.T. 197.
62. [1985] A.C. 835 at 851.
63. 'Legitimate' expectation seems to be preferred to 'reasonable' expectation. See *Council of Civil Service Unions v. Minister for the Civil Service* [1985] A.C. 374 at 401

and 408–9. A bibliography is to be found in Craig, P.P. (1992). Legitimate Expectations: a conceptual analysis. *Law Quarterly Review* 108 79–98, note.

64. *R. v. Inland Revenue Commissioners, ex parte Preston* [1985] A.C. 835 at 836 and 867, per Lord Templeman.
65. *Attorney-General of Hong Kong v. Ng Yuen Shiu* [1983] 2 A.C. 629.
66. Brennan J. in *Attorney-General for New South Wales v. Quin* (1990) 170 C.L.R. 1 at 40.

Chapter 15 Reasonableness

1. There had, in this case, been no proper investigation of allegations on the basis of which the dismissal took place.
2. *R. v. Higher Education Funding Council, ex parte Institute of Dental Surgery* [1994] I W.L.R. 242.
3. *R. v. Commonalty and Citizens of the City of London and Another, ex parte Matson* [1996] 8 Admin. L.R. 49 at 50.
4. Lord Irvine of Lairg (1996). Judges and decision-makers: the theory and practice of Wednesbury Review. *Public Law* 59 at 65–6.
5. Published in *Cambridge University Reporter*, 22 October 1997.
6. *Doody v. Secretary of State for the Home Department* [1994] 1 A.C. 531; [1993] 3 W.L.R. 154, H.L.; [1993] 3 All E.R. 92 at 106.
7. Craig, P.P. (1994). The common law, reasons and administrative justice. *Cambridge Law Journal* 53: 282–302 at 283–4.
8. *Norton Tool Co. Ltd v. Tewson* [1973] 1 W.L.R. 45.
9. On the 'abuse of power' argument, see Craig, op. cit., at 289.
10. See my article, Having and giving reasons: the Cambridge promotions controversy. *Law and Justice*, 134 (1998), 22–38.
11. *R. v. Lancashire County Council, ex parte Huddleston* [1986] All E.R. 941 at 945, Cf. *R. v. Kensington and Chelsea Royal Borough Council, ex parte Assiter, per* Sedley, S.
12. Professor M. Pepper, *Cambridge University Reporter*, 1996–7, p. 678.
13. *Cambridge University Reporter*, 1996–7, p. 681.
14. Ibid., p. 683.
15. Ibid., p. 678.
16. *R. v. City of London Corp, ex parte Matson* (1995) 8 Admin. L.R. 49, C.A. at 61.
17. *R. v. Higher Education Funding Council, ex parte Institute of Dental Surgery* [1994] I All E.R. 651 at 655.

    Meier, G.M. (1994). Review of Development Research in the UK: Report to the Development Studies Association. *Journal of International Development 6* 465–517 at 509.

    Ibid., at 508.

    Ibid., at 510.

    R. v. Mayor, Commonalty and Citizens of the City of London and another, ex parte Matson (1996) 8 Admin. L.R. 49 at 71, *per* Swinton Thomas, L.J.
18. This is officially acknowledged in many institutions. See my *Prospects of promotion: towards a common code of practice* (1994). Council for Academic Freedom and Academic Standards. *Report No. 3.* Oxford is an exception. It has now made the decision to award titles in recognition of distinction without accompanying pay rises.
19. Wade, W.H.R. (1995). *Administrative Law.* 7th edn. Oxford. Oxford University Press. pp. 391–2.

20. *R. v. Higher Education Funding Council, ex parte Institute of Dental Surgery* [1994] I All E.R. 651 at 668.
21. *R. v. Higher Education Funding Council, ex parte Institute of Dental Surgery* [1994] I W.L.R. 242 at 259.
22. Craig, op. cit., at 299–300.
23. *Lloyd v. McMahon* [1987] A.C. 625 at 702, *per* Lord Bridge.
24. *R. v. Secretary of State for the Home Department, ex parte Asif Mahmood Khan* [1984] 1 W.L.R. 1337 at 1352.
25. [1992] I.C.R. 816, 828F.
26. W.L.R. [1994] 256.
27. *R. v. Higher Education Funding Council, ex parte Institute of Dental Surgery* [1994] I All E.R. 651 at 669.
28. *1996 Research Assessment Exercise: Conduct of the Exercise: RAE Manager's Report* (HEFCE May 1997), RAE 96 1/97 (60).
29. Ibid., (19).
30. Ibid., (6).
31. Ibid., (6).
32. Ibid., (39).
33. Ibid., (40).
34. Ibid., (49).
35. Ibid., (52).
36. Ibid., (52).
37. Ibid., (94).
38. Ibid., (95).
39. Ibid., (96).
40. *R. v. Lancashire County Council, ex parte Huddleston* [1986] 2 All E.R. 941.
41. Scott, Sir Richard (1996). Ministerial accountability. *Public Law* 410 at 416. Cf. Ministerial Accountability and Responsibility (1995–6) HC 313, para. 26.
42. 'Setting . . . rare cases aside, the proposition that it is unacceptable for a minister to give an answer that is deliberately incomplete is one which, in my opinion, is inconsistent with the requirements of the constitutional principle of ministerial accountability.'
43. Scott, Sir Richard op. cit., at 422.
44. Ibid., at 424.
45. Ibid., at 426.
46. Farrington, J.D. (1994). *The Law of Higher Education.* London. Butterworths. 5.38.
47. On reckoning and explaining, see Wagner, R.B. (1989). *Accountability in Education: a Philosophical Enquiry.* New York. p. 8 ff.
48. See *Prospects of Promotion,* op. cit.
49. Craig, op. cit., at 300.
50. *R. v. Lancashire County Council, ex parte Huddleston* [1986] 2 All E.R. 941 at 947.
51. Justice-All Souls (1998). *Administrative Justice: some Necessary Reforms.* Oxford. Oxford University Press.
52. *R. v. Secretary of State for the Home Department, ex parte Doody* [1994] 1 A.C. 531 at 564.
53. *R. v. Secretary of State for the Home Department, ex parte Doody* [1994] 1 A.C. 531 at 565.
54. *R. v. Mayor, Commonalty and Citizens of the City of London and another, ex parte Matson* (1996) 8 Admin L.R. 49 at 63–4.
55. *Institute of Dental Surgery* case at 257–58.
56. *Times Higher Education Supplement* 16 January 1998.

Conclusion

1. Scott, Sir Richard (1996). Ministerial accountability. *Public Law* 410 at 413.
2. Ibid., at 415, cf. The Public Service Committee in its Second Report, *Ministerial Accountability and Responsibility* (1995–6) HC 313, para. 26.
3. House of Commons Debates, col. 1285 (20 July 1954).
4. Pelikan, J. (1992). *The idea of a university: a Reexamination.* Yale. Yale University Press. p. 46.
5. Ibid., p. 51.

Selective Bibliography

Advisory Board for the Research Councils (1976). *Second Report.* London, HMSO.

Advisory Board for the Research Councils (1987). *A Strategy for the Science Base.* London, HMSO.

Advisory Council on Applied Research and Development (1986).

Applied Research and Development (1983). *Improving Links between Higher Education and Industry.* London, HMSO.

Advisory Council on Scientific Policy (1962). *Exploitable Areas of Science.* London HMSO.

Advisory Council on Scientific Policy (1964). *Annual Report* 1961–62. London, HMSO.

Aitken, Sir Robert (1969). The Vice-Chancellors' Committee and the UGC. *Universities Quarterly,* 23(2): 165–71.

Allocation of the Science Budget, Office of Science and Technology, 15 January 1997.

Armytage, W.H.G. (1955). *Civic Universities.* London, Ernest Benn.

Aspen, P. (1985). Oxford Blasts Cutbacks. *The Times Higher Education Supplement*, 13 December.

Bainbridge, D. (1996). *Introduction to Computer Law.* 3rd edn. London, Pitman.

Bainbridge, D. (1994). *Software Copyright Law.* London, Pitman.

Baker, J.H. (1990). The third university of England: the Inns of Court and the Common Law tradition, *Selden Society Lecture.* London.

Bantock, G.H. (1965). T.S. Eliot and Education. *Universities Quarterly,* 19(2): 109–14.

Baskerville, E.A. (1986). Oxford and the Schools. Nuffield College, Oxford, 17 October.

Beloff, Lord (1990). Universities and the Public Purse: An Update. *Higher Education Quarterly,* 44(I), 3–19.

Benson, G.C.S. (1994). Codes of ethics and whistleblowing, in G. Vinten (ed.) *Whistleblowing: Subversion or Corporate Citizenship.* London, Paul Chapman.

Berdahl, R.O. (1959). *British Universities and the State.* Cambridge, Cambridge University Press.

Blackstone's *Commentary* (1797), 10th edn.

Bone, R.G. (1995). Lon Fuller's Theory of Adjudication and the false dichotomy between Dispute Resolution and the Public Law models of Litigation. *Boston University Law Review,* 75: 1274–1324.

Boydell, C. and Gaunt, R. (1995). Patents and Innovation. *Oxford Innovation News,* 15: 8–11.

Boys Smith, J.S. (1959). The College Accounts: An Explanatory Note. Cambridge, St John's College.

Bridges, J.W. (1970). Keeping Peace in the Universities: the role of the visitor. *Law Quarterly Review*, 86: 531 at 534–5.

Bullock, Lord (1986). Reminiscences of a Former Vice-Chancellor. Nuffield College, Oxford, 24 October.

Caldwell, J.L. (1981). Judicial Review of Universities – the Visitor and the visited. *97 Canterbury LR 307.*

Cambridge Tutorial Representatives (1984). *Sixth Term Examination for Admission to Cambridge.* Cambridge, CTR.

Cambridge Tutorial Representatives (1985). *Final Report of the Working Party on Admission to Cambridge.* Cambridge, CTR.

Cambridge Tutorial Representatives (1990). *Cambridge: Admissions Prospectus, 1991–92.* Cambridge, CTR.

Carnwath, R. (1996). The reasonable limits of local authority powers. *Public Law,* 244.

Carr, C.T. (1921). *Delegated legislation.* Cambridge, Cambridge University Press.

Carswell, J. (1985). *Government and the Universities in Britain.* Cambridge, Cambridge University Press.

Cass, R.A. (1995). Judging: norms and incentives of restrospective decision-making. *Boston University Law Review,* 75: 941–96.

Central Advisory Council for Education (England) (1959). 15 to 18, vol. I (*The Crowther Report*). London, HMSO.

Christie, J. (1976). The power to award degrees. *Public Law,* 358–96.

Churchill, E.F. (1920). The dispensing power of the Crown in ecclesiastical affairs. *Law Quarterly Review,* 38: 297.

Clark, B.R. (1983). Governing the Higher Education System, in M. Shattock (ed.) *The Structure and Governance of Higher Education.* Society for Research into Higher Education Monographs. Guildford. 19–45.

Clarkson, C.M.V. (1996). Kicking corporate bodies and damning their souls. *Modern Law Review,* 59: 557.

Committee of Vice-Chancellors and Principals (1985). *Report of the Steering Committee for Efficiency.* Studies in Universities. London, CVCP.

Committee of Vice-Chancellors and Principals (1989). *The Teaching Function: Quality Assurance.* London, CVCP.

Committee on Higher Education (1963). *Report (Robbins).* London, HMSO.

Committee on Standards in Public Life (1996). *Second Report.* London.

Committee on Undergraduate Admissions (1983). *Report (Dover).* Oxford, Oxford Colleges Admissions Office.

Copyright, Designs and Patents Act 1988.

Cornford, F.M. (1908, repr. 1994). *Microcosmographia Academica.* Cambridge, Cambridge University Press.

Council for Scientific Policy (1966). *Report on Science Policy.* London, HMSO.

Council for Scientific Policy (1967). *Report on Science Policy.* London, HMSO.

Council for Scientific Policy (1971). *The Future of the Research Council System.* London, HMSO.

Cover, M. and Humphreys, G. (1994). Whistleblowing in English Law, in G. Vinten (ed.) *Whistleblowing: Subversion or Corporate Citizenship.* London, Paul Chapman.

Crequer, N. (1986). The Strengths and the Weaknesses. *The Times Higher Education Supplement,* 30 May, 4–6.

Crequer, N. (1989). The Passing of the Education Reform Act. *Higher Education Quarterly*, 43(1): 3–19.

Crompton, J. (1961). Fasciculi Zizaniorum. *Journal of Ecclesiastical History*, 12: 35–45, 155–6.

Cross, C. and Bailey, S. (1986). *Local Government Law* (7th edn). London, Sweet and Maxwell.

Curzon, Lord (1909). *Principles and Methods of University Reform.* Oxford, Clarendon Press.

Department of Education and Science (1970a). *Education Planning Paper No. 1: Ouput Budgeting for the DES.* London, HMSO.

Department of Education and Science (1970b). *Education Planning Paper No. 2: Student Numbers in Higher Education in England and Wales.* London, HMSO.

Department of Education and Science (1972). *Education: A Framework for Expansion.* London, HMSO.

Department of Education and Science (1975–76). *The Education (Mandatory Awards) Regulations.* London, DES.

Department of Education and Science (1985). *The Development of Higher Education into the 1990s.* London, HMSO.

Department of Education and Science (1985–86). *The Education (Mandatory Awards) Regulations.* London, DES.

Department of Education and Science (1987). *Higher Education: Meeting the Challenge.* London, HMSO.

Department of Education and Science (n.d.). *Tuition Fees and College Dues Claimed by Cambridge University Colleges for Sessions 1968–69, 1969–70 and 1970–71.* London, DES.

Department of Education and Science (n.d.). *Tuition Fees and College Dues Claimed by Oxford University Colleges for Sessions 1968–69, 1969–70 and 1970–71.* London, DES.

Dodds, H.W. *et al.* (1952). *Government Assistance to Universities in Great Britain.* New York, Columbia University Press.

Dorey, W. (1986). The University Administration, Nuffield College, Oxford, 21 November.

Ducor, P. (1997). Are patents and research compatible? *Nature*, 387: 13–14.

Education Reform Act 1988.

Edwards, A.W.F. (1981). 1963: The Downfall of Cambridge's Constitution. *The Cambridge Review*, 23 October, 4–10.

Engel, A.J. (1983). *From Clergyman to Don: The Rise of the Academic Profession in Nineteenth Century Oxford.* Oxford, Clarendon Press.

Epistolae Academicae Oxoniensis (1898) (Registrum F): I (1421–57) H. Anstey (ed.). Oxford, Oxford University Press.

Evans, G.R. and Moloney, K. (1996). *Upward Appraisal.* Council for Academic Freedom and Academic Standards, Report No. 5.

Evans, G.R. (1983). *Old Arts and new Theology.* Oxford, Oxford University Press.

Evans, G.R. (1992). *Problems of Authority in the Reformation Debates.* Cambridge, Cambridge University Press.

Evans, G.R. (1994). *Prospects of promotion: towards a common code of practice.* Council for Academic Freedom and Academic Standards, Report No. 3.

Farrington, J.D. (1994). *The Law of Higher Education.* London, Butterworths.

Fasciculi Zizaniorum (1858) W. Waddington Shisley. Rolls Series, London, HMSO.

Ferns, H.S. (1969). *Towards an Independent University.* Occasional Paper No. 25. London, Institute of Economic Affairs.

Final Report of Labour's Policy Review for the 1990s. London, Labour Party.

Franks, Lord (1986). The Franks Report in Retrospect. Nuffield College, Oxford, 31 January.

Fredman, S. and Morris, G. (1991). Public or private? State Employees and Judicial Review. *Law Quarterly Review,* 107: 298.

Gilbert of Poitiers (1969). *Commentaries on Boethius by Gilbert of Poitiers,* N.M. Häring (ed.) Toronto, Pontifical Institute of Mediaeval Studies.

Gilbert, R.J. and Shapiro, C. (1996). An economic analysis of unilateral refusals to license intellectual property. *Proceedings of the National Academy of Science USA,* 93: 12749–12755.

Gilson, M.K. (1997). Letter, *Science* 275, 3 January.

Giugni, G. (1969). The Public and Private Ordering of Dispute-Settlement procedures. *Dispute Settlement Procedures in Five Western European Countries* 24–31. Los Angeles Institute of Industrial Relations.

Griffith, J. (1989). Universities and the State: the next steps. Council for Academic Freedom and Democracy. November.

Griffiths, S. (1991). UFC Quality Ratings Ignored. *The Times Higher Education Supplement,* 1. 12 April.

Guide for College Governors (1995). Further Education Funding Council for England.

Guide for Governing Bodies of Universities and Colleges in England and Wales (1995). Committee of University Chairmen.

Hall, G. (1996). *Staff communication review at Southampton Institute.* November.

Halsey, A.H. (1961a). British Universities and Intellectual Life. In A.H. Halsey, J. Floud and C. Arnold (eds) *Education, Culture, Economy and Society.* New York, Free Press.

Halsey, A.H. (1961b). The Changing Functions of Universities, in *Education, Culture, Economy and Society.* New York, Free Press.

Halsey, A.H. (1969). The Universities and the State. *Universities Quarterly,* 23: 128–48.

Halsey, A.H. and Trow, M.A. (1971). *The British Academics.* Cambridge, Mass. Harvard University Press.

Halsey, A.H. (1979). Are the British Universities Capable of Change? *New Universities Quarterly,* 33(4): 402–16.

Halsey, A.H. (1984). Oxford's Power Game. *The Times Higher Education Supplement,* 14, 6 January.

Hamilton, Sir William (1852). *Discussions on Philosophy and Literature, Education and University Reform.* Edinburgh, MacLachlan and Stewart.

Hansard (Lords) (1923). Vol. 53, Col. 745, 19 April.

Hansard (Commons) (1981). Written Answers, Cols 449–50, 2 July.

Hansard (Commons) (1986a). Written Answers, Cols 443–4, 13 January.

Hansard (Commons) (1986b). Written Answers, Cols 15–16, 9 June.

Harlow, C. (1976). Administrative reaction to judicial review. *Public Law,* 116–33.

Haskins, G.L. (1941). The University of Oxford and the *Ius ubique docendi. English Historical Review,* 56: 281.

Holdaway, S. (1994). Academic Whistleblowing on the beat, in G. Vinten (ed.) *Whistleblowing: Subversion or Corporate Citizenship.* London, Paul Chapman.

Holdsworth, Sir William, *A History of English Law* (1926). London.

Holmes, O.W. (1881). *The Common Law.* Boston, Boston University.

Howells, G.G. (1989). Employment disputes within universities. *Civil Justice Quarterly,* 8: 152.

Hudson, A. (1986). Wycliffism in Oxford, 1381–1411, in A. Kenny (ed.) *Wyclif in his Times*, 67–84. Oxford, Oxford University Press.

Jaeger, W. (1939). *Paedeia*, G. Highet (tr.). Oxford, Oxford University Press.

Joint Research Equipment Initiative: HEFCE and DENI Awards. HEFCE circular, February 1997.

Kedourie, E. (1988). *Diamonds into Glass.* London, Centre for Policy Studies.

Ker, I. and Gornall, T. (eds) vol. I (1978). *Letters and Diaries.* Oxford, Oxford University Press.

Khan, A.N. (1990). The university visitor revisited, I. *Education and the law* 2.

Khan, A.N. (1991). The university visitor revisited, II. *Education and the law* 3 179.

Labour Party (1973). *Higher and Further Education.* London, Labour Party.

Labour Party (1990). *Meet the Challenge, Make the Change: A New Agenda for Britain.* London, Labour Party.

Lamb, J. (ed.) (1838). *A Collection of Letters, Statutes and other Documents.*

Landis, J.M. (1960). *Report on Regulatory Agencies to the President-Elect* 41–5. December. Reprinted in *Subcommittee on administrative practice and procedure*, Senate Committee on the Judiciary, 81st Cong. 2D Sess. Report on Regulatory Agencies to the President-Elect 41–5 (Comm Print 1960).

Laws, J. (1995). Law and Democracy. *Public Law* 72.

Lee, D. (1972). *Entry and Performance at Oxford and Cambridge, 1966–71.* London, Schools Council Research Studies.

Letwin, O., Minford, P. and Sexton, S. (eds) (1988). *Higher Education: Freedom and Finance.* London, Institute of Economic Affairs.

Lewis, R. (1995). Disciplinary dismissals and redundancies in higher and further education. *Education and the law*, 7(4): 211–19.

Lockwood, G. (1986). Efficiency Measures. *The Times Higher Education Supplement*, 15, 28 February.

London Guildhall University (1997). The Articles of Association.

London's Liberties; of a learned argument of law and reason upon Saturday, December 14, 1650, before the Lord Mayor, Court of Aldermen, and Common Councell at Guild Hall, London. London, 1650.

Lord Irvine of Lairg (1996). Judges and decision-makers: the theory and practice of Wednesbury Review. *Public Law* 59.

Lovell, A. and Robertson, C. (1994). Charles Robertson: in the eye of the storm, in G. Vinten (ed.) *Whistleblowing: Subversion or Corporate Citizenship.* London, Paul Chapman.

Lucas, J.R. (1987). In Place of the CUF. *Oxford Magazine*, No. 27: 8.

McHale, J.V. (1993). *Medical confidentiality and legal privilege.* London, Routledge.

McHale, J. (1994). Whistleblowing in American Health Care, in G. Hunt (ed.) *Whistleblowing in the Health Service.* London, Arnold.

McKendrick, E. (1990/1994). *Contract Law.* London, Basingstoke, Macmillan.

McKenzie, P., Mitchell, P. and Oliver, P. (eds) (1995). *Competence and accountability in education.* Aldershot, Arena.

Maitland, F.W. (1901). *English Law and the Renaissance.* Cambridge, Cambridge University Press.

Martin, J.P. (1985). *Hospitals in Trouble.* Oxford, Blackwell.

Mason, D. (1986). *University Challenge.* London, Adam Smith Institute.

Maynard, A. (1975). *Experiment with Choice in Education.* London, Institute of Economic Affairs.

Meier, G.M. (1994). Review of Development Research in the UK: Report to the Development Studies Association. *Journal of International Development*, 6: 465–517.

Ministry of Education (1956). *Technical Education*. London, HMSO.

Ministry of Education (1958). *Education in 1958*. London, HMSO.

Moberly, Sir Walter (1949). *Crisis in the University*. London, SCM Press.

Neale, A.D. and Goyder, D.G. (1960). *The Antitrust Laws of the United States of America*. Cambridge, Cambridge University Press. 3rd edn. 1980.

Neave, G. (1983). Regionalization in Higher Education Governance and the Regional Dimension: Some Considerations from a European perspective, in M. Shattock (ed.) *The Structure and Governance of Higher Education*, 133–49. Society for Research into Higher Education Monographs.

Newman, J.H. (1996). *The Idea of a University*, F.M. Turner (ed.). Yale, Yale University Press.

1996 Research Assessment Exercise: Conduct of the Exercise: RAE Manager's Report. HEFCE, May 1997.

Owen, T.A. (1972). The power to grant degrees. *Universities Quarterly*, 26: 271–82.

Palfreyman, D. (1997). Find the Visitor. *Oxford Magazine*, 142: 3–4.

Pelikan, J. (1992). *The idea of a university: a Reexamination*. Yale, Yale University Press.

Petrus Abaelardus, A. (1967). *Historia Calamitatum*, G. Monfrin (ed.). Paris, Cerf.

Picarda, H. (1995). *The law and practice relating to charities*. 2nd edn. London, Butterworths.

Pilgrim, D. (1994). Explaining abuse and inadequate care, in G. Hunt (ed.) *Whistleblowing in the Health Service*. London, Arnold.

Pincoffs, E.L. (1973). Educational accountability. *Studies in Philosophy and Education*, 8.

Pollitt, C. (1990). Doing business in the Temple? Managers and Quality Assurance in the Public Services. *Public Administration*, 68(4): 435–52.

Reeves, M. (1969). The European University in Mediaeval Times, in W.R. Niblett (ed.) *Higher Education: Demand and Response*. London, Quail Roost Conference Centre.

Report of the Machinery of Government Committee (*The Haldane Report*). London, HMSO.

Ricquier, E. (1978). The University Visitor. *Dalhousie Law Journal*, 4: 647.

Rowe, P. (ed.) (1997). *Review of Institutional Lessons to be Learned 1994–6*. University of Lancaster.

Sadler, R.J. (1981). *The University Visitor: Visitorial Precedent and Procedure in Australia*. Uni of Tas LR 7: 2.

Salmond, J.W. (1902). *Jurisprudence*.

Salter, H.E. (ed.) (1920). *Mediaeval Archives of the University of Oxford*. Oxford, Oxford University Press.

Sayers, D. (1935). *Gaudy Night* (London, reprinted Bath, Chivers, 1988).

Scott, Sir Richard (1996). Ministerial accountability. *Public Law* 410.

Sedley, S. (1995). Human Rights: a Twenty-First Century Agenda. *Public Law* 386.

Shattock, M. (ed.) (1983). *The Structure and Governance of Higher Education*. Society for Research into Higher Education Monographs.

Shattock, M. (1994). *Derby College: Wilmorton Report of an Enquiry into the Governance and Management of the College*. FEFCE.

Shattock, M. (1994). *The UGC and the Management of British Universities*. Buckingham. Society for Research into Higher Education and Open University Press.

Special Digest Report of the CVCP on submissions to Dearing (1997). London.

Standards and Criteria in Higher Education (1986). G.C. Moodie (ed.). London.
Sunstein, C.R. (1993). *Democracy and the problem of free speech.*
The Cambridge Case, being an Exact narrative of all the proceedings against the Vice-Chancellor and delegates of the University for refusing to admit Alban Francis . . . to the Degree of Master of Arts (London, 1669). New York, The Free Press.
The Guardian (1986). 29 May.
The Guardian (1991). 29 January.
Tillotson, J. (1995). *Contract Law in Perspective.* London, Cavendish.
Trani, E.P. (1997). The changing American college presidency. *Perspectives,* 1: 34–39.
Veblen, T. (1918). *The Higher Learning in America: A Memorandum on the Conduct of Universities by Businessmen* repr. London, 1994.
Vinten, G. (ed.) (1994). *Whistleblowing: Subversion or Corporate Citizenship.* London, Paul Chapman.
Wade, Sir William (1955). The basis of legal sovereignty. *Cambridge Law Journal* 172.
Wade, H.W.R. (1969). Judicial Control of Universities. *Law Quarterly Review,* 85: 468.
Wade, W.H.R. (1994). *Administrative Law.* (1994). Oxford, Oxford University Press.
Wagner, R.B. (1989). *Accountability in Education: a Philosophical Enquiry.* New York.
Wall, A. and Rowden, R. (1994). Managerial accountability, in G. Hunt (ed.) *Whistleblowing in the Health Service.* London, Arnold.
Warner, D. and Palfreyman, D. (eds) (1997). *Higher Education Management: the key elements.* Society for Research into Higher Education.
Wenneras, C. and Wold, A. (1997). *Nature,* 387: 341–4 (22 May).
Whalley, P.W.F. and Price, D.M. (1994). 'Mischievous anachronism' or a 'swift, cheap and final' form of alternative dispute resolution for universities? *ABCD* 114: 7–11.
Whalley, P.W.F. and Price, D.M. (1996). Noblesse oblige – a role for the Visitor? *ABCD* 124: 48–53.
Whincup, M.H. (1993). The exercise of university disciplinary powers. *Education and the Law,* 5(1): 19–31.
White, G.E. (1993). *Justice Oliver Wendell Holmes.* Oxford/New York, Oxford University Press.
Williams, G. and Fry, H. (1994). *Longer Term Prospects for Higher Education.* CVCP Report, Institute of Education, University of London.
Williams, S. (1977). Robbins plus Twenty. *Foundation Oration.* Birkbeck College, London.
Zemsky, R. and Massy, W.F. (1995). Toward an understanding of our current predicaments. *Change.* November/December, 41–9.

Case List

Adam v. Ward [1917] A.C. 309
Amalgamated Society of Railway Servants v. Osborne [1910] A.C. 87
Anismic v. Foreign Compensation Commission [1969] 2 All E.R. 208
Ashbury Railway Carriage Co v. Riche (1875) L.R. 7 H.L. 653
Associated Provincial Picture Houses Ltd v. Wednesbury Corporation [1948] 1 K.B. 228
Attorney-General for New South Wales v. Quin (1990) 170 C.L.R. 1 40
Attorney-General of Hong Kong v. Ng Yuen Shiu [1983] 2 A.C. 629
Attorney-General v. Dedham School [1857] 23 Beav. 350, 53 E.R. 138
Attorney-General v. Great Eastern Railway (1880) 5 App. Cas. 473
Attorney-General v. Guardian Newspapers (No. 2) [1988] W.L.R. 776 H.L.
Attorney-General v. North Metropolitan Tramways Co [1892] 3 Ch. 70; (1895) 72 L.T. 340
Attorney-General v. Talbot (1748) 1 Ves. Sen. 78
AUT v. University of Newcastle [1987] I.C.R. 317
Bagg's Case (1615) 11 Co. Rep. 93b
Blasser v. Royal Institute for the Advancement of Learning [1985] 24 D.L.R. (4th) 507
Board of Curators of University of Missouri v. Horowitz, 435 U.S. 78; 55 L. Ed. 3d 124 (Sup. Ct.)
Bonham's Case (1610) Co. Rep. 113b
Commonwealth of Australia v. John Fairfax (1980) 147 C.L.R. 39
Council of Civil Service Unions v. Minister for the Civil Service [1985] A.C. 374
Czarnikow v. Roth Schmidt and Co [1922] 2 K.B. 478
D v. National Society for the Prevention of Cruelty to Children [1977] 1 All E.R. 589, [1978] A.C. 171
Doe v. University of Michigan, 721 F. Supp. 852 (ED Mich. 1989)
Eden v. Foster (1726) 2 P. Wms. 325
Ex parte Duncan (1904) 4 S.R. (N.S.W.) 217
Ex parte Forster re University of Sydney [1963] N.S.W.R. 723
Faccenda Chicken Ltd v. Fowler [1986] 1 All E.R. 617 C.A.
Foster v. British Gas plc [1990] 3 All E.R. 897
Fyfe and McGrouther Ltd v. Byrne [1977] I.R.L.R. 29
Glynn v. Keele University and another [1971] 2 All E.R. 89
Hammond v. Hutt Valley and Bays Metropolitan Milk Board [1958] N.Z.L.R. 720.
Hines v. Birkbeck College [1985] 3 All E.R. 156

Horrocks v. Lowe [1975] A.C. 135
Kane v. Board of Governors of the University of British Columbia (1980) 110 D.L.R. (3d) 311
King v. University of Saskatchewan [1969] 6 D.L.R. (3d) 120; [1969] S.C.R. 678
Leech v. Governor of Parkhurst Prison [1988] A.C. 533
Lloyd v. McMahon [1987] A.C. 625; [1987] All E.R. 1118
Ludden v. Choyce and others [1975] W.L.R. 422
Murdoch University v. Bloom [1980] W.A.R. 193
Norrie v. Senate of the University of Auckland [1984] 1 N.Z.L.R. 129
Oakes v. Sidney Sussex College, Cambridge [1988] 1 All E.R. 1005
Page v. Visitor of Hull University [1993] 1 All E.R. 97
Patel v. University of Bradford Senate [1979] 2 All E.R. 582 C.A.
Pergamon Press Ltd [1971] 1 Ch. 388
Philips v. Bury (1694) Skin. 447 H.L.; 90 E.R. 198; Holt K.B. 715
R. v. Bishop of Ely (1788) 2 Term Rep. 290
R. v. Board of Education [1910] 2 K.B. 165
R. v. Civil Service Appeal Board, ex parte Cunningham [1991] 4 All E.R. 319
R. v. Dunsheath, ex parte Meredith [1951] 1 K.B. 127
R. v. Hertford College [1878] 3 Q.B.D. 693
R. v. Higher Education Funding Council, ex parte Institute of Dental Surgery [1994] I All E.R. 651
R. v. Home Secretary, ex parte Ruddock [1988] 1 W.L.R. 1482
R. v. Inland Revenue Commissioners, ex parte National Federation of Self-Employed and Small Businesses Ltd [1982] A.C. 617
R. v. Inland Revenue Commissioners, ex parte Preston [1985] A.C. 835
R. v. Lambeth LBC, ex parte Thompson, The Independent (30 October 1995).
R. v. Liverpool Corporation, ex parte Liverpool Taxi Fleet Operators' Association [1972] 2 Q.B. 299
R. v. Mayor, Commonalty and Citizens of the City of London and another, ex parte Matson (1996) 8 Admin. L.R. 49
R. v. Oxford University, ex parte Bolchover, The Times (7 October 1970)
R. v. Secretary of State, ex parte McQuillan [1995] 4 All E.R. 400
R. v. Secretary of State for Health, ex parte United States Tobacco International Inc, The Independent (4 January 1991).
R. v. Secretary of State for the Home Department, ex parte Asif Mahmood Khan [1984] 1 W.L.R. 1337
R. v. Senate of University of Aston, ex parte Roffey [1969] 2 Q.B. 538; [1969] 2 All E.R. 964
R. v. Stepney Corporation [1902] 1 K.B. 317
R. v. Visitors to Lincoln's Inn, ex parte Cale and *Same v. Same, ex parte Persaud* [1992] W.L.R. 994
R. v. Westminster City Council ex parte Ermakov [1996] 2 All E.R. 302
Re Bezeau and Ontario Institute for Studies in Education [1982] 134 D.L.R. (3d) 99
Re Civil Service Salaries: EC Commission v. EC Council [1973] C.M.L.R. 639
Re Coney v. Choyce and others [1975] W.L.R. 422
Re Handy's Crown Brewery [1910] 2 K.B. 257
Re Harelkin and University of Regina (1979) 96 D.L.R. (3d) 14
Re Paine and University of Toronto [1981] 131 D.L.R. 325
Re Schabas and Caput of University of Toronto [1975] 52 D.L.R. 497
Re University of Melbourne, ex parte de Simone [1981] V.R. 378

Re Wisling's application [1984] N.I. 163
Rigg v. University of Waikato (Commissaries' Report) [1984] 1 N.Z.L.R. 149
Robinson v. Crompton Parkinson Ltd [1978] I.C.R. 401
Rooke's Case [1598] 5 Co. Rep. 99b
S v. Lasker 1991 (1) S.A. 558 (C)
Schmidt v. Secretary of State for Home Affairs [1969] 2 Ch. 149
Sharpe v. Wakefield [1891] A.C. 173
St David's College, Lampeter v. Ministry of Education SI 1948, No. 1655 at 561
St John's College, Cambridge v. Todington (1757), 1 Burr 158
The Prince's Case (1606) 8 Co. Rep. 1a, 166
Thomas v. Bradford University [1987] 1 A.C. 795
Thomson v. University of London (1864) 33 L.J. Ch. 625
Thorne v. University of London [1966] 2 Q.B. 237; [1966] 2 All E.R. 338
UNM Post, Inc v. Bd of Regents, 774 F. Supp. 1163 (ED Wis. 1991)
Vaneck v. Governors of University of Alberta [1975] 5 W.W.R. 429
Vidyodaya University of Ceylon and others v. Silva [1964] 3 All E.R. 865
R. v. Home Secretary, ex parte Bhajan Singh [1976] Q.B. 198
Woods v. Secretary of State for Scotland [1991] S.L.T. 197

Index

The Society for Research into Higher Education

The Society for Research into Higher Education exists to stimulate and coordinate research into all aspects of higher education. It aims to improve the quality of higher education through the encouragement of debate and publication on issues of policy, on the organization and management of higher education institutions, and on the curriculum and teaching methods.

The Society's income is derived from subscriptions, sales of its books and journals, conference fees and grants. It receives no subsidies, and is wholly independent. Its individual members include teachers, researchers, managers and students. Its corporate members are institutions of higher education, research institutes, professional, industrial and governmental bodies. Members are not only from the UK, but from elsewhere in Europe, from America, Canada and Australasia, and it regards its international work as among its most important activities.

Under the imprint *SRHE & Open University Press*, the Society is a specialist publisher of research, having over 70 titles in print. The Editorial Board of the Society's Imprint seeks authoritative research or study in the above fields. It offers competitive royalties, a highly recognizable format in both hardback and paperback and the worldwide reputation of the Open University Press.

The Society also publishes *Studies in Higher Education* (three times a year), which is mainly concerned with academic issues, *Higher Education Quarterly* (formerly *Universities Quarterly*), mainly concerned with policy issues, *Research into Higher Education Abstracts* (three times a year), and *SRHE News* (four times a year).

The society holds a major annual conference in December, jointly with an institution of higher education. In 1995 the topic was 'The Changing University' at Heriot-Watt University in Edinburgh. In 1996 it was 'Working in Higher Education' at University of Wales, Cardiff and in 1997, 'Beyond the First Degree' at the University of Warwick. The 1998 conference will be on the topic of globalization at the University of Lancaster.

The Society's committees, study groups and networks are run by the members. The networks at present include:

- Access
- Curriculum Development
- Disability
- Eastern European
- Funding
- Legal Education
- Mentoring
- Postgraduate Issues
- Quality
- Quantitative Studies
- Student Development
- Vocational Qualifications

Benefits to members

Individual

Individual members receive

- *SRHE News*, the Society's publications list, conference details and other material included in mailings.
- Greatly reduced rates for *Studies in Higher Education* and *Higher Education Quarterly*.
- A 35 per cent discount on all SRHE & Open University Press publications.
- Free copies of the Precedings – commissioned papers on the theme of the Annual Conference.
- Free copies of *Research into Higher Education Abstracts*.
- Reduced rates for the annual conference.
- Extensive contacts and scope for facilitating initiatives.
- Free copies of the *Register of Members' Research Interests*.
- Membership of the Society's networks.

Corporate

Corporate members receive:

- Benefits of individual members, plus.
- Free copies of *Studies in Higher Education*.
- Unlimited copies of the Society's publications at reduced rates.
- Reduced rates for the annual conference.
- The right to submit applications for the Society's research grants.
- The right to use the Society's facility for supplying statistical HESA data for purposes of research.

Membership details: SRHE, 3 Devonshire Street, London W1N 2BA, UK. Tel: 0171 637 2766. Fax: 0171 637 2781.
email: srhe@mailbox.ulcc.ac.uk
World Wide Web: http://www.srhe.ac.uk./srhe/
Catalogue: SRHE & Open University Press, Celtic Court, 22 Ballmoor, Buckingham MK18 1XW. Tel: 01280 823388. Fax: 01280 823233. email: enquiries@openup.co.uk

GOVERNING UNIVERSITIES
CHANGING THE CULTURE?

Catherine Bargh, Peter Scott and David Smith

The governance of higher education in the UK was regarded until recently as the 'dignified' element within the constitution of the academy. University councils were trustees rather than directors. But governance is now a contested area and, in particular, lay governors are seen as key change agents, responsible for reforming the old donnish culture of elite higher education. *Governing Universities* explores who governors are, how they conceive of their new roles, and what they think about higher education policy. It examines whether governing bodies have become more actively engaged in setting institutional policies; and whether governors have changed the old culture or gone 'native'. It sets university governance in the large context of the massification and 'marketization' of higher education; and draws comparisons both with other parts of the public sector and the private sector, and with governance in North America and the rest of Europe.

This is the first full-length research-based study of UK higher education governance and is essential reading for all those involved with and interested in university governance.

Contents

208pp 0 335 19538 5 (Paperback) 0 335 19539 3 (Hardback)

ACADEMIC WOMEN

Ann Brooks

> Dr Brooks is able to document the structural basis of power, patronage and prejudice . . . should be read and valued by a wide audience.
>
> Ann Oakley

- How and why have women academics experienced patterns of exclusion, segregation and discrimination in higher education?
- To what extent are academic relationships characterized by endemic sexism in defence of male privilege?
- What parallels are there in patterns of discrimination and disadvantage for academic women in different cultural contexts?

Academic Women explores these questions and investigates the relationships between gender, power and the academy through an analysis of the position of academic women in higher education in the UK and New Zealand. It considers the gap between the models of equality and academic fairness which are said to characterize academic life and the sexist reality of the academy. Ann Brooks combines new and original data drawn from statistical evidence and from the results of questionnaires and interviews with British and New Zealand women academics; and this evidence is located within a wider framework of historical evidence on the position of academic women in both countries.

Contents

192pp 0 335 19599 7 (Paperback) 0 335 19600 4 (Hardback)